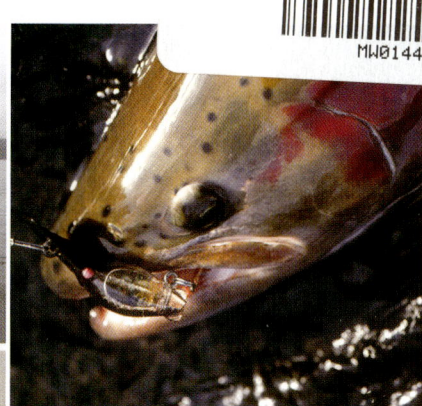

OREGON
RIVER MAPS
&
FISHING GUIDE

Frank Amato Publications

OREGON
RIVER MAPS & FISHING GUIDE

Not for navigation / Always wear a lifevest

		Page				Page				Page
1	Necanicum River	14	14	Umpqua River, Upper	40	26	Molalla River	64
2	Nehalem River	16	15	Coos River & Bay	42	27	Santiam River, North	66
3	Tillamook Bay	18	16	Coquille River	44	28	Santiam River, South	68
4	Kilchis River	20	17	Sixes River	46	29	McKenzie River, Lower	70
5	Wilson River	22	18	Elk River	48	30	McKenzie River, Upper	72
6	Trask River	24	19	Rogue River, Lower	50	31	Middle Fork Willamette River	74
7	Nestucca River	26	20	Rogue River, Middle	52	32	Deschutes River, Lower	76
8	Siletz River	28	21	Rogue River, Upper	54	33	Deschutes River, Lower	78
9	Yaquina Bay	30	22	Chetco River	56	34	Metolius River	80
10	Alsea River	32	23	Willamette River, Lower	58	35	Crooked River	82
11	Siuslaw River	34	24	Sandy River	60	36	Grande Ronde River	84
12	Smith River	36	25	Clackamas River	62	37	John Day River, Lower	86
13	Umpqua River, Lower	38				38	John Day River, Lower	88

Note: Numbers refer to detailed maps inside

Contents

Oregon Sportfish	4-5	Fly-Fishing Techniques	9-10
Hatches	6	Gear-Fishing Techniques	11-12
Fly Patterns	7	Fishing Knots	13
Fishing Tackle	8	River Maps	14-88

IMPORTANT CONTACT INFORMATION

- **Oregon Department of Fish and Wildlife,** (503) 947-6000 or (800) 720-6339, www.dfw.state.or.us
- **United States Coast Guard, Emergencies:** Dial 911 or call the Coast Guard on Marine Channel 16, www.uscg.mil/d13/msuportland
- **Tide Chart,** www.or.usharbors.com/monthly-tides
- **Oregon State Parks,** (503) 986-0707, **Reservations:** (800) 452-5687, **Information:** (800) 551-6949, www.oregonstateparks.org
- **US Forest Service,** www.fs.fed.us/recreation/
- **Oregon Bureau of Land Management,** (503) 375-5646, www.blm.gov/or
- **U.S. Bureau of Land Management,** www.blm.gov/or
- **Oregon Department of Forestry,** www.odf.state.or.us
- **State Park Reservations,** www.reserveamerica.com
- **Turn In Poachers, Oregon Program,** (800) 452-7888
- **Oregon State Park Reservations,** www.reserveamerica.com

- **Oregon State Parks,** www.stateparks.com
- **Guide to Oregon's Central Coast,** www.newportnet.com
- **Boat Escape: Oregon's Ultimate Boating Resource,** www.boatescape.com
- **Oregon Information,** www.visiteasternoregon.com
- **Oregon Parks Association,** www.orparks.org
- **RV Park Finder,** www.rvparkfinder.net
- **Oregon Fishing Guides Organization,** www.oregonfishingguides.org
- **Oregon Shellfish Areas,** www.dfw.state.or.us/mrp/shellfish
- **Oregon Fly Fishing,** www.oregononthefly.com
- **Northwest Fly Fishing,** www.west-fly-fishing.com
- **Oregon Fly Fishing Shops,** www.askaboutflyfishing.com
- **RV Park Reviews,** www.rvparkreviews.com/regions/oregon
- **Southern Oregon Fishing,** www.southernoregonfishingreports.com

WARNING! IMPORTANT NOTICES

Boating: This book is not meant for navigational purposes. Before proceeding down any river or stretch of river, boaters should visually check the water first. It should be remembered that all the rivers in this book are subject to floods and high water and their currents and courses change frequently. Extreme caution is advised at all times, as is the use of Coast Guard-approved personal floatation devices (pfds).

Fishing Regulations: Fishing regulations often change, especially due to the complexities of managing steelhead and salmon populations. Check the Oregon Sport-Fishing Regulations booklet before each season, and before fishing a new piece of water.

Editor: Doug Rose • **Book Design & Maps:** Esther Poleo-Appel Design, 503-641-8079
Cover Photo: Ted Richter • **Illustrations:** Loren Smith, Jeff Dayne and Dürten Kampmann
Hatches, Fly Patterns & Fishing Tackle photographs: Jim Schollmeyer

Frank Amato Publications

All inquiries should be addressed to:
PO Box 82112 • Portland, Oregon 97282 • (503) 653-8108
Softbound ISBN-13: 978-1-57188-514-2 • Softbound ISBN-10: 1-57188-513-7 • Softbound UPC: 0-81127-00365-5
Printed in Singapore
©2014 Frank Amato Publications, Inc.

All rights reserved. No part of this book may be photocopied, electronically stored, or manner without the written consent of the publisher.

OREGON RIVER MAPS & FISHING GUIDE

OREGON SPORTFISH

Spawning Chinook Salmon, Male

Chum Salmon

Rainbow Trout

Bull Trout

Brown Trout

Steelhead

White Sturgeon

4 Fish Charts for Sale at Windsor Nature Discov

OREGON SPORTFISH

Bright Chinook Salmon, Female

Coho Salmon

Shad

Brook Trout

Smallmouth Bass

Coastal Cutthroat

Striped Bass

Green Sturgeon

www.nature-discovery.com or call 1-800-635-4194

Hatches

Insect Hatches *(freshwater)*	Jan	Feb	Mar	Apr	May	Jun	Jul	Aug	Sep	Oct	Nov	Dec
1. Blue-winged olive *(Baetis spp.)*	•	•	•	•	•	•	•	•	•	•	•	•
2. March brown *(Rhithrogena morrisoni)*			•	•	•							
3. Pale morning dun *(Ephemerella inermis & infrequens)*					•	•	•	•				
4. Green drake *(Drunella grandis & doddsi)*						•	•					
5. Mahogany dun *(Paraleptophlebia spp.)*				•	•			•	•	•		
6. Little yellow may *(Epeorus spp.)*					•	•	•	•	•			
7. Salmonfly *(Pteronarcys spp.)*					•	•	•					
8. Yellow Sally *(Isoperla spp.)*						•	•	•	•			
9. Golden stone *(Hesperoperla pacifica & Calineuria californica)*					•	•	•					
10. Green rockworm *(Rhyacophila spp.)*					•	•	•	•	•	•		
11. Spotted sedge *(Hydropsyche spp.)*						•	•	•	•	•		
12. Turtle-cased caddis *(Glossosoma spp.)*				•	•							
13. Fall caddis *(Dicosmoecus spp.)*									•	•	•	•
14. American grannom *(Brachycentrus spp.)*				•	•		•	•	•			
15. Green caddis *(Arctopsyche spp.)* not shown					•	•						
16. Midges *(Chironomidae)*	•	•	•	•	•	•	•	•	•	•	•	•

1. Blue-winged olive *(Baetis spp.)*
2. March brown *(Rhithrogena morrisoni)* 
3. Pale morning dun *(Ephemerella inermis & infrequens)* 
4. Green drake *(Drunella grandis & doddsi)* 
5. Mahogany dun *(Paraleptophlebia spp.)* 
6. Little yellow may *(Epeorus spp.)* 
7. Salmonfly *(Pteronarcys spp.)* 
8. Yellow Sally *(Isoperla spp.)* 
9. Golden stone *(Hesperoperla pacifica & Calineuria californica)* 
10. Green rockworm *(Rhyacophila spp.)* 
11. Spotted sedge *(Hydropsyche spp.)* 
12. Turtle-cased caddis *(Glossosoma spp.)* 
13. Fall caddis *(Dicosmoecus spp.)* 
14. American grannom *(Brachycentrus spp.)* 
16. Midges *(Chironomidae)* 

Jim Schollmeyer photographs

Fly Patterns / Trout

Jim Schollmeyer photographs

Adams	Parachute Adams	Yellow Humpy	Yellow Wulff	Royal Coachman	March Brown
Green Drake	Compara-dun (PMD)	Elk Hair Caddis (black)	Elk Hair Caddis (brown)	Bucktail Caddis (orange)	Goddard Caddis
Tent-Wing Caddis	Stimulator (yellow)	MacSalmon (golden)	MacSalmon (salmonfly)	Hopper	Chernobyl Ant
Humpy Midge	Bead-Head Hare's Ear Nymph	AP Nymph (black)	AP Nymph (gray)	Zug Bug	Prince Nymph
Midge Pupa (pheasant tail)	Caddis Larva (tan)	Bead-head Caddis Pupa	Bitch Creek	Damsel Nymph	Mickey Finn
Muddler Minnow	Woolly Bugger (brown)	Carey Bugger (black)	Carey Bugger (olive)	Crystal Muddler (white)	Clouser Minnow

Steelhead & Salmon

Bunny Leech	Egg Sucking Leech	Popsicle	General Practitioner	Signal Light	Green Butt Skunk
Polar Shrimp	Babine Special	Freight Train	Glo Bug	Micro Egg	Waller's Waker

7

FISHING TACKLE

Jim Schollmeyer photographs

PLUGS
1. Flatfish™
2. Kwikfish™
3. Fatfish™
4. Wiggle Wart™
5. Hot Shot Special Edition™
6. Tadpolly™
7. Hot Shot™

SPOONS
1. Alvin™ (wobbler)
2. Pixee™
3. Little Cleo™
4. BC Steel™
5. Mor-Tac™
6. Stee-Lee™

SPINNERS
1. Rooster Tail™
2. Aglia™
3. Vibrax™
4. Rainbow Spinner™

DIVERS
5. Hot-n-Tot™ (modified)
6. E-Z Diver™
7. Jet Diver™

FLASHERS
1. Dodger™
2. Flasher

DRIFT BOBBERS
1. Birdie™
2. Spin-N-Glo™
3. Winged Cheater™
4. Lil' Corkie™

JIGS
1. Beau Mac™ (steelhead)
2. Crippled Herring™ (salmon)
3. Scampi™ (ling cod)

BOBBERS
1. Fixed Bobber
2. Sliding Bobber

HOOKS
1. Octopus
2. Siwash
3. Circle

SWIVELS
1. Barrel Swivel
2. Snap Swivel
3. Slider
4. Bead-chain Swivel
5. Spreader

WEIGHTS
1. Cannonball
2. Bank Sinker
3. Pyramid Sinker
4. In-line Sinker

BAITS
1. Roe (salmon eggs)
2. Sand Shrimp
3. Herring
4. Anchovy
5. Prawn
6. Pink Worm
7. Gooey Bob™
8. Smelt
9. Sardine

STRIKE INDICATORS
1. Bobber-style
2. Poly-yarn Style

Fly-Fishing Techniques

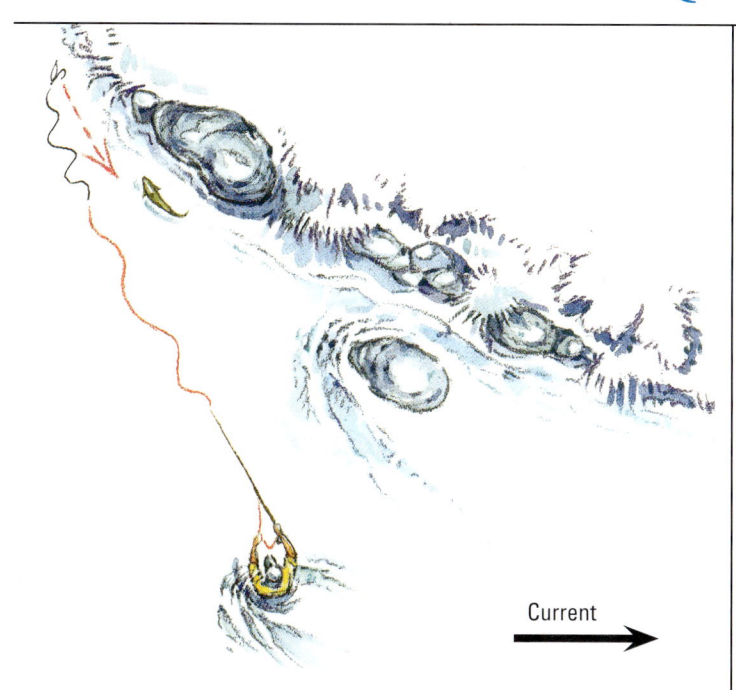

DRY FLY, DEAD DRIFT

Cast your dry fly well upstream of a rising fish and let it drift with the current. Usually, as the fly moves downstream, it is necessary to strip in excess line to keep slack line to a minimum. When a fish rises to the fly, set the hook immediately, and keep tension on the fish throughout the fight.

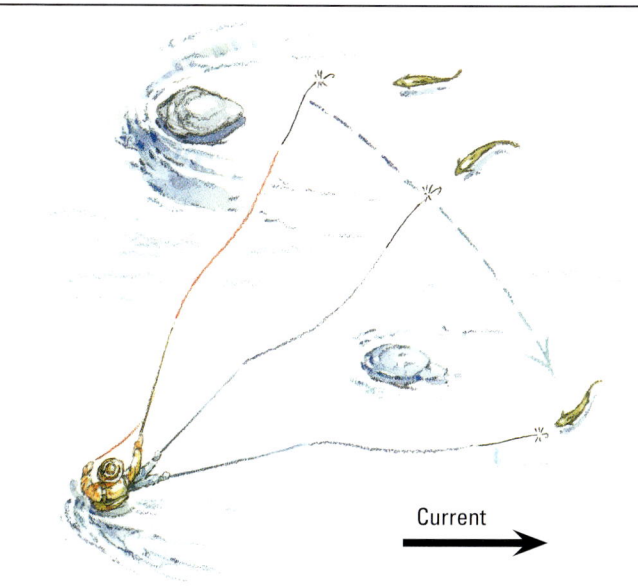

DRY FLY, SWUNG

Cast your dry fly across the river and slightly downstream, then let the current *"swing"* the fly until it is hanging directly downstream. Take a couple of steps downstream between casts to cover all of the water where fish could be holding. The best dry flies for this style of presentation are buoyant enough to skate along the surface throughout the swing. Adding a *"riffle hitch"* to the head of a fly will help keep it riding on the surface. A riffle hitch is simply a half-hitch that is secured around the head of the fly, usually about ¼" behind the eye of the hook.

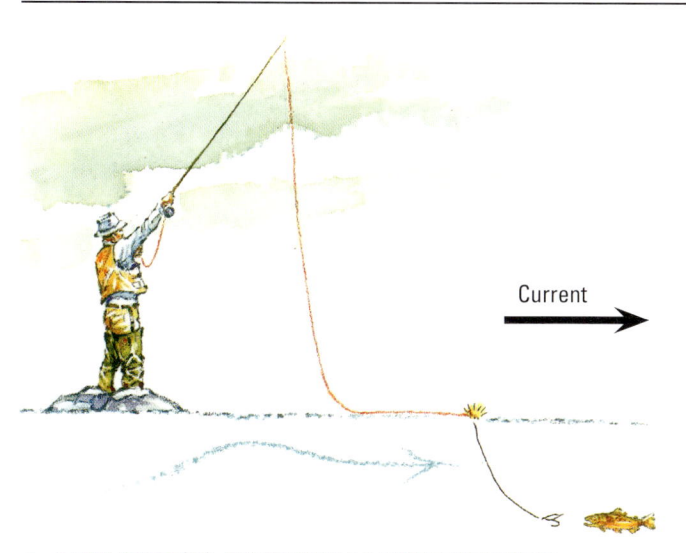

a. POLY-YARN INDICATOR

1. NYMPH(S) LIGHTLY WEIGHTED

Nymphs are sinking flies that are drifted with the current. Cast well upstream of the fish you are targeting, and allow the fly to drift naturally with the current. For lightly weighted nymphs, your fly line should be buoyant enough to keep the fly from catching on the bottom.

2. NYMPH(S) WEIGHTED WITH INDICATOR

For heavily weighted nymphs, a strike indicator is recommended **(Figures a & b)**. Use the same drifting technique as described. Strike indicators help keep your nymph(s) from hanging up on the bottom and alert you when a fish has taken your fly.

b. BOBBER-STYLE INDICATOR

Illustrations by Loren Smith

Fly-Fishing Techniques

Wade fishing or fishing from a boat

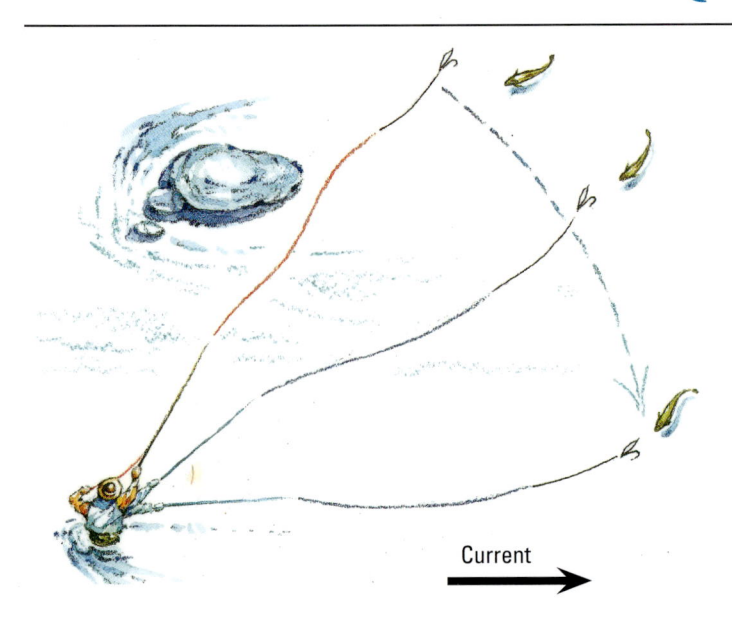

1. WET FLY, SWUNG NEAR SURFACE

Cast your wet fly across and slightly downstream, then let the current *"swing"* the fly until it is hanging directly downstream. Take a couple of steps downstream between each swing, thereby covering all of the water where fish could be holding.

2. WET FLY, SWUNG DEEP

Using the same *"swinging"* technique described above, add heavier flies and/or sinking lines to get your fly as deep as is necessary to find fish.

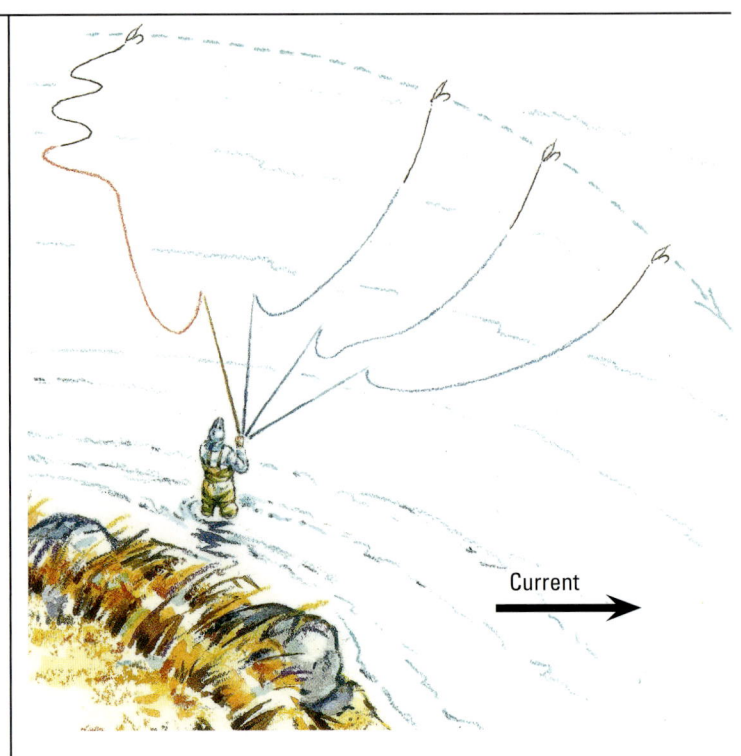

DEEP-DRIFTED FLY, WITH OR WITHOUT STRIKE INDICATOR

Using a lightly weighted fly, cast slightly upstream and let the fly drift naturally downstream with the current. To extend the drift, pay out fly line as the fly drifts downstream. This can be done with or without a strike indicator.

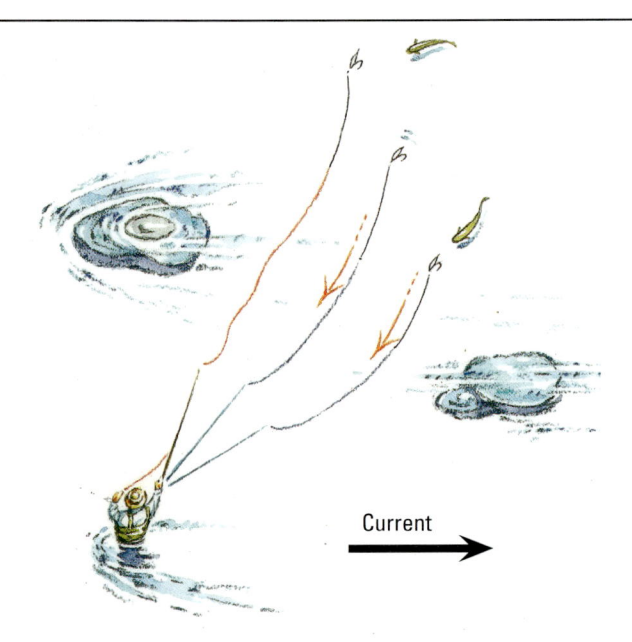

WEIGHTED STREAMER WITH FAST RETRIEVE

Cast across the current, either upstream or downstream, and retrieve your wet fly by stripping in the fly line. Try stripping in the fly line with short, fast strips and long, slow strips to determine which method attracts the most fish.

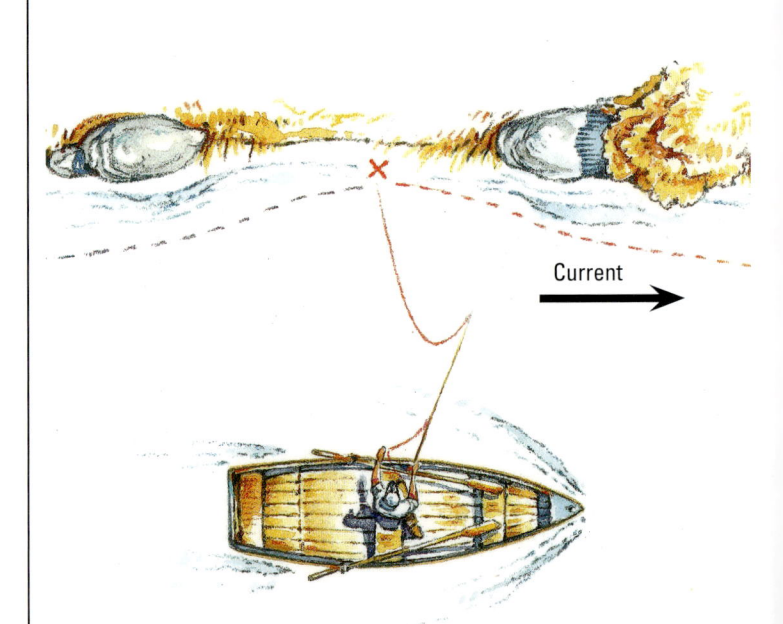

FLOAT-FISHING FROM A BOAT

Cast weighted fly to the side of the boat and let it drift. When fly gets ahead of or too far back, recast. Set back when strike indicator goes under.

Illustrations by Loren Smith

GEAR-FISHING TECHNIQUES
Shore fishing

DRIFT FISHING

Cast slightly upstream and let your sinker bounce downstream with the current through the most likely holding water. You can lengthen your drift by slowly letting out line, but only enough line to keep your bait bouncing downstream. When you feel a bite, set the hook and stay tight to your fish.

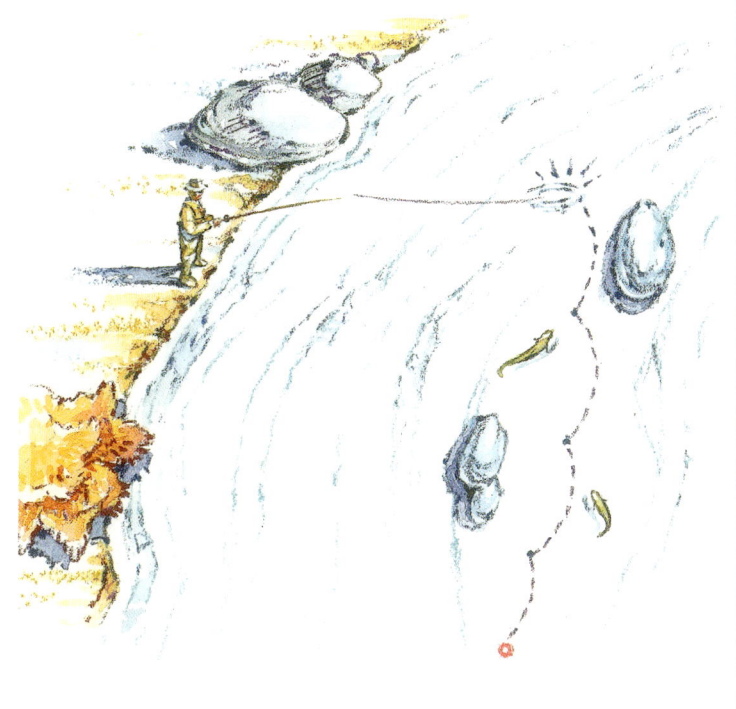

DRIFT-FISHING RIG

CASTING SPINNERS, SPOONS, AND PLUGS

Cast and retrieve your lure at varying depths and speeds. Cover all of the suitable water.

FLOAT-FISHING

Cast well upstream of the fish you want to catch and let the bait drift down to the fish at the speed of the current. A natural dead-drift is often the only way to fool a wary fish. The two most popular types of float-fishing are with jigs and with bait.

FLOAT & JIG RIG

FLOAT & BAIT RIG

11

GEAR-FISHING TECHNIQUES

Fishing from a boat

ANCHOR FISHING

From an anchor position, back lures or bait (usually with a sinker & dropper line) down into the current until the sinker is touching lightly on the bottom, or until your bait is suspended at the depth of the fish. Usually salmon and steelhead hold between 8 and 25 feet deep.

PLUNKING

PLUNKING AND PLUNKING RIG

Cast your bait and sinker out to the desired spot, let it settle to the bottom, and set your rod in a sturdy place (preferably a rod holder) where you can watch for a bite.

PLUNKING RIG

JIGGING

Lift and drop your jig or lure to give it a lively action. This action is known as *"jigging."* From a boat, it is usually best to jig directly under the boat. From the bank, lift and drop the jig, reeling in a few feet of line before or after each lift.

Illustrations by Loren Smith

FISHING KNOTS

CLINCH KNOT

DOUBLE SURGEON'S KNOT

PALOMAR KNOT

BLOOD KNOT

NAIL, OR TUBE, KNOT

ALBRIGHT KNOT

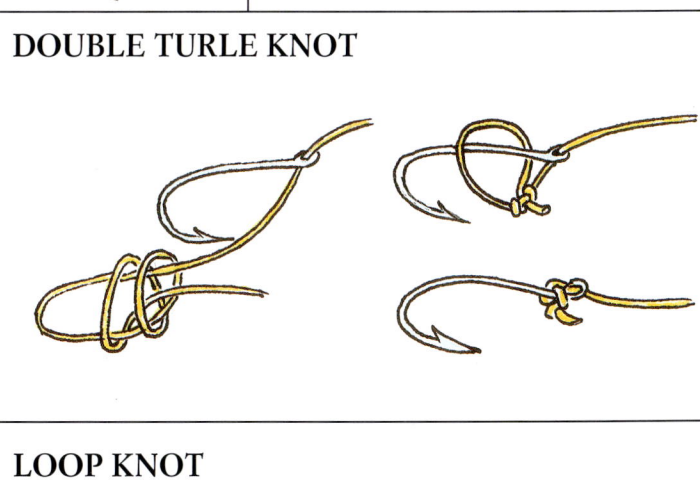

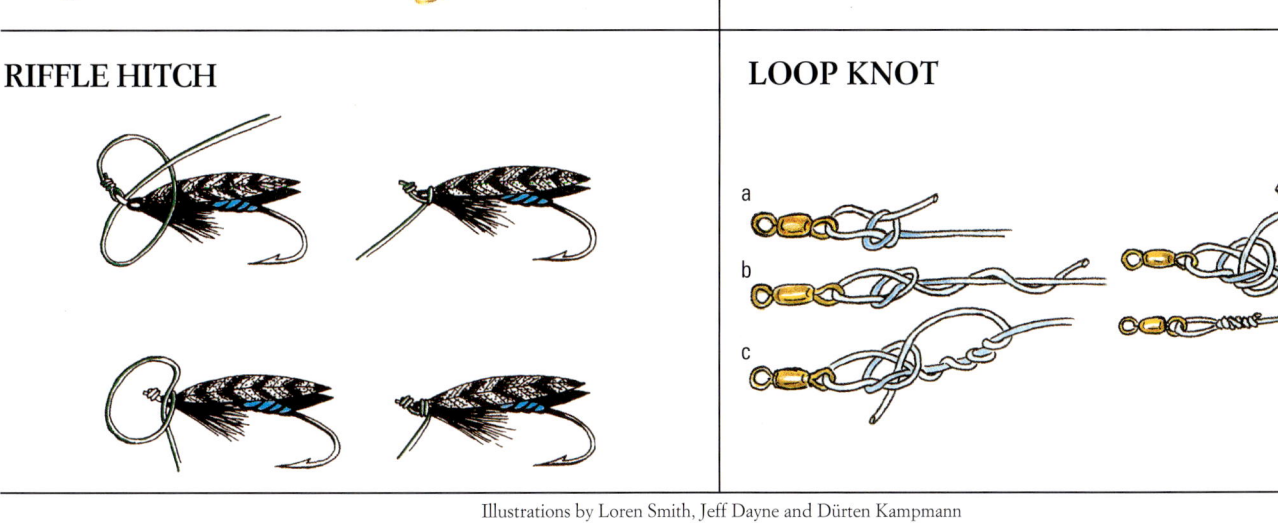

PERFECTION LOOP

DOUBLE TURLE KNOT

RIFFLE HITCH

LOOP KNOT

a
b
c
d
e

Illustrations by Loren Smith, Jeff Dayne and Dürten Kampmann

Oregon River Maps & Fishing Guide

Necanicum River

The Necanicum River is a small but productive salmon and steelhead river in the far northwest of Oregon. It holds the distinction as the first coastal river to clear after a heavy rain, and it is one of the smallest navigable rivers for drift boats. It flows just over 20 miles from Saddle Mountain to the busy coastal town of Seaside.

Winter steelhead are the main focus for anglers on the Necanicum. Early hatchery fish arrive from late November through January, while native fish peak in February and March. Boaters drift the lower river, from Klootchie Creek to Seaside, where private land restricts bank access. Above Klootchie Creek, most reaches of the river are accessible. Drift fishing and casting float/jig combinations are the most successful fishing methods.

There is a small fall Chinook run on the Necanicum, thanks to a limited hatchery program. These fish congregate in tidewater and the lower river from late September until the first fall rains. Float-fishing with bait, casting spinners and fly-fishing are the most successful techniques. Native coho are closed to fishing and should be released unharmed.

Cutthroat trout are spread throughout the Necanicum drainage. Late summer and fall offer the best opportunity for finding fishable numbers of sea-runs, but resident fish live throughout the river year-round. Fly-fishing with small streamers or casting small lures are the best trout techniques.

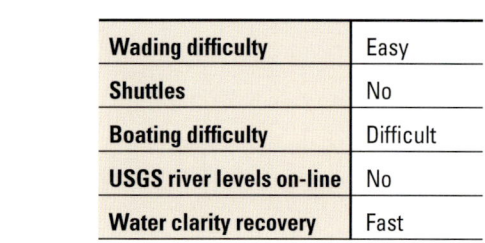

Wading difficulty	Easy
Shuttles	No
Boating difficulty	Difficult
USGS river levels on-line	No
Water clarity recovery	Fast

LOCATION:
Clatsop County

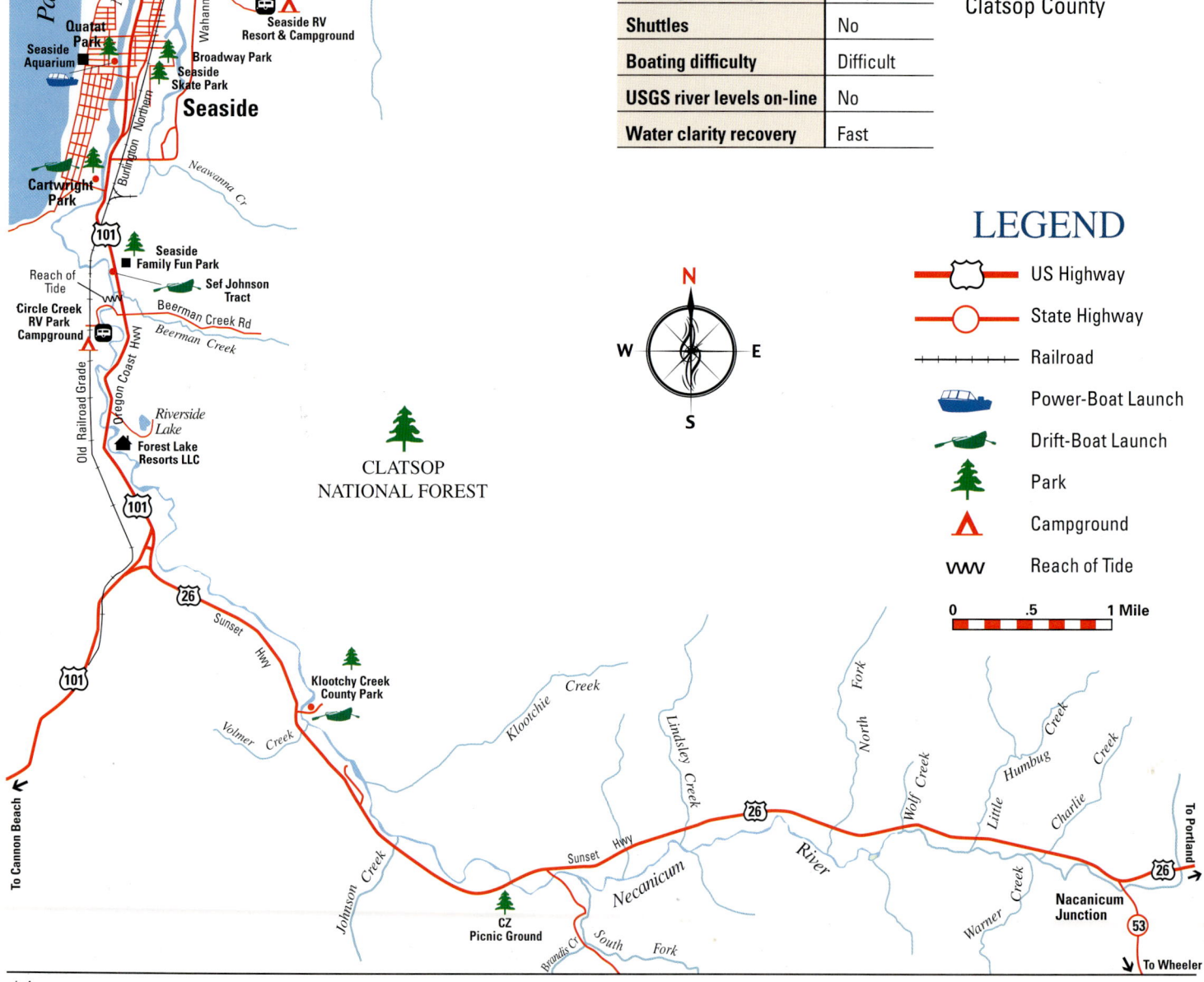

LEGEND

- US Highway
- State Highway
- Railroad
- Power-Boat Launch
- Drift-Boat Launch
- Park
- Campground
- Reach of Tide

Necanicum River

SERVICES

CAMPING/PARKS
- **Saddle Mountain State Natural Area,** Hwy. 26, (primitive), Info: (800) 551-6949, Park: (503) 368-5943
- **Bud's RV Park,** Gearhart, 97138, (800) 730-6855, (503) 738-6855, www.budsrv.com
- **Cartwright City Park,** Seaside, 97138, (503) 738-5511 (ramp – no camping)
- **Quatat City Park,** Seaside, 97138, (503) 738-5511 (ramp – no camping)
- **Klootchy Creek County Park,** (503) 325-9306 (ramp – no camping)
- **Circle Creek RV Park Campground,** Seaside, 97138, (503) 738-6070, www.circlecreekrv.com

ACCOMMODATIONS
- **The Gilbert Inn,** Seaside, 97138, (800) 410-9770, (503) 738-9770, www.gilbertinn.com
- **Rivertide Suites,** Seaside, 97138, (503) 717-1100, (877) 871-8433, www.rivertidesuites.com
- **The Lanai at the Cove,** Seaside, 97138, (503) 738-6343, www.seasidelanai.com
- **A Loafer's Paradise,** Seaside, 97138, (503) 968-2525, www.loafersparadise.com

TACKLE SHOPS
- **Trucke's One-Stop,** Seaside, 97138, (1-503)-738-8863, www.shopseaside.com/trucke
- **Bud's RV Park (& Tackle),** Gearhart, 97138, (800) 730-6855, (503) 738-6855

VISITOR INFORMATION
- **Seaside Visitors Bureau,** Seaside, 97138, (888) 306-2326, (503) 738-3097, www.seasideor.com

BEST GEAR-FISHING TECHNIQUES & ESTIMATED HOOKUPS IN AN AVERAGE YEAR

	Jan	Feb	Mar	Apr	May	Jun	Jul	Aug	Sep	Oct	Nov	Dec
Winter Steelhead 1500	1,2 3,4	1,2 3,4	1,2 3,4								1,2,3,4	1,2 3,4
Fall Chinook 200									2,3,6	1,2,3 4,5,6	1,2,3 4,5,6	
Coho 200											1,2,3 4,5	1,2,3 4,5
Sea-Run Cutthroat			2					2	2	2		

1. Drift fishing (from bank or boat, with or without bait)
2. Casting spinners, spoons, plugs
3. Float fishing (with jigs or bait)
4. Back-trolling (plugs or diver-and-bait)
5. Back-bouncing (boat)
6. Trolling (boat only)
7. Anchor fishing
8. Plunking
9. Jigging

BEST FLY-FISHING TECHNIQUES

	Jan	Feb	Mar	Apr	May	Jun	Jul	Aug	Sep	Oct	Nov	Dec
Winter Steelhead	4,6,7	4,6,7	4,6,7								4,6,7	1,2 3,4
Fall Chinook								6,7,9	4,6 7,9	4,6 7,9		
Coho											3,4 7,8	3,4 7,8
Sea-Run Cutthroat			2,6 8,9					2,6 8,9	2,6 8,9	2,6 8,9		

1. Dry fly, dead-drift
2. Dry fly, swung
3. Wet fly, swung near surface
4. Wet fly, swung deep
5. Nymph(s), lightly weighted
6. Nymph(s), weighted with indicator
7. Deep drifted fly (with or without indicator)
8. Wet fly retrieved near surface
9. Deep swing with retrieve

A fresh winter steelhead glows in the first rays of morning sun.

Photo by Nick Amato

OREGON RIVER MAPS & FISHING GUIDE

Nehalem River

The largest river on Oregon's north coast, the Nehalem drains over 850 square miles of rainforest, flowing over 100 miles to Nehalem Bay. The river and bay are known for their excellent summer and fall Chinook salmon fishing. The Nehalem also supports strong wild runs of coho salmon, winter steelhead and sea-run cutthroat trout. In addition, Nehalem Bay is a popular crabbing and clamming destination through most of the year.

Chinook salmon are the dominant fish in the mainstem of the Nehalem River, running from July through November, with peaks in August, September and October. Until the first heavy rains of autumn, Chinook move in stages up the bay toward reach-of-tide. From the jaws of the bay to the town of Nehalem, trolling herring is most popular. From Nehalem upstream to Mohler, trolling spinners and float fishing with bait are best.

Winter steelhead run up the Nehalem from December through April, with peaks in February and March. Fly-fishing, casting spinners, drift fishing and back-trolling plugs are the best steelheading techniques.

Native coho run strong in the Nehalem in November and December, but are closed to fishing. Chinook anglers commonly catch these acrobatic fish, which must be released unharmed.

From August through October, sea-run cutthroat trout move through the Nehalem estuary and into the river. Trolling small plugs through tidewater, casting spinners, and fly-fishing with small streamers are the best trout techniques.

LOCATION:
Clatsop, Tillamook Counties

LEGEND

- US Highway
- State Highway
- Railroad
- Power-Boat Launch
- Drift-Boat Launch
- Park
- Campground
- Reach of Tide

0 .5 1 Mile

Wading difficulty	Moderate-Difficult
Shuttles	Yes
Boating difficulty	Difficult
USGS river levels on-line	Yes (mainstem only)
Water clarity recovery	Slow
Best river levels	3'-6' (mainstem)

NEHALEM RIVER

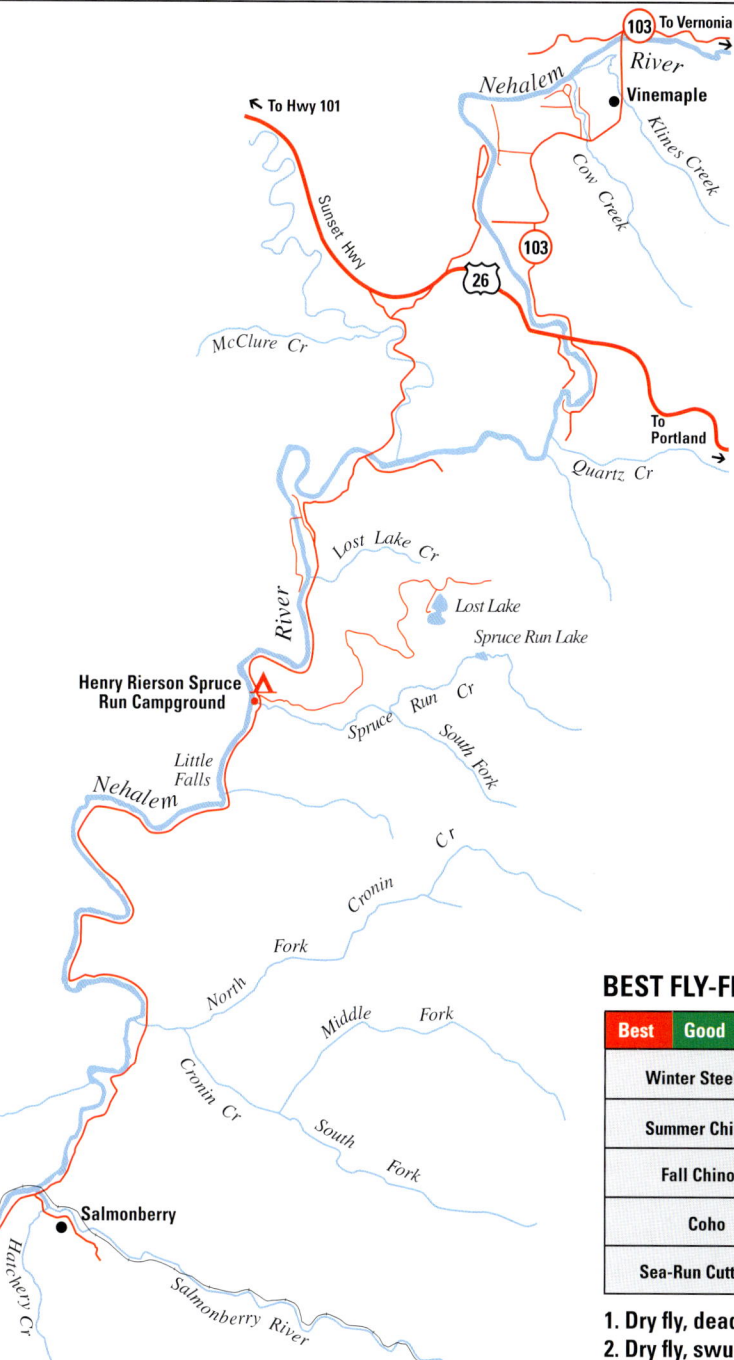

SERVICES

CAMPING/PARKS
- **North Fork Nehalem County Park,** (503) 322-3522, www.co.clatsop.or.us/page/156
- **Wheeler on the Bay Lodge & Marina,** Wheeler, 97147, (503) 368-5780, www.wheelermarina.net
- **Henry Rierson Spruce Run Campground,** Seaside, 97138, (503) 325-5451, www.oregon.gov
- **Paradise Cove Resort & Marina,** Rockaway Beach, 97136, (503) 368-6581
- **Nehalem Bay State Park,** Manzanita, Info: (800) 551-6949, Park: (503) 368-5154, www.oregonstateparks.org
- **Nehalem Falls Campground,** Nehalem, (503) 842-2545, www.oregon.gov/odf
- **The Jetty Fishery,** Rockaway Beach, 97136, (800) 821-7697 or (503) 368-5746, www.jettyfishery.com
- **Roy Creek County Park,** Roy Creek Park, (503) 322-3522, www.co.tillamook.or.us/gov
- **Kelly's Brighton Marina,** Rockaway Beach, 97136, (503) 368-5745, www.kellyscrabs.com

ACCOMMODATIONS
- **Zen Garden Bed and Breakfast,** Manzanita, 97130, (503) 368-6697, www.zengardenbedandbreakfast.com
- **Old Wheeler Hotel,** Wheeler, 97147, (877) 653-4683, (503)368-6000, www.oldwheelerhotel.com
- **Wheeler on the Bay Lodge & Marina,** (800) 469-3204, (503) 368-5858, www.wheeleronthebay.com

TACKLE SHOPS
- **Wheeler Marina,** Wheeler, 97147, (503) 368-5780
- **Barview Jetty Store,** Garibaldi, 97118, (503) 322-2644

VISITOR INFORMATION
- **Tillamook State Forest,** Tillamook, 97141, (503) 842-2545, www.oregon.gov/odf/tillamookstateforest
- **Oregon Coast Visitors Association,** Wheeler, 97147, (888) 628-2101, (541) 574-2679, www.visittheoregoncoast.com
- **Tillamook Area Chamber Of Commerce,** Tillamook, 97141, (503) 842-7525, www.tillamookchamber.org

BEST FLY-FISHING TECHNIQUES

Best / Good / Slow	Jan	Feb	Mar	Apr	May	Jun	Jul	Aug	Sep	Oct	Nov	Dec
Winter Steelhead	4,6,7	4,6,7	4,6,7	4,6,7 / 4,6,7							4,6,7	4,6,7
Summer Chinook							6,7,9	6,7,9	6,7,9			
Fall Chinook									6,7,9	4,6,7,9	4,6,7,9	
Coho									3,4,7,8	3,4,7,8	3,4,7,8	3,4,7,8
Sea-Run Cutthroat	2,6 8,9	2,6 8,9	2,6 8,9	2,6 8,9	2,6 8,9	2,6 8,9	2,6 8,9	2,6 8,9	2,6 8,9	2,6 8,9	2,6 8,9	2,6 8,9

1. Dry fly, dead-drift
2. Dry fly, swung
3. Wet fly, swung near surface
4. Wet fly, swung deep
5. Nymph(s), lightly weighted
6. Nymph(s), weighted with indicator
7. Deep drifted fly (with or without indicator)
8. Wet fly retrieved near surface
9. Deep swing with retrieve

BEST GEAR-FISHING TECHNIQUES & ESTIMATED HOOKUPS IN AN AVERAGE YEAR

Best / Good / Slow	Jan	Feb	Mar	Apr	May	Jun	Jul	Aug	Sep	Oct	Nov	Dec
Winter Steelhead 3500	1,2 3,4	1,2 3,4	1,2 3,4	1,2 3,4	1,2 3,4						1,2 3,4	1,2 3,4
Summer Chinook 1000							1,2,3,4,5,6	1,2,3 4,5,6	1,2,3 4,5,6			
Fall Chinook (Tide water) 2500									2,3,6	2,3,6	2,3,6	
Fall Chinook (River) 2000										1,2,3 4,5,6	1,2,3 4,5,6	
Coho 2000									1,2,3 4,5,6	1,2,3 4,5,6	1,2,3 4,5,6	1,2,3 4,5,6
Sea-Run Cutthroat 2000	2,6	2,6	2,6	2,6	2,6	2,6	2,6	2,6	2,6	2,6	2,6	2,6
Sturgeon	8	8	8	8	8	8	8	8	8	8	8	8
Crabs												

1. Drift fishing (from bank or boat, with or without bait)
2. Casting spinners, spoons, plugs
3. Float fishing (with jigs or bait)
4. Back-trolling (plugs or diver-and-bait)
5. Back-bouncing (boat)
6. Trolling (boat only)
7. Anchor fishing
8. Plunking
9. Jigging

Oregon River Maps & Fishing Guide

Tillamook Bay

LOCATION: Tillamook County

Tillamook Bay is one of the largest estuaries in Oregon, second only to Coos Bay in size. The historic fishing village of Garibaldi sits on the north end of the bay, and the agricultural community of Tillamook rests on the south end. A small commercial fleet and a handful of sportfishing charter boats call Garibaldi home, using the Tillamook bar to access the rich ocean fisheries off shore. Salmon, sturgeon, halibut, rockfish and lingcod are abundant.

1. JB & Water Sport Fishing
2. Harborview Inn & RV Park
3. Port of Garibaldi
4. Siggi-G Ocean Charters
5. Kerri Lin Charters
6. Garibaldi Marina
8. Tillamook Bay Boat House
7. Biak By the Sea RV Park
9. Old Mill RV Park & Event Center

LEGEND

- US Highway
- State Highway
- Hiking Trail
- Power-Boat Launch
- Drift-Boat Launch
- Park
- Campground
- Reach of Tide

0 .5 1 Mile

TILLAMOOK BAY

BEST FLY-FISHING TECHNIQUES

	Jan	Feb	Mar	Apr	May	Jun	Jul	Aug	Sep	Oct	Nov	Dec
Spring Chinook				9	9	9						
Fall Chinook									9	9	9	
Coho									8,9	8,9	8,9	

Legend: Best / Good / Slow

1. Dry fly, dead-drift
2. Dry fly, swung
3. Wet fly, swung near surface
4. Wet fly, swung deep
5. Nymph(s), lightly weighted
6. Nymph(s), weighted with indicator
7. Deep drifted fly (with or without indicator)
8. Wet fly retrieved near surface
9. Deep swing with retrieve

BEST GEAR-FISHING TECHNIQUES & ESTIMATED HOOKUPS IN AN AVERAGE YEAR

	Jan	Feb	Mar	Apr	May	Jun	Jul	Aug	Sep	Oct	Nov	Dec
Spring Chinook 800				6	6	6	6					
Fall Chinook 7000									6	6	6	6
Coho 1000									6	6		
Ocean Salmon 15000							6	6	6	6	6	
Sturgeon	7	7	7	7	7	7	7	7	7	7	7	7
Ling Cod				9	9	9						
Crabs												

Legend: Best / Good / Slow

1. Drift fishing (from bank or boat, with or without bait)
2. Casting spinners, spoons, plugs
3. Float fishing (with jigs or bait)
4. Back-trolling (plugs or diver-and-bait)
5. Back-bouncing (boat)
6. Trolling (boat only)
7. Anchor fishing
8. Plunking
9. Jigging

Photo by Nick Amato

Tillamook Bay is world famous for its giant fall chinook salmon.

Within the bay, there is legendary salmon fishing from April through June, and again from September to November. Anglers troll herring, spinners, wobblers and plugs along the channels that weave through the bay for kings and coho. Sturgeon are present throughout the bay, and are most often caught with sand shrimp or mud shrimp fished on the bottom. Crabbing, clamming and sturgeon fishing are also popular within the bay year-round.

SERVICES

CAMPING/PARKS
- **Barview Jetty County Campground,** Barview, 97118, (503) 322-3522, www.co.tillamook.or.us
- **The Old Mill RV Park & Event Center (Marina),** Garibaldi, 97118, (503) 322-0322, www.oldmill.us
- **Pacific Campground & Overnight Trailer Park,** Tillamook, 97141, (503) 842-5201, www.gotillamook.com
- **Garibaldi Marina,** Garibaldi, 97118, (800) 383-3828, (503) 322-3312, www.garibaldimarina.com

ACCOMMODATIONS
- **Cape Lookout B&B,** Tillamook, 97141, (503) 807-6764, www.capelookoutbnb.com
- **Zen Garden Bed and Breakfast,** Manzanita, 97130, (503) 368-6697, www.zengardenbedandbreakfast.com
- **Wheeler on the Bay Lodge and Marina,** (800) 469-3204, (503) 368-5858, www.wheeleronthebay.com
- **Ashley Inn of Tillamook,** Tillamook, 97141, (503) 842-7599, www.ashleyinntillamook.com

TACKLE SHOPS
- **Tillamook Sporting Goods,** Tillamook, 97141, (503) 842-4334, www.tillamooksportinggoods.com
- **Tillamook Bait Company,** Tillamook, 97141, (503) 842-5031, www.tillamookbait.com

VISITOR INFORMATION
- **Tillamook State Forest,** Tillamook, 97141, (503) 357-2191, www.oregon.gov/odf
- **Oregon Department of Fish and Wildlife,** Salem, 97303, (503) 947-6000 or (800) 720-6339, www.dfw.state.or.us
- **United States Coast Guard,** Dial 911 or call the Coast Guard on Marine Channel 16, www.uscg.mil/d13/msuportland
- **Tide Chart,** www.or.usharbors.com/monthly-tides
- **Tillamook Area Chamber of Commerce,** Tillamook, 97141, (503) 842-7525, www.tillamookchamber.org

OREGON RIVER MAPS & FISHING GUIDE

Kilchis River

The Kilchis River is one of Tillamook's smaller streams, flowing only about twenty-five miles from headwaters in the Tillamook State Forest to Tillamook Bay. For its size, it is one of the most productive salmon and steelhead fisheries on Oregon's northern coast. Fall and winter Chinook, coho and chum salmon, winter steelhead and cutthroat trout all have strong wild runs.

Salmon arrive in tidewater just before the first fall rains in early October. Chinook, coho and chum run at the same time, from October through January, peaking in November. Float fishing with bait or jigs is very popular for all salmon species on the Kilchis. Bank access is excellent along the upper river. Boaters back-troll plugs or back-bounce bait in the lower river.

Chum salmon return in good numbers to the Kilchis in October and November, attracting crowds of people, especially approaching the closure on November 15th. Fly-fishing, drift fishing and float fishing with jigs are the most popular methods. Best colors for attracting chum salmon are fluorescent green, pink, purple and red.

Winter steelhead run from November through March on the Kilchis. They are mainly wild, with a small number of hatchery fish planted annually, and returning early in the season. Wild fish peak in February and March. All methods of steelhead fishing are effective.

Sea-run cutthroat are present in the Kilchis in spring and fall, especially in tidewater and the lower river. They are commonly caught by salmon and steelhead anglers. Fly fishing with streamers, casting spinners and fishing bait on the bottom are the most popular fishing methods.

LOCATION:
Tillamook County

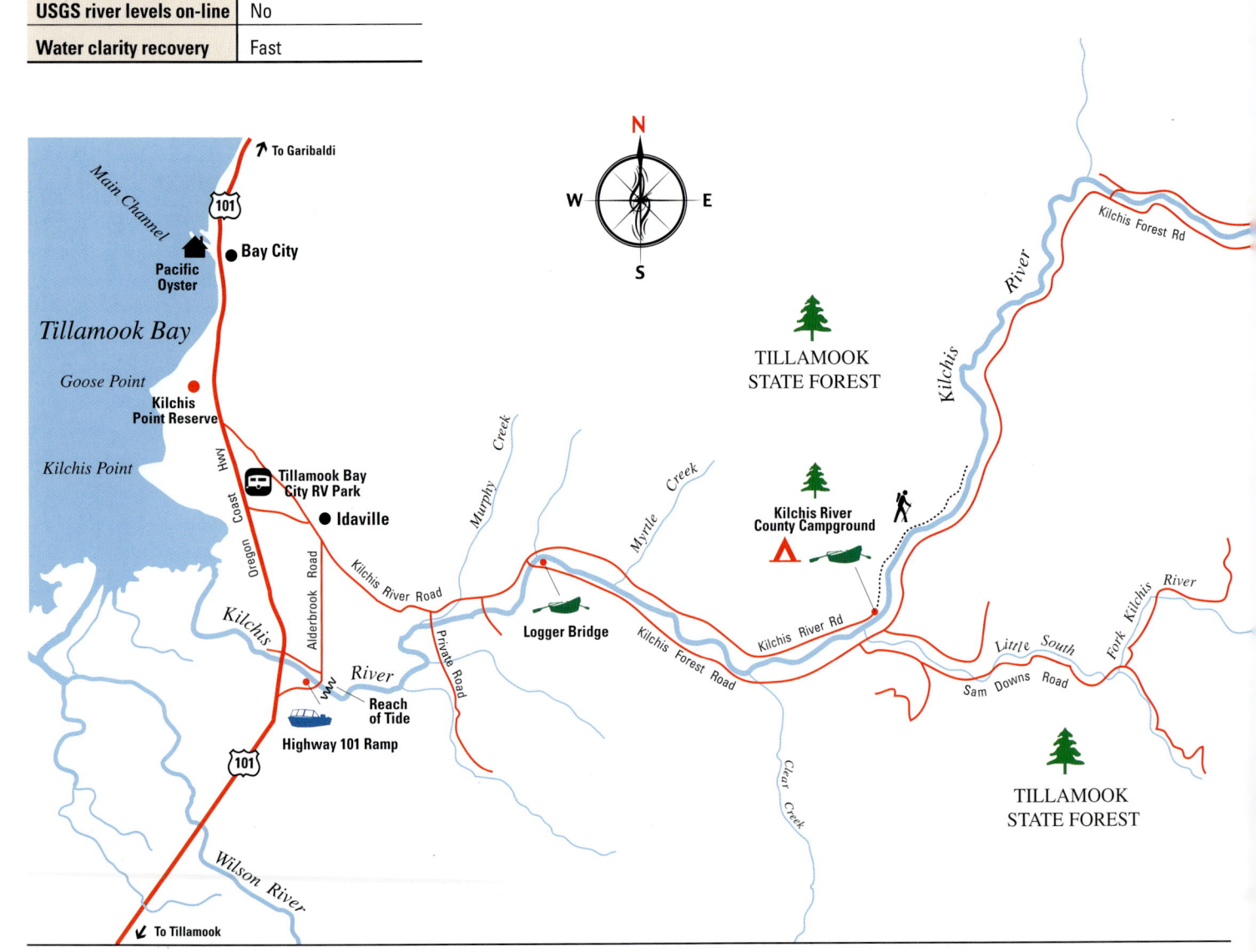

Wading difficulty	Easy
Shuttles	Yes
Boating difficulty	Moderate
USGS river levels on-line	No
Water clarity recovery	Fast

KILCHIS RIVER

BEST FLY-FISHING TECHNIQUES

	Jan	Feb	Mar	Apr	May	Jun	Jul	Aug	Sep	Oct	Nov	Dec
Winter Steelhead	4,6,7 (Good)	4,6,7 (Best)	4,6,7 (Good)								4,6,7 (Slow)	4,6,7 (Good)
Summer Steelhead					2,3,4 5,6,7	2,3,4 5,6,7	2,3,4 5,6,7	2,3,4 5,6,7	2,3,4 5,6,7	2,3,4 5,6,7		
Fall Chinook										6,7,9	4,6,7,9	4,6,7,9
Coho										3,4,7,8	3,4,7,8	
Chum										4,6,7,9	4,6,7,9	
Sea-Run Cutthroat					2,6 8,9	2,6 8,9	2,6 8,9		2,6 8,9	2,6 8,9	2,6 8,9	2,6 8,9

Legend: Best / Good / Slow

1. Dry fly, dead-drift
2. Dry fly, swung
3. Wet fly, swung near surface
4. Wet fly, swung deep
5. Nymph(s), lightly weighted
6. Nymph(s), weighted with indicator
7. Deep drifted fly (with or without indicator)
8. Wet fly retrieved near surface
9. Deep swing with retrieve

BEST GEAR-FISHING TECHNIQUES & ESTIMATED HOOKUPS IN AN AVERAGE YEAR

	Jan	Feb	Mar	Apr	May	Jun	Jul	Aug	Sep	Oct	Nov	Dec
Winter Steelhead 500	1,2 3,4	1,2 3,4	1,2 3,4								1,2,3,4	1,2 3,4
Summer Steelhead 75					1,2 3,4	1,2 3,4	1,2 3,4	1,2 3,4	1,2 3,4			
Fall Chinook 500										2,3,6	1,2,3 4,5,6	1,2,3 4,5,6
Coho 50										1,2,3 4,5	1,2,3 4,5	
Chum 1000										1,2,4,6	1,2,4,5	
Sea-Run Cutthroat				2	2	2		2	2	2	2	

1. Drift fishing (from bank or boat, with or without bait)
2. Casting spinners, spoons, plugs
3. Float fishing (with jigs or bait)
4. Back-trolling (plugs or diver-and-bait)
5. Back-bouncing (boat)
6. Trolling (boat only)
7. Anchor fishing
8. Plunking
9. Jigging

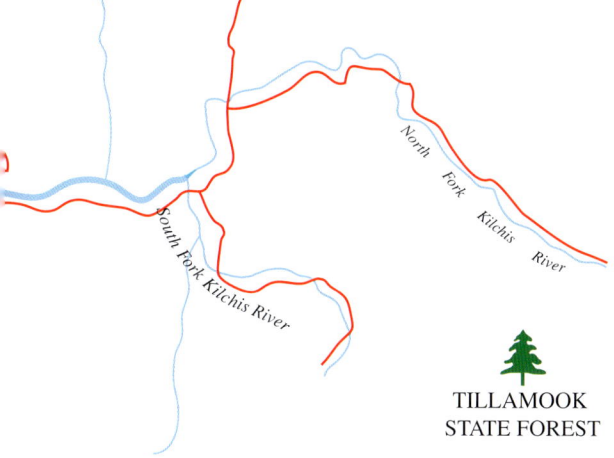

LEGEND

- US Highway
- State Highway
- Hiking Trail
- Power-Boat Launch
- Drift-Boat Launch
- Park
- Campground
- Reach of Tide

0 — .5 — 1 Mile

SERVICES

CAMPING/PARKS
- **Kilchis River County Park,** Tillamook, 97141, (503) 842-6694, www.co.tillamook.or.us/gov
- **Barview Jetty County Campground,** Barview, 97118, (503) 322-3522, www.co.tillamook.or.us/gov
- **Cape Lookout State Park,** Tillamook, 97141, Info: (800) 551-6949, Park: (503) 842-4981, www.oregonstateparks.org
- **The Old Mill RV Park and Event Center (Marina),** Garibaldi, 97118, (503) 322-0322, www.oldmill.us/html/campground.html
- **Pacific Campground & Overnight Trailer Park,** Tillamook, 97141, (503) 842-5201, www.gotillamook.com
- **Carnahan Park, (boat launch),** Tillamook, 97141, www.tillamookor.gov

ACCOMMODATIONS
- **Cape Lookout B&B,** Tillamook, 97141, (503) 807-6764, www.capelookoutbnb.com
- **Zen Garden B&B,** Manzanita, 97130, (503) 368-6697, www.zengardenbedandbreakfast.com
- **Wheeler on the Bay Lodge and Marina,** (800) 469-3204, (503) 368-5858, www.wheeleronthebay.com

TACKLE SHOPS
- **Tillamook Sporting Goods,** Tillamook, 97141, (503) 842-4334, www.tillamooksportinggoods.com
- **Tillamook Bait Company,** Tillamook, 97141, (503) 842-5031, www.tillamookbait.com

VISITOR INFORMATION
- **Tillamook State Forest,** Tillamook, 97141, (503) 357-2191, www.oregon.gov/odf
- **Oregon Department of Fish and Wildlife,** Salem, 97303, (503) 947-6000 or (800) 720-6339, www.dfw.state.or.us
- **United States Coast Guard, Emergencies:** Dial 911 or call the Coast Guard on Marine Channel 16, www.uscg.mil/d13/msuportland
- **Tide Chart,** www.or.usharbors.com/monthly-tides
- **Tillamook Area Chamber of Commerce,** Tillamook, 97141, (503) 842-7525, www.tillamookchamber.org

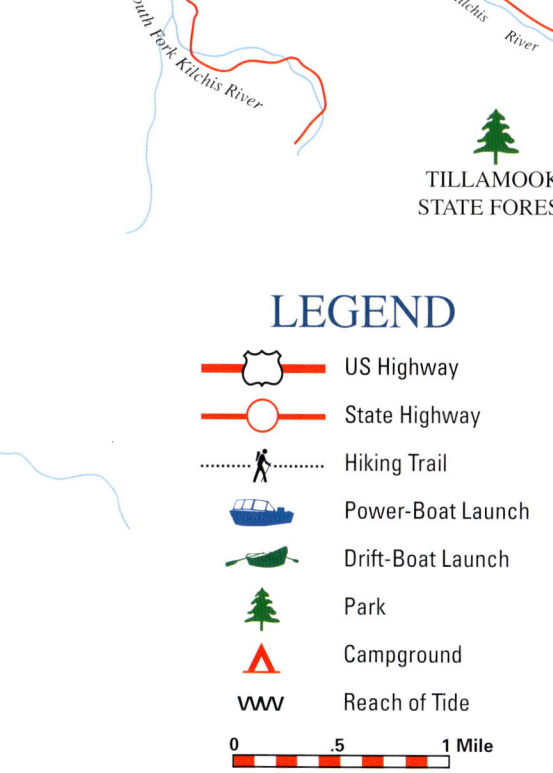

Oregon River Maps & Fishing Guide

Wilson River

The Wilson River is the largest and most accessible of the five rivers feeding Tillamook Bay. Consequently, it receives the most fish, and fishermen, of any Tillamook-area river. It has strong runs of winter and summer steelhead, as well as spring, fall and winter Chinook salmon. The Wilson is also home to lesser runs of coho and chum salmon, as well as sea-run cutthroat trout. The lowest ten miles offer good drift-boating when the river is between 2.5 and 6 feet, with five launch sites along the way (beware of the Mine Field, just below Siskeyville, when the river drops below 3.5 feet). The entire river offers good bank access, up to the fishing deadline at Rivermile 33, where the Devil's Lake Fork and the South Fork meet.

Spring Chinook and summer steelhead arrive together each spring. The first few appear in April with the last of the winter steelhead. The runs build to their peaks in early June, and ramp down through July. Every method of angling can catch these fish. Through late summer, spring Chinook turn dark and are less desirable, whereas summer steelhead continue to offer excellent sport through October.

Fall Chinook draw the most attention from anglers because of their sheer size. Wilson River kings average 25 pounds but reach over 60 pounds. They accumulate in tidewater through September and October, then move into the river to spawn with the first hard rains of autumn. Winter Chinook arrive in November and run through January (the season closes Dec. 31st). In low water, float fishing with bait, casting spinners and fly-fishing are the best techniques. In higher water, drift fishing from shore, with or without bait, is very effective. From a boat, back-bouncing bait and back-trolling plugs are the preferred methods. Coho and chum salmon maintain small, remnant runs, but must be released unharmed.

Winter steelhead enter the Wilson River from December through April. Along with the Wilson's strong wild run of winters, hatchery steelhead run throughout the season, peaking in February and March. Steelhead average eight pounds, but can reach over twenty-five. All methods of steelheading are effective, with drift fishing the most popular.

Cutthroat trout are numerous throughout the Wilson year-round. Sea-run cutts migrate in and out of the lower river, with peaks from March through May, and again from August through September. Casting lures and fly fishing with streamers are the best techniques.

LOCATION: Tillamook County

BEST FLY-FISHING TECHNIQUES

	Jan	Feb	Mar	Apr	May	Jun	Jul	Aug	Sep	Oct	Nov	Dec
Winter Steelhead	4,6,7	4,6,7	4,6,7	4,6,7							4,6,7	4,6,7
Summer Steelhead				2,3,4 5,6,7	2,3,4 5,6,7	2,3,4 5,6,7	2,3,4 5,6,7	2,3,4 5,6,7	2,3,4 5,6,7	2,3,4 5,6,7		
Fall Chinook									6,7,9	4,6 7,9	4,6 7,9	4,6 7,9
Spring Chinook				4,6 7,9	4,6 7,9	4,6 7,9	4,6 7,9					
Coho									3,4 7,8	3,4 7,8	3,4 7,8	
Cutthroat Trout			2,3 8,9	2,3 8,9	2,3 8,9	2,3 8,9	2,3 8,9	2,3 8,9	2,3 8,9	2,3 8,9		

Legend: Best / Good / Slow

1. Dry fly, dead-drift
2. Dry fly, swung
3. Wet fly, swung near surface
4. Wet fly, swung deep
5. Nymph(s), lightly weighted
6. Nymph(s), weighted with indicator
7. Deep drifted fly (with or without indicator)
8. Wet fly retrieved near surface
9. Deep swing with retrieve

WILSON RIVER

BEST GEAR-FISHING TECHNIQUES & ESTIMATED HOOKUPS IN AN AVERAGE YEAR

	Jan	Feb	Mar	Apr	May	Jun	Jul	Aug	Sep	Oct	Nov	Dec
Winter Steelhead 2500	1,2 3,4	1,2 3,4	1,2 3,4	1,2 3,4							1,2 3,4	1,2 3,4
Summer Steelhead 500			1,2 3,4	1,2 3,4	1,2 3,4	1,2 3,4	1,2 3,4	1,2 3,4	1,2 3,4	1,2 3,4		
Fall Chinook tide water 1500									2,3,6	2,3,6	2,3,6	
Fall Chinook river 1500										1,2,3 4,5,6	1,2,3 4,5,6	1,2,3 4,5,6
Spring Chinook 200				1,2,3 4,5	1,2,3 4,5	1,2,3 4,5	1,2,3 4,5					
Coho 150										1,2,3 4,5	1,2,3 4,5	
Cutthroat Trout			2	2	2	2	2	2	2	2		

Legend: Best (red), Good (green), Slow (yellow)

1. Drift fishing (from bank or boat, with or without bait)
2. Casting spinners, spoons, plugs
3. Float fishing (with jigs or bait)
4. Back-trolling (plugs or diver-and-bait)
5. Back-bouncing (boat)
6. Trolling (boat only)
7. Anchor fishing
8. Plunking
9. Jigging

Wading difficulty	Moderate-Difficult
Shuttles	Yes
Boating difficulty	Moderate to easy
USGS river levels on-line	Yes
Water clarity recovery	Moderate
Best levels	3'-6'

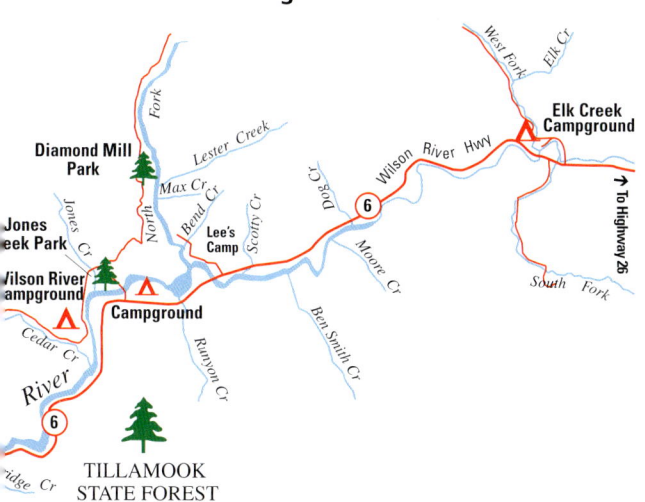

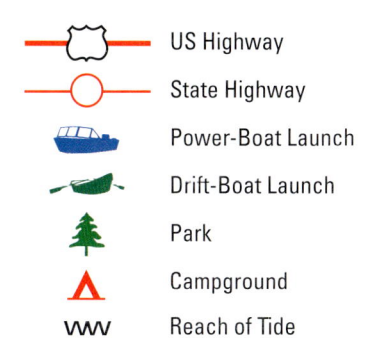

SERVICES

CAMPING/PARKS
- **Barview Jetty County Campground,** Barview, 97118, (503) 322-3522, www.co.tillamook.or.us
- **Cape Lookout State Park,** Tillamook, 97141, Info: (800) 551-6949, Park: (503) 842-4981, www.oregonstateparks.org
- **The Old Mill RV Park and Event Center (Marina),** Garibaldi, 97118, (503) 322-0322, www.oldmill.us/html/campground.html
- **Pacific Campground & Overnight Trailer Park,** Tillamook, 97141, (503) 842-5201, www.gotillamook.com
- **Wilson River RV Park,** Tillamook, 97141, (503) 842-2750, www.wilsonriver.com
- **Kilchis River County Park,** Tillamook, 97141, (503) 842-6694 or (503) 322-3522, www.wilsonriver.com
- **Keenig Creek Campground, (rustic),** Tillamook Recreation Unit, (503) 842-2545, www.oregon.gov/odf
- **Elk Creek Campground, (rustic),** Forest Grove Recreation Unit, (503) 357-2191, www.oregon.gov/odf
- **Jones Creek Campground, (rustic),** Tillamook Recreation Unit, (503) 842-2545, www.oregon.gov/odf
- **Diamond Mill State Park, (rustic),** Tillamook Recreation Unit, (503) 842-2545, www.oregon.gov/odf

ACCOMMODATIONS
- **Cape Lookout B & B,** Tillamook, 97141, (503) 807-6764, www.capelookoutbnb.com
- **Zen Garden Bed and Breakfast,** Manzanita, 97130, (503) 368-6697, www.zengardenbedandbreakfast.com
- **Wheeler on the Bay Lodge and Marina,** (800) 469-3204, (503) 368-5858, www.wheeleronthebay.com

TACKLE SHOPS
- **Tillamook Sporting Goods,** Tillamook, 97141, (503) 842-4334, www.tillamooksportinggoods.com
- **Tillamook Bait Company,** Tillamook, 97141, (503) 842-5031, www.tillamookbait.com

VISITOR INFORMATION
- **Tillamook State Forest,** Tillamook, 97141, (503) 357-2191, www.oregon.gov/odf
- **Oregon Department of Fish and Wildlife,** Salem, 97303, (503) 947-6000 or (800) 720-6339, www.dfw.state.or.us
- **United States Coast Guard, Emergencies:** Dial 911 or call the Coast Guard on Marine Channel 16, www.uscg.mil/d13/msuportland
- **Tide Chart,** www.or.usharbors.com/monthly-tides
- **Tillamook City Parks,** Tillamook, 97141, www.tillamookor.gov
- **Tillamook County Parks,** Tillamook, 97141, www.co.tillamook.or.us/gov/parks
- **Tillamook Area Chamber of Commerce,** Tillamook, 97141, (503) 842-7525, www.tillamookchamber.org

LEGEND
- US Highway
- State Highway
- Power-Boat Launch
- Drift-Boat Launch
- Park
- Campground
- Reach of Tide

OREGON RIVER MAPS & FISHING GUIDE

Trask River

Draining the wettest mountains in the state (over 200 inches of rainfall annually), the Trask flows westward over 50 miles to the town of Tillamook and Tillamook Bay. The Trask is a legendary fall Chinook river, known for producing many fish over 50 pounds. It also hosts a superb run of wild winter steelhead, small runs of spring Chinook and hatchery coho salmon, and a respectable run of sea-run cutthroat.

Chinook salmon enter the Trask River from April through June (spring-run) and from September through November (fall-run). Boaters concentrate on the lower river, from Loren's Drift to Highway 101, where there is virtually no bank access besides the quarter-mile stretch adjacent to Loren's Drift. Bank access is best from the fish hatchery up to Trask Park. Drifting bait under a float, or along the bottom is the most popular fishing method. Casting lures is also productive. Boaters have the best success back-bouncing bait and back-trolling plugs.

Winter steelhead run from November through April in the Trask. There are no hatchery steelhead planted in the river, but strays from nearby rivers occur frequently. Drift fishing is the most popular fishing method, but all methods of steelheading are productive on the Trask. Boaters can choose the upper or lower river floats. The upper drift, from Stone's Camp to Upper Peninsula (or Last Chance for more advanced boaters) is excellent in high water, and the lower drift, from Loren's Drift to Highway 101 is best in low water.

Coho are primarily hatchery-raised on the Trask, and run from late September through November. Few anglers target these fish because of their tendency not to bite. Casting spinners and spoons, or stripping flashy streamer flies are the best fishing methods. Only fin-clipped coho can be taken.

Cutthroat trout, both resident and sea-run, inhabit every reach of the Trask throughout the year. In the spring and again in late summer, fly-fishing for these aggressive trout can be very good. Bait fishing is allowed, but discouraged.

LOCATION: Tillamook County

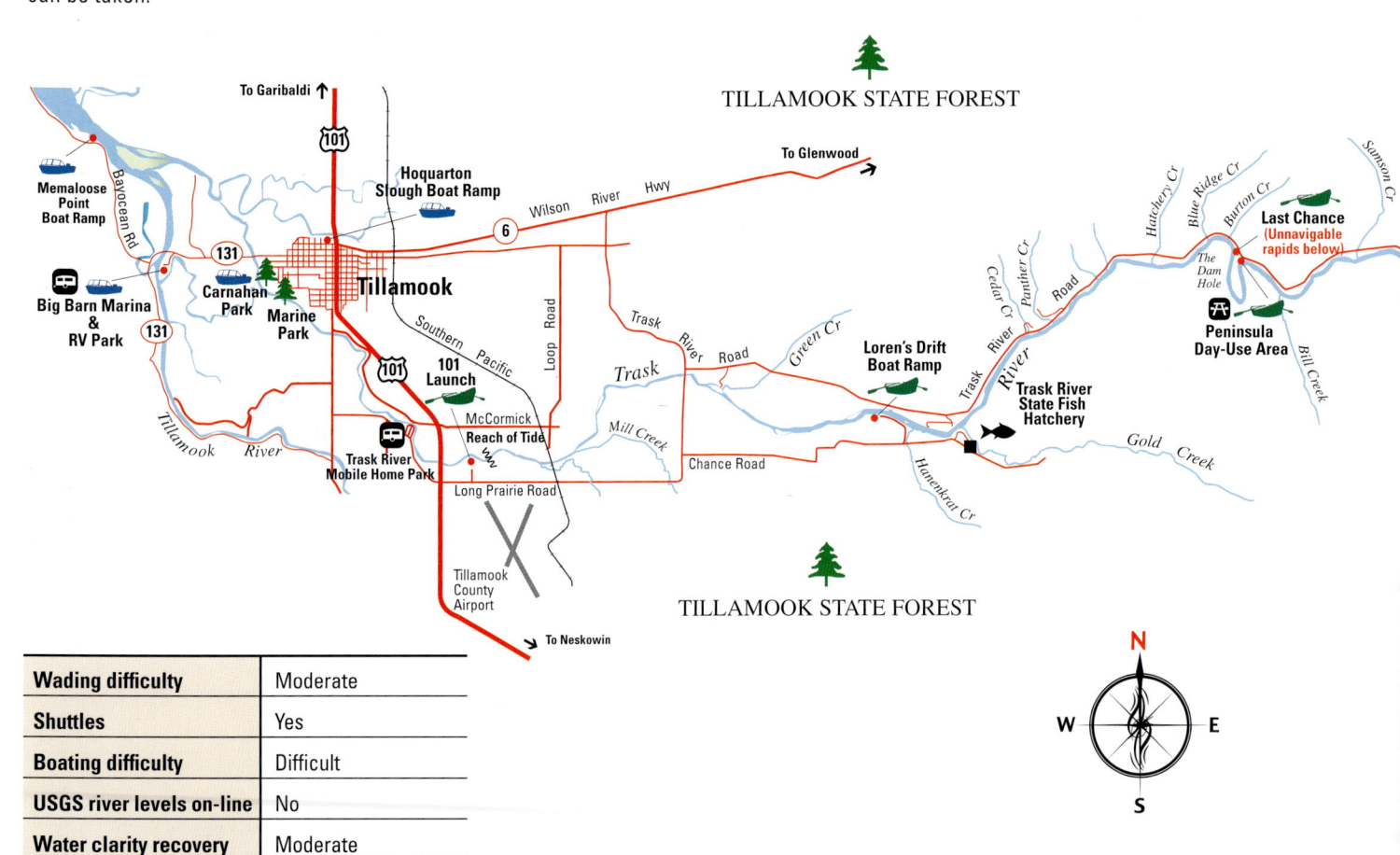

LEGEND

- US Highway
- State Highway
- Railroad
- Power-Boat Launch
- Drift-Boat Launch
- Park
- Campground
- Fish Hatchery
- Reach of Tide

0   .5   1 Mile

Wading difficulty	Moderate
Shuttles	Yes
Boating difficulty	Difficult
USGS river levels on-line	No
Water clarity recovery	Moderate

24

Trask River

BEST GEAR-FISHING TECHNIQUES & ESTIMATED HOOKUPS IN AN AVERAGE YEAR

	Jan	Feb	Mar	Apr	May	Jun	Jul	Aug	Sep	Oct	Nov	Dec
Winter Steelhead 1000	1,2 3,4	1,2 3,4	1,2 3,4	1,2 3,4							1,2,3,4	1,2 3,4
Summer Steelhead 200					1,2 3,4	1,2 3,4	1,2 3,4	1,2 3,4	1,2 3,4	1,2 3,4		
Fall Chinook (Tidewater) 3000									2,3,6	1,2,3 4,5,6	1,2,3 4,5,6	1,2,3 4,5,6
Fall Chinook (River) 2000										1,2,3 4,5,6	1,2,3 4,5,6	1,2,3 4,5,6
Spring Chinook 1000				1,2,3 4,5,6	1,2,3 4,5	1,2,3 4,5	1,2,3 4,5					
Coho 1000									1,2,3 4,5,6	1,2,3 4,5,6	1,2,3 4,5,6	1,2,3 4,5,6
Sea-Run Cutthroat		2,6	2,6	2,6	2,6		2,6	2,6	2,6	2,6		

Legend: Best / Good / Slow

1. Drift fishing (from bank or boat, with or without bait)
2. Casting spinners, spoons, plugs
3. Float fishing (with jigs or bait)
4. Back-trolling (plugs or diver-and-bait)
5. Back-bouncing (boat)
6. Trolling (boat only)
7. Anchor fishing
8. Plunking
9. Jigging

BEST FLY-FISHING TECHNIQUES

	Jan	Feb	Mar	Apr	May	Jun	Jul	Aug	Sep	Oct	Nov	Dec
Winter Steelhead	4,6,7	4,6,7	4,6,7	4,6,7							4,6,7	4,6,7
Summer Steelhead					2,3,4 5,6,7	2,3,4 5,6,7	2,3,4 5,6,7	2,3,4 5,6,7	2,3,4 5,6,7	2,3,4 5,6,7		
Fall Chinook									6,7,9	4,6 7,9	4,6 7,9	
Spring Chinook				4,6,7,9	4,6 7,9	4,6 7,9	4,6 7,9					
Coho									3,4,7,8	3,4 7,8	3,4 7,8	3,4 7,8
Sea-Run Cutthroat		2,6 8,9	2,6 8,9	2,6 8,9	2,6 8,9		2,6 8,9	2,6 8,9	2,6 8,9	2,6 8,9		

1. Dry fly, dead-drift
2. Dry fly, swung
3. Wet fly, swung near surface
4. Wet fly, swung deep
5. Nymph(s), lightly weighted
6. Nymph(s), weighted with indicator
7. Deep drifted fly (with or without indicator)
8. Wet fly retrieved near surface
9. Deep swing with retrieve

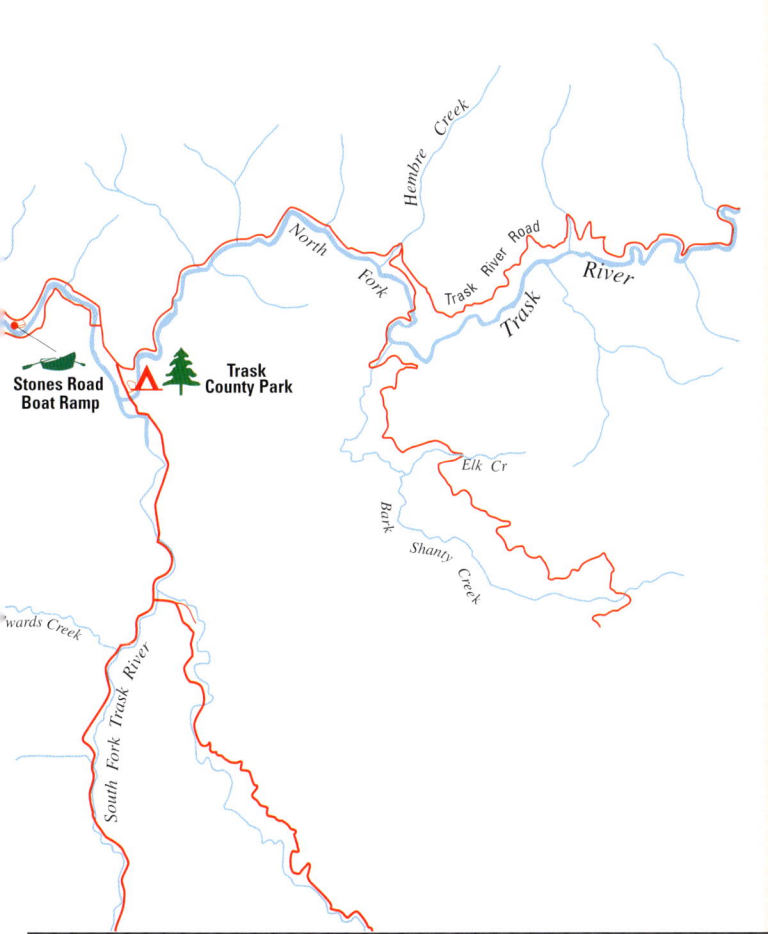

SERVICES

CAMPING/PARKS

- **Trask Park County Campground,** Tillamook, 97141, (503) 842-4559, www.co.tillamook.or.us/gov
- **Barview Jetty County Campground,** Barview, 97118, (503) 322-3522, www.co.tillamook.or.us
- **Cape Lookout State Park,** Tillamook, 97141, **Info:** (800) 551-6949, **Park:** (503) 842-4981, www.oregonstateparks.org
- **The Old Mill RV Park and Event Center (Marina),** Garibaldi, 97118, (503) 322-0322, www.oldmill.us
- **Pacific Campground & Overnight Trailer Park,** Tillamook, 97141, (503) 842-5201, www.gotillamook.com
- **Carnahan Park (boat launch),** Tillamook, 97141, www.tillamookor.gov

ACCOMMODATIONS

- **Cape Lookout B & B,** Tillamook, 97141, (503) 807-6764, www.capelookoutbnb.com
- **Zen Garden B&B,** Manzanita, 97130, (503) 368-6697, www.zengardenbedandbreakfast.com
- **Wheeler on the Bay Lodge and Marina,** (800) 469-3204, (503) 368-5858, www.wheeleronthebay.com

TACKLE SHOPS

- **Tillamook Sporting Goods,** Tillamook, 97141, (503) 842-4334, www.tillamooksportinggoods.com
- **Tillamook Bait Company,** Tillamook, 97141, (503) 842-5031, www.tillamookbait.com

VISITOR INFORMATION

- **Tillamook State Forest,** Tillamook, 97141, (503) 357-2191, www.oregon.gov/odf
- **Tillamook City Parks,** Tillamook, 97141, www.tillamookor.gov
- **Tillamook Area Chamber of Commerce,** Tillamook, 97141, (503) 842-7525, www.tillamookchamber.org

OREGON RIVER MAPS & FISHING GUIDE

Nestucca River

The Nestucca is one of the most productive salmon and steelhead rivers in Oregon, boasting strong runs of fall and spring Chinook, summer and winter steelhead, and sea-run cutthroat trout. Flowing from deep in the coastal rainforest, the Nestucca River meanders 60 miles to Nestucca Bay and the idyllic community of Pacific City.

Kiwanda Beach, on the ocean-side of Nestucca Bay's North Spit, is the landing for the historic Pacific City dory fleet. This small but famous group of commercial and sportfishing boats works the near-shore waters during the summer months for salmon, rockfish, lingcod and various other species of ocean fish.

Nestucca Bay and tidewater is heavily fished in May and June for spring Chinook, and again from August through October for fall Chinook. Trolling herring, spinners and plugs is a popular tactic throughout the estuary. Float fishing with roe and sand shrimp is also productive. Fishing from a boat is desirable, but the boat launches along Nestucca Bay offer excellent access for bank anglers. From the bank, casting spinners is the traditional fishing method.

In the river, Chinook salmon are present from May through July (spring-run) and again from September through December (fall- & winter-run).

Drift boats can safely navigate from 4th bridge to Cloverdale, with five boat landings in between. Back-trolling plugs, back-bouncing bait, drift fishing and casting lures are the most successful techniques. Boat launches offer the best bank access, where drift fishing, casting lures, and float fishing with bait are best.

Steelhead are present year-round in the Nestucca, but there are periods in the year that offer the best success. Winter steelhead run from November through April, with peak times in December and January, and again in February and March. Summer steelhead run from April through October, with peak times in May and June, and again in October. All methods of steelhead fishing can be successful. Boating is best from October through May. Low water makes boating difficult in summer months.

Resident and sea-run cutthroat trout are present throughout the Nestucca most of the year. Fly-fishing with small to medium-sized streamers is the best fishing method, but bait-fishing is still popular. Best times for cutthroat are spring (April-May) and late summer (August-October).

LOCATION: Tillamook, Yamhill Counties

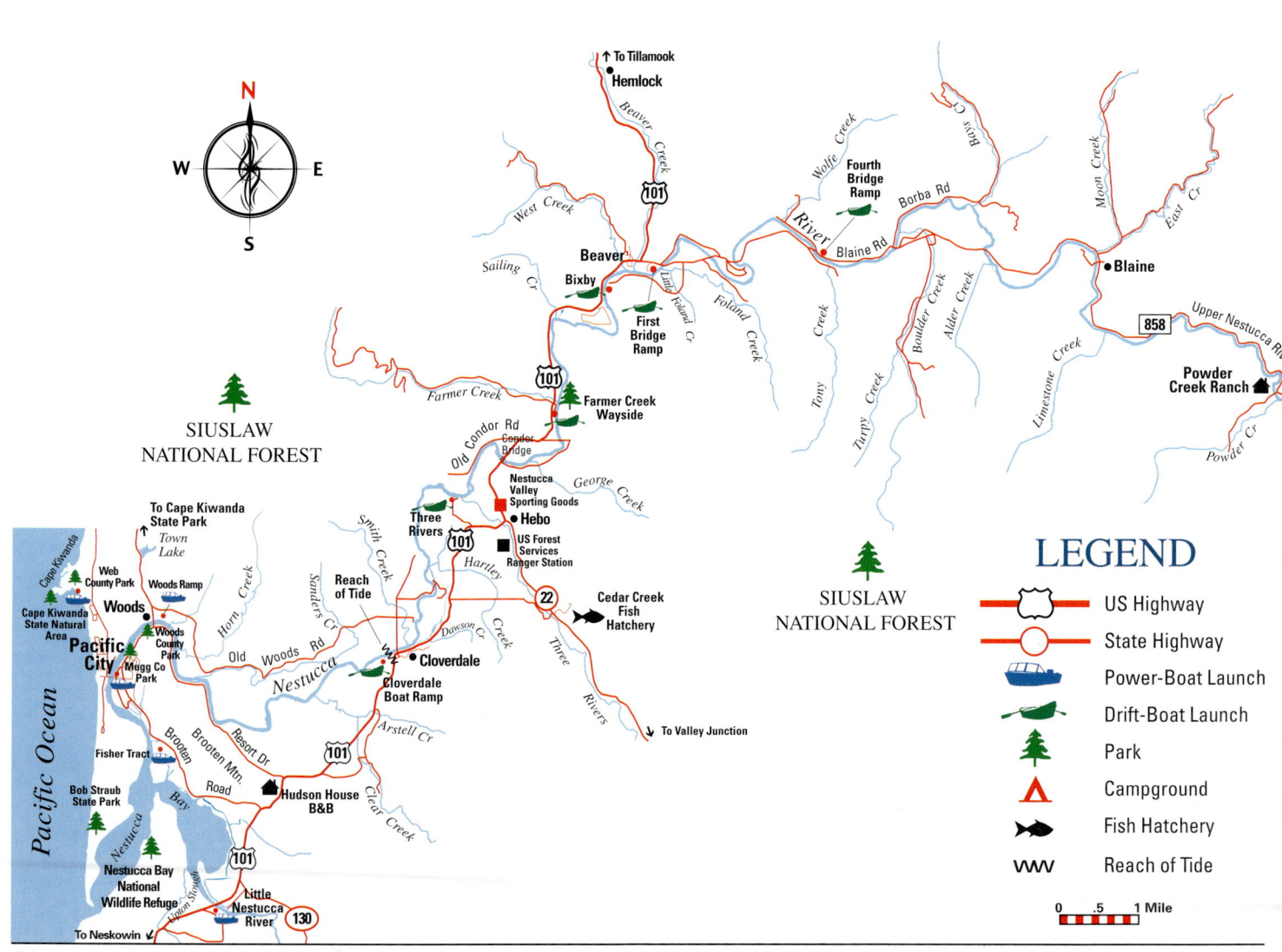

LEGEND

- US Highway
- State Highway
- Power-Boat Launch
- Drift-Boat Launch
- Park
- Campground
- Fish Hatchery
- Reach of Tide

0 .5 1 Mile

NESTUCCA RIVER

BEST GEAR-FISHING TECHNIQUES & ESTIMATED HOOKUPS IN AN AVERAGE YEAR

	Jan	Feb	Mar	Apr	May	Jun	Jul	Aug	Sep	Oct	Nov	Dec
Winter Steelhead 2000	1,2 3,4	1,2 3,4	1,2 3,4	1,2 3,4							1,2,3,4	1,2 3,4
Summer Steelhead 1500					1,2,3,4 1,2,3,4	1,2 3,4	1,2 3,4	1,2 3,4	1,2 3,4	1,2 3,4	1,2 3,4	
Fall Chinook (Tidewater) 3000								2,3,6	2,3,6	1,2,3 4,5,6	1,2,3 4,5,6	
Fall Chinook (River) 1000									1,2,3 4,5	1,2,3 4,5	1,2,3 4,5	1,2,3 4,5
Spring Chinook 1000				1,2,3 4,5	1,2,3 4,5	1,2,3 4,5	1,2,3 4,5					
Coho 500									1,2,3 4,5	1,2,3 4,5	1,2,3 4,5,6	1,2,3 4,5,6
Sea-Run Cutthroat				2,6	2,6	2,6	2,6	2,6	2,6	2,6		
Perch			1	1	1							
Crabs												

1. Drift fishing (from bank or boat, with or without bait)
2. Casting spinners, spoons, plugs
3. Float fishing (with jigs or bait)
4. Back-trolling (plugs or diver-and-bait)
5. Back-bouncing (boat)
6. Trolling (boat only)
7. Anchor fishing
8. Plunking
9. Jigging

Wading difficulty	Moderate
Shuttles	Yes
Boating difficulty	Difficult
USGS river levels on-line	No
Water clarity recovery	Moderate

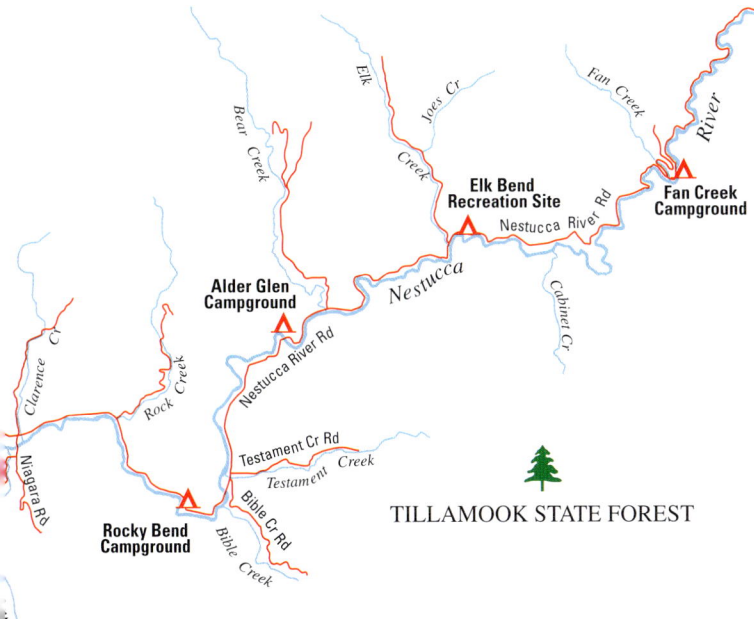

SERVICES

CAMPING/PARKS
- **Woods County Campground/Park,** Pacific City, 97135, (503) 965-5001, www.co.tillamook.or.us
- **Alder Glen Campground (BLM), Elk Bend Campground (BLM), Fan Creek Campground (BLM),** Salem, 97306, (503) 375-5646, www.blm.gov/or
- **Rocky Bend Campground,** Beaver, 97108, www.oregoncoasttravel.net

ACCOMMODATIONS
- **The Craftsman B&B,** Pacific City, 97135, (503) 965-4574, www.craftsmanbb.com
- **Hudson House B&B,** Cloverdale, 97112, (503) 392-3533, www.hudsonhouse.com
- **Powder Creek Ranch,** Beaver, 97108, (503) 398-5348, www.powdercreekranch.com

TACKLE SHOPS
- **Nestucca Valley Sporting Goods,** Hebo, 97122, (503) 392-4269, www.nestuccariveroutfitters.com

VISITOR INFORMATION
- **Siuslaw National Forest,** Tidewater, 97390, (541) 750-7000, www.fs.usda.gov/siuslaw
- **Newport Internet's: A Guide to Oregon's Central Coast,** www.newportnet.com
- **Boat Escape: Oregon's Boating Resource,** www.boatescape.com
- **Pacific City Oregon Visitor's Guide,** www.pacificcity.org/fishing
- **Tillamook Area Chamber of Commerce,** Tillamook, 97141, (503) 842-7525, www.tillamookchamber.org

BEST FLY-FISHING TECHNIQUES

	Jan	Feb	Mar	Apr	May	Jun	Jul	Aug	Sep	Oct	Nov	Dec
Winter Steelhead	4,6 7,9	4,6 7,9	4,6 7,9	4,6 7,9							4,6,7,9	4,6 7,9
Summer Steelhead					2,3,4 5,6,7	2,3,4 5,6,7	2,3,4 5,6,7	2,3,4 5,6,7	2,3,4 5,6,7	2,3,4 5,6,7	2,3,4 5,6,7	
Fall Chinook								6,7,9	6,7,9	4,6 7,9	4,6 7,9	
Spring Chinook				4,6 7,9	4,6 7,9	4,6 7,9	4,6 7,9					
Coho									3,4 7,8	3,4 7,8	3,4 7,8	3,4 7,8
Sea-Run Cutthroat					2,6 8,9	2,6 8,9	2,6 8,9	2,6 8,9	2,6 8,9	2,6 8,9		
Perch			9	9	9							

1. Dry fly, dead-drift
2. Dry fly, swung
3. Wet fly, swung near surface
4. Wet fly, swung deep
5. Nymph(s), lightly weighted
6. Nymph(s), weighted with indicator
7. Deep drifted fly (with or without indicator)
8. Wet fly retrieved near surface
9. Deep swing with retrieve

OREGON RIVER MAPS & FISHING GUIDE

Siletz River

One of Oregon's largest, most productive salmon and steelhead rivers, the Siletz is famous for its long estuary, stretching over 17 miles from the bay to reach-of-tide. The waters of the Siletz originate in the heart of Oregon's coastal rainforest, draining over 700 square miles, and flowing almost 80 miles to the ocean. The Siletz also boasts the only native run of summer steelhead on Oregon's north coast.

Chinook salmon are the dominant fish in the Siletz. Before the first heavy rains of fall, anglers pursue these fish in the lower 10 miles of tidewater, especially from Kernville up to Echo Creek. Trolling herring, spinners, wobblers and plugs is the traditional way to catch tidewater kings.

Winter steelhead fishing on the Siletz is superb. The run begins in December, but is strongest from January through April. Drift fishing with roe is the most popular fishing method here, but all steelheading methods are effective. Boating is the best way to access the river below Moonshine Park, but there is good bank access above and below.

BEST GEAR-FISHING TECHNIQUES & ESTIMATED HOOKUPS IN AN AVERAGE YEAR

Best / Good / Slow	Jan	Feb	Mar	Apr	May	Jun	Jul	Aug	Sep	Oct	Nov	Dec
Winter Steelhead 3000	1,2 3,4	1,2 3,4	1,2 3,4	1,2 3,4							1,2 3,4	1,2 3,4
Summer Steelhead 2000				1,2 3,4	1,2 3,4	1,2 3,4	1,2 3,4	1,2 3,4	1,2 3,4	1,2 3,4		
Fall Chinook 2500									2,3,6	2,3,6	1,2,3 4,5,6	1,2,3 4,5,6
Summer Chinook 300							2,3,6	2,3,6	2,3,6	1,2,3 4,5,6		
Coho 400									1,2,3 4,5,6	1,2,3 4,5,6	1,2,3 4,5,6	1,2,3 4,5,6
Sea-Run Cutthroat			2,6	2,6	2,6	2,6	2,6	2,6	2,6	2,6		

1. Drift fishing (from bank or boat, with or without bait)
2. Casting spinners, spoons, plugs
3. Float fishing (with jigs or bait)
4. Back-trolling (plugs or diver-and-bait)
5. Back-bouncing (boat)
6. Trolling (boat only)
7. Anchor fishing
8. Plunking
9. Jigging

BEST FLY-FISHING TECHNIQUES

Best / Good / Slow	Jan	Feb	Mar	Apr	May	Jun	Jul	Aug	Sep	Oct	Nov	Dec
Winter Steelhead	4,6,7	4,6,7	4,6,7	4,6,7 4,6,7							4,6,7	4,6,7 4,6,7
Summer Steelhead				2,3,4 5,6,7	2,3,4 5,6,7	2,3,4 5,6,7	2,3,4 5,6,7	2,3,4 5,6,7	2,3,4 5,6,7	2,3,4 5,6,7		
Fall Chinook								6,7,9	6,7,9	4,6 7,9	4,6 7,9	4,6 7,9
Coho									3,4 7,8	3,4 7,8	3,4 7,8	3,4 7,8
Sea-Run Cutthroat				2,6 8,9	2,6 8,9	2,6 8,9	2,6 8,9	2,6 8,9	2,6 8,9	2,6 8,9		

1. Dry fly, dead-drift
2. Dry fly, swung
3. Wet fly, swung near surface
4. Wet fly, swung deep
5. Nymph(s), lightly weighted
6. Nymph(s), weighted with indicator
7. Deep drifted fly (with or without indicator)
8. Wet fly retrieved near surface
9. Deep swing with retrieve

SERVICES

CAMPING/PARKS
- **Jack Morgan County Park & Campground,** Siletz River, 97380, (541) 574-1215, www.co.lincoln.or.us
- **Moonshine County Park,** Siletz River, 97380, (541) 444-1326, www.co.lincoln.or.us
- **Coyote Rock RV Resort & Marina,** Lincoln City, 97367, (541) 996-6824,
- **Siletz Moorage,** Lincoln City, 97367, (541) 996-3671, www.siletzmoorage.com
- **Chinook Bend RV Resort,** Lincoln City, 97367, (541) 996-2032, www.chinookbend.com
- **Sportsman's Landing RV Park,** Lincoln City, 97367, (541) 996-4225, www.newportnet.com

ACCOMMODATIONS
- **Brey House Ocean View B&B,** Lincoln City, 97367, (541) 994-7123, (877) 994-7123, www.breyhouse.com
- **Baywood Shores B&B,** Lincoln City, 97367, (800) 327-0486, (541) 996-6700, www.baywoodshores.com

TACKLE SHOPS
- **Knight's Tackle Box,** Otis, 97368, (541) 994-8137
- **Sunset Landing RV Park,** Lincoln City, 97367, (541) 994-8880

VISITOR INFORMATION
- **Siuslaw National Forest,** Tidewater, 97390, (541) 750-7000, www.fs.usda.gov/siuslaw
- **Lincoln County Parks,** Newport, 97365, (541) 574-1215, www.co.lincoln.or.us
- **A Guide to Oregon's Central Coast,** www.newportnet.com
- **Oregon's Boating Resource,** www.boatescape.com
- **Lincoln City Chamber of Commerce,** Lincoln City, 97367, (541) 994-3070, www.lcchamber.com

LOCATION: Lincoln County

Wading difficulty	Moderate
Shuttles	Yes
Boating difficulty	Moderate
USGS river levels on-line	Yes
Water clarity recovery	Moderate

Siletz River

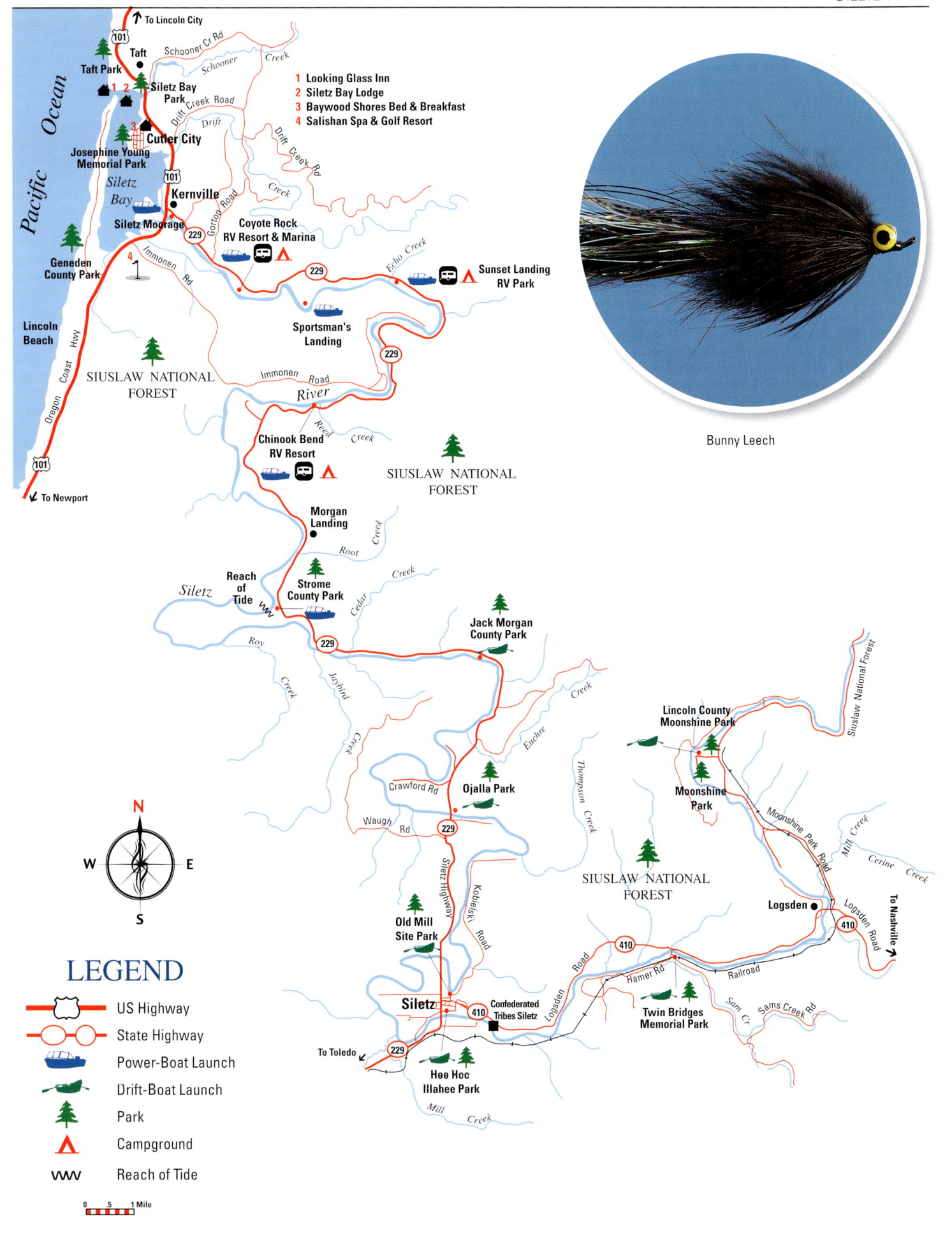

1. Looking Glass Inn
2. Siletz Bay Lodge
3. Baywood Shores Bed & Breakfast
4. Salishan Spa & Golf Resort

Bunny Leech

LEGEND
- US Highway
- State Highway
- Power-Boat Launch
- Drift-Boat Launch
- Park
- Campground
- Reach of Tide

0 .5 1 Mile

29

Oregon River Maps & Fishing Guide

Yaquina Bay

Yaquina Bay flows through the town of Newport. Its source is the Yaquina River, home to a modest run of salmon and steelhead, and a good number of cutthroat trout. The bay's popularity is due mainly to the access it provides to excellent saltwater fisheries including halibut, rockfish, lingcod and salmon. Crabbing can also be good year-round from the jetties up to the public dock at Southbeach.

Chinook and coho salmon enter the bay in September and October, then move into the Yaquina River in October November. Most salmon anglers troll spinners, herring, or spinner/bait combinations in the bay and tidewater. Float fishing with bait is also popular in tidewater before the fall rains arrive. After the first rains of autumn, anglers follow Chinook salmon into the river, drift fishing with bait or casting lures. Coho must be released unharmed.

Winter steelhead are present from December through March, and are found in the Yaquina River and its major tributaries, Big and Little Elk creeks. Hatchery steelhead run early in the Yaquina system, peaking in December and January. A small wild run peaks in February and March.

LOCATION: Lincoln County

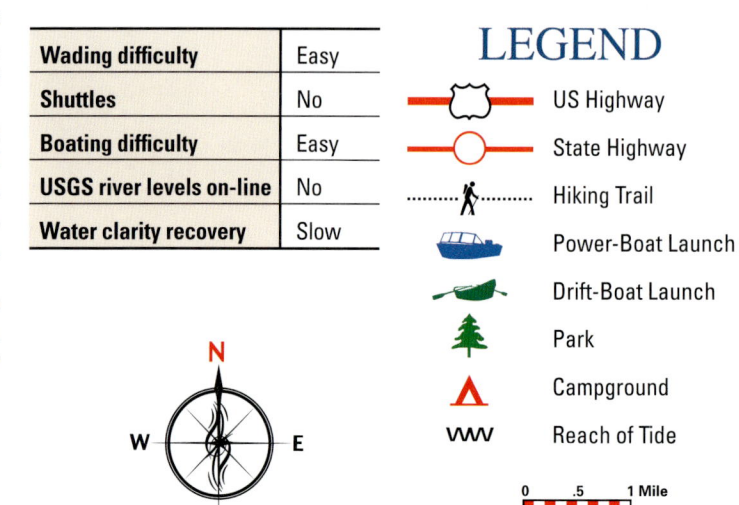

Wading difficulty	Easy
Shuttles	No
Boating difficulty	Easy
USGS river levels on-line	No
Water clarity recovery	Slow

LEGEND

- US Highway
- State Highway
- Hiking Trail
- Power-Boat Launch
- Drift-Boat Launch
- Park
- Campground
- Reach of Tide

1. Port of Newport, RV Park
2. Embarcadero Resort Hotel & Marina
3. Charter Fishing Newport Oregon
4. Troyer's Marine Supply
5. Hatfield Marine Science Center OSU
6. Captains Reel Deep Sea Fishing

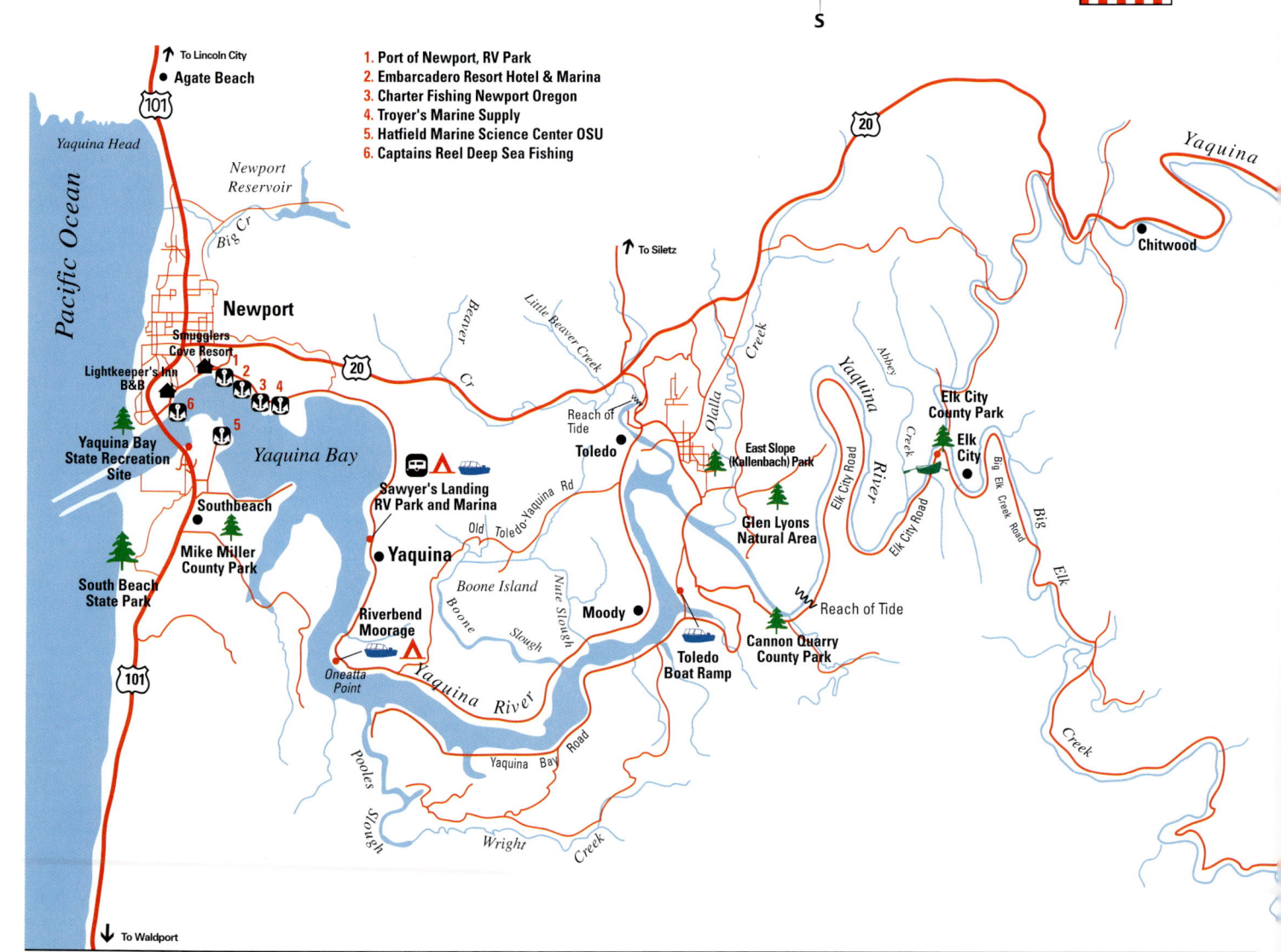

YAQUINA BAY

BEST GEAR-FISHING TECHNIQUES & ESTIMATED HOOKUPS IN AN AVERAGE YEAR

	Jan	Feb	Mar	Apr	May	Jun	Jul	Aug	Sep	Oct	Nov	Dec
Winter Steelhead 400	1,2 3,4	1,2 3,4	1,2 3,4	1,2 3,4							1,2 3,4	1,2 3,4
Spring Chinook 100			1,2,3 4,5,6	1,2,3 4,5,6	1,2,3 4,5,6	1,2,3 4,5,6						
Fall Chinook 2000									2,3,6	1,2,3 4,5,6	1,2,3 4,5,6	1,2,3 4,5,6
Ocean Salmon 5000					6	6	6	6	6	6		
Coho 2000									2,6	1,2 4,6	1,2 4,6	
Halibut			8	8	8	8	8					
Lingcod		9	9	9	9	9	9					
Sturgeon		8	8	8	8	8	8	8				
Crabs												
Sea-Run Cutthroat			2,6	2,6	2,6	2,6	2,6	2,6	2,6	2,6 2,6	2,6	

Legend: Best / Good / Slow

1. Drift fishing (from bank or boat, with or without bait)
2. Casting spinners, spoons, plugs
3. Float fishing (with jigs or bait)
4. Back-trolling (plugs or diver-and-bait)
5. Back-bouncing (boat)
6. Trolling (boat only)
7. Anchor fishing
8. Plunking
9. Jigging

BEST FLY-FISHING TECHNIQUES

	Jan	Feb	Mar	Apr	May	Jun	Jul	Aug	Sep	Oct	Nov	Dec
Winter Steelhead	4,6,7	4,6,7	4,6,7	4,6,7							4,6,7	4,6,7
Spring Chinook			4,6 7,8	4,6 7,8	4,6 7,8	4,6 7,8						
Fall Chinook									4,6 7,8	4,6 7,8	4,6 7,8	4,6 7,8
Coho									3,4,7 8,9	3,4,7 8,9	3,4,7 8,9	
Sea-Run Cutthroat			1,2,3 4,8,9	1,2,3 4,8,9	1,2,3 4,8,9	1,2,3 4,8,9	1,2,3 4,8,9	1,2,3 4,8,9	1,2,3 4,8,9	1,2,3 4,8,9	1,2,3 4,8,9	

1. Dry fly, dead-drift
2. Dry fly, swung
3. Wet fly, swung near surface
4. Wet fly, swung deep
5. Nymph(s), lightly weighted
6. Nymph(s), weighted with indicator
7. Deep drifted fly (with or without indicator)
8. Wet fly retrieved near surface
9. Deep swing with retrieve

SERVICES

CAMPING/PARKS
- **Sawyer's Landing RV Park & Marina,** Newport, 97365, (541) 265-3907,
- **Harbor Village RV Park,** Newport, 97365, (541) 265-5088, www.harborvillagervpark.com
- **River Bend Moorage,** Newport, 97365, (541) 265-9243
- **Sawyer's Landing,** Newport, 97365, (541) 265-3907, www.newportchamber.org
- **Captains Reel Deep Sea Fishing,** Newport, 97365, (541) 265-7441, www.captainsreel.com
- **Port of Newport RV Parks,** Newport 97365, (541) 867-3321, www.portofnewport.com

ACCOMMODATIONS
- **Ocean House B&B,** Newport, 97365, (866) 495-3888 or (541) 265-3888, www.oceanhouse.com
- **Embarcadero Resort Hotel & Marina,** Newport, 97365, (541) 265-8521, www.embarcadero-resort.com
- **The Lightkeeper's Inn,** Newport, 97365, (541) 265-5642, www.thelightkeepersinnbb.com

TACKLE SHOPS
- **Harry's Bait & Tackle,** Newport, 97365, (541) 265-2407
- **Troyer's Marine Supply,** Newport, (541) 265-6653
- **Englund Marine,** Newport, 97365, (541) 265-9275, www.englundmarine.com

VISITOR INFORMATION
- **Siuslaw National Forest,** Tidewater, 97390, (541) 750-7000, www.fs.usda.gov/siuslaw
- **Lincoln County Parks,** Newport, 97365, (541) 574-1215, www.co.lincoln.or.us
- **A Guide to Oregon's Central Coast,** www.newportnet.com
- **Oregon's Boating Resource,** www.boatescape.com
- **Newport Chamber of Commerce,** Newport, 97365, (541) 265-8801, (800) 262-7844, www.newportchamber.org

OREGON RIVER MAPS & FISHING GUIDE

Alsea River

Meeting the Pacific Ocean at the picturesque town of Waldport, the Alsea is an important mid-sized salmon and steelhead river. It hosts superb runs of fall Chinook and winter steelhead, as well as respectable runs of coho and sea-run cutthroat. Alsea Bay also offers excellent dungeness crabbing most of the year.

From the reach-of-tide at the town of Tidewater to the bay at Waldport, anglers target early-season fall Chinook from August through October. Trolling spinners, herring or plugs in this reach is effective. In recent years, float fishing with bait (cured salmon roe and sand shrimp) has eclipsed all other methods for catching these tidewater kings. Coho are numerous in the tidal stretch in September and October. Hatchery coho are no longer released in the Alsea, and targeting the remaining native coho is prohibited.

Once the first heavy rains of autumn bring the river level up, anglers shift their focus to the main river, from the town of Alsea to Tidewater. Drift boats are the best way to access the main river, but there is fair bank access at the parks and boat launches along the way. Back-trolling plugs, back-bouncing bait, drift fishing and casting lures are most popular methods for salmon.

Winter steelhead run strong in the Alsea. Hatchery steelhead are released in the North Fork Alsea and Fall Creek, providing a good early run from late November through January. Native steelhead start to arrive in January and build through February and March. Drift fishing with simple rigs (like a single pink or red "corkie") is generally most effective, however, when the water is low and clear, float-and-jig fishing is best.

Sea-run cutthroat, once a renowned fishery on the Alsea, are coming back from a decade-long slump. From April through May, cutthroat are spread throughout the river and are caught on lures of every variety. Fly fishing with streamers is also very effective. In late summer and fall (July through September), trolling small flatfish in upper tidewater, or fly-casting streamers in the lowest reaches of the river, can yield the largest trout of the season.

LOCATION: Lincoln County

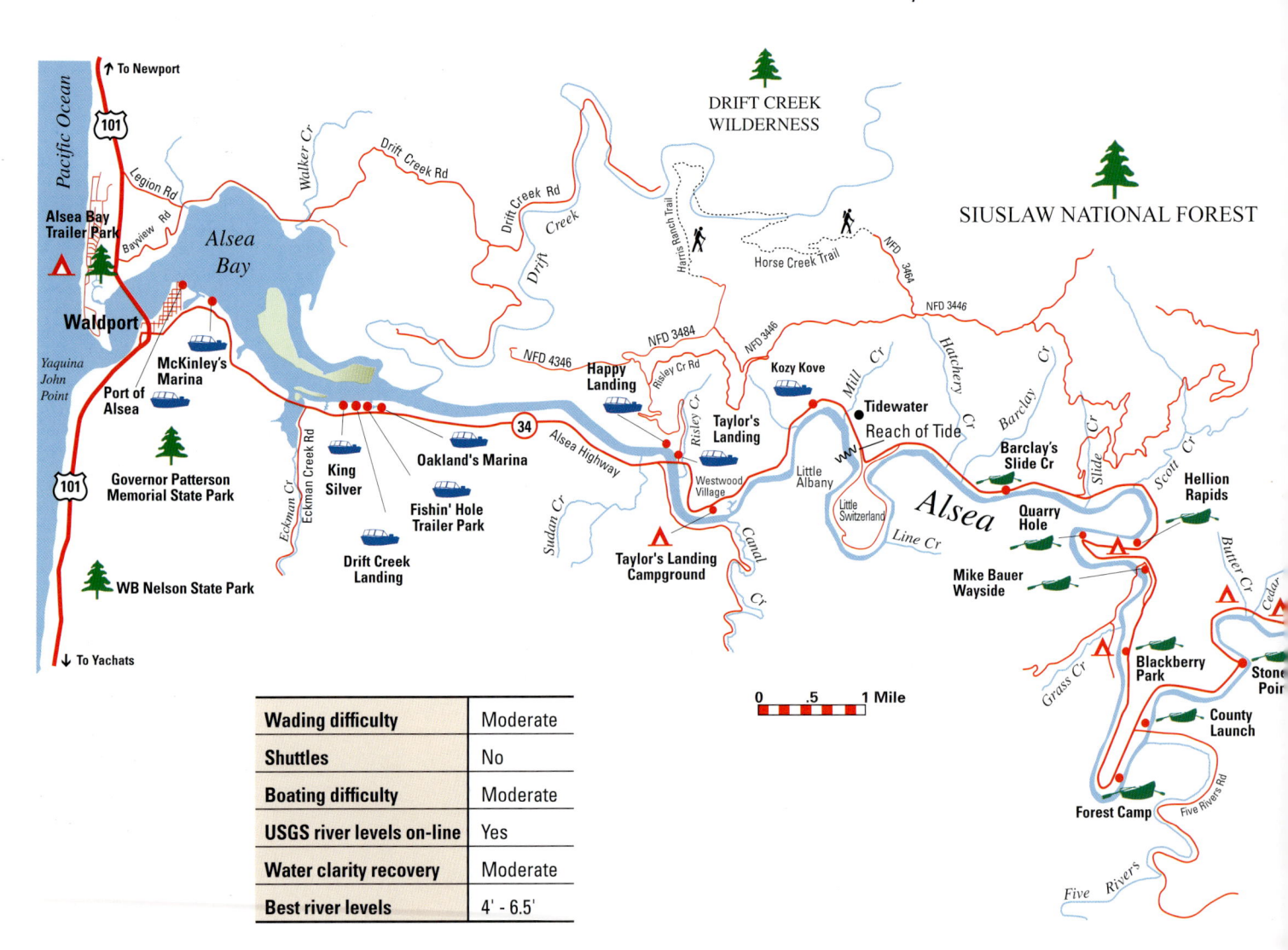

Wading difficulty	Moderate
Shuttles	No
Boating difficulty	Moderate
USGS river levels on-line	Yes
Water clarity recovery	Moderate
Best river levels	4' - 6.5'

ALSEA RIVER

BEST GEAR-FISHING TECHNIQUES & ESTIMATED HOOKUPS IN AN AVERAGE YEAR

Best / Good / Slow	Jan	Feb	Mar	Apr	May	Jun	Jul	Aug	Sep	Oct	Nov	Dec
Winter Steelhead 2000	1,2 3,4	1,2 3,4	1,2 3,4								1,2 3,4	1,2 3,4
Summer Steelhead 100					1,2 3,4	1,2 3,4	1,2 3,4	1,2 3,4	1,2 3,4	1,2 3,4	1,2 3,4	
Spring Chinook 50				1,2,3 4,5	1,2,3 4,5	1,2,3 4,5						
Fall Chinook (tidewater) 2000								2,3,6	2,3,6	2,3,6	2,3,6	
Fall Chinook (river) 2000									1,2,3 4,5	1,2,3 4,5	1,2,3 4,5	1,2,3 4,5
Coho 1000									1,2,3 4,5	1,2,3 4,5	1,2,3 4,5	
Sea-Run Cutthroat				2	2	2		2	2	2		

1. Drift fishing (from bank or boat, with or without bait)
2. Casting spinners, spoons, plugs
3. Float fishing (with jigs or bait)
4. Back-trolling (plugs or diver-and-bait)
5. Back-bouncing (boat)
6. Trolling (boat only)
7. Anchor fishing
8. Plunking
9. Jigging

BEST FLY-FISHING TECHNIQUES

Best / Good / Slow	Jan	Feb	Mar	Apr	May	Jun	Jul	Aug	Sep	Oct	Nov	Dec
Winter Steelhead	4,6,7	4,6,7	4,6,7								4,6,7	4,6,7
Summer Steelhead					2,3,4 5,6,7	2,3,4 5,6,7	2,3,4 5,6,7	2,3,4 5,6,7	2,3,4 5,6,7	2,3,4 5,6,7	2,3,4 5,6,7	
Spring Chinook				4,7,8	4,7,8	4,7,8						
Fall Chinook								6,7,9	4,6 7,9	4,6 7,9	4,6,7,9	
Sea-Run Cutthroat				2,6 8,9	2,6 8,9	2,6 8,9		2,6,8,9	2,6 8,9	2,6 8,9		
Coho									3,4 7,8	3,4 7,8	3,4 7,8	

1. Dry fly, dead-drift
2. Dry fly, swung
3. Wet fly, swung near surface
4. Wet fly, swung deep
5. Nymph(s), lightly weighted
6. Nymph(s), weighted with indicator
7. Deep drifted fly (with or without indicator)
8. Wet fly retrieved near surface
9. Deep swing with retrieve

SERVICES

CAMPING/PARKS
- **Happy Landing RV Park & Marina,** Waldport, 97394, (541) 528-3300, www.facebook.com
- **Blackberry Campground,** Tidewater, 97390, (541) 547-3679, www.reserveamerica.com
- **Waldport/Newport KOA,** Waldport, 97394, (541) 563-2250, www.koa.com
- **Taylor's Landing,** Waldport, 97394, (541) 528-3388
- **Alsea River RV Park & Marina,** Waldport, 97394, (541) 563-3401, www.alsearivrpark.com
- **Drift Creek Landing,** Waldport, 97394, (541) 563-3610, www.driftcreeklandingrv.com

ACCOMMODATIONS
- **Ambrosia Gardens B & B,** Yachats, 97498, (541) 547-3013, www.ambrosia-gardens.com
- **Resting on the Rock B & B,** Seal Rock, 97376, (800) 313-5171 or (541) 563-2643, www.restingontherock.com

TACKLE SHOPS
- **Waldport Ace Hardware,** Waldport, 97394, (541) 563-3199
- **John Boy's Alsea Mercantile & Shuttle Service,** Alsea, 97324, (541) 487-4462, www.alseavalley.com/mercantile.htm

VISITOR INFORMATION
- **Siuslaw National Forest,** Tidewater, 97390, (541) 750-7000, www.fs.usda.gov/siuslaw
- **Lincoln County Parks,** Newport, 97365, (541) 574-1215, www.co.lincoln.or.us
- **A Guide to Oregon's Central Coast,** www.newportnet.com
- **Oregon's Boating Resource,** www.boatescape.com
- **Newport Chamber of Commerce,** Newport, 97365, (541) 265-8801, (800) 262-7844, www.newportchamber.org

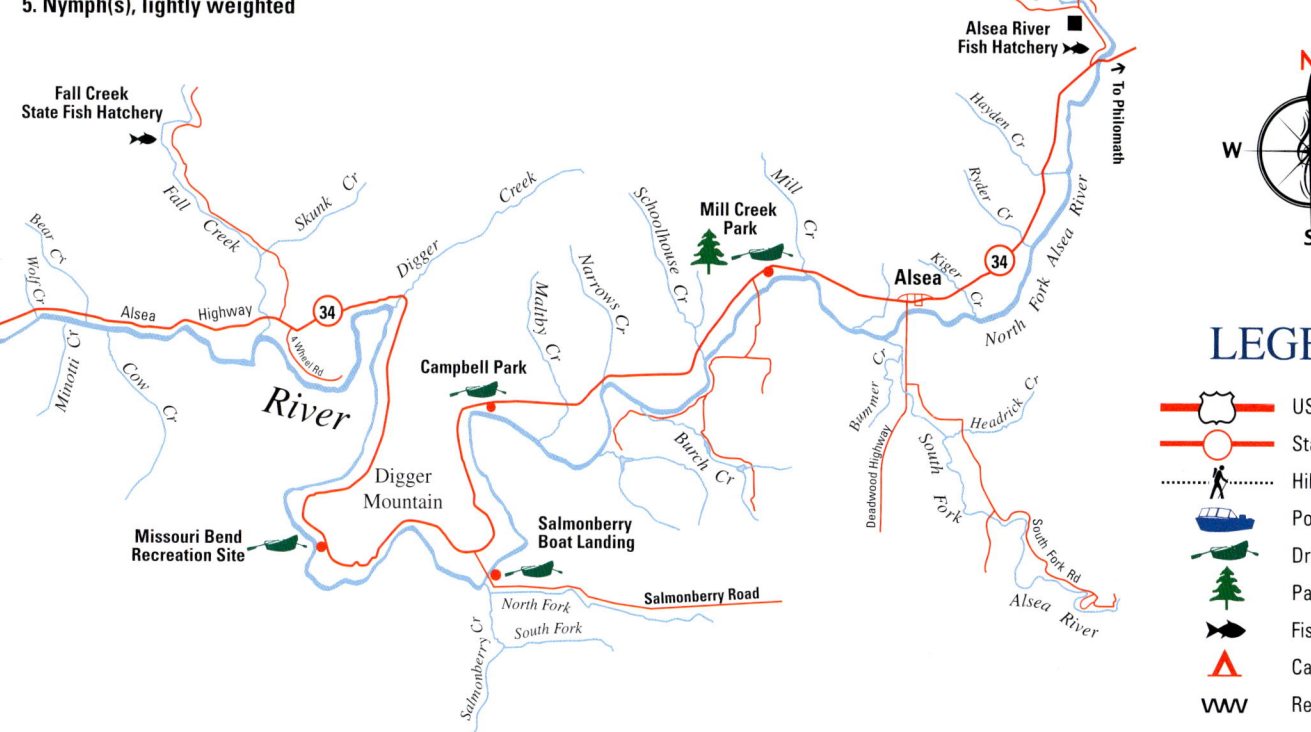

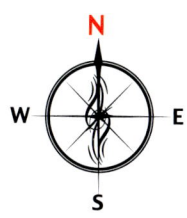

LEGEND

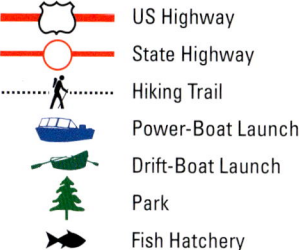

- US Highway
- State Highway
- Hiking Trail
- Power-Boat Launch
- Drift-Boat Launch
- Park
- Fish Hatchery
- Campground
- Reach of Tide

Oregon River Maps & Fishing Guide

Siuslaw River

The Siuslaw is a major river draining a large portion of the central coast range. It flows over 100 miles from its mountain headwaters to its bay at the coastal town of Florence. Like most coastal rivers, the Siuslaw is known for its fall chinook and winter steelhead. It also hosts a respectable population of sea-run cutthroat, and the uppermost reaches hold resident coastal cutthroat. Coho salmon have dwindled to a small remnant run of wild fish which must be released unharmed.

Fall chinook are the mainstay of the Siuslaw, with most fish caught within the tidewater reaches from Tide Wayside to Cushman RV Park. Chinook begin arriving in late August and continue accumulating in tidewater until the first major rains in late October or November. Trolling spinners, herring and spinner/bait combinations is a popular style of fishing in the tidal reaches, but in recent years, float fishing with cured salmon roe and sand shrimp has become most popular.

Winter steelhead are native throughout the Siuslaw system, and hatchery winter steelhead are planted in Lake Creek. From late November through March, winter steelhead course through the system, intercepted by anglers using all types of fishing styles.

Cutthroat trout, both sea-run and resident, live throughout the Siuslaw, from the uppermost tributaries to the estuary. Spring and fall are the best times for sea-runs, summer and early fall for the up-river residents.

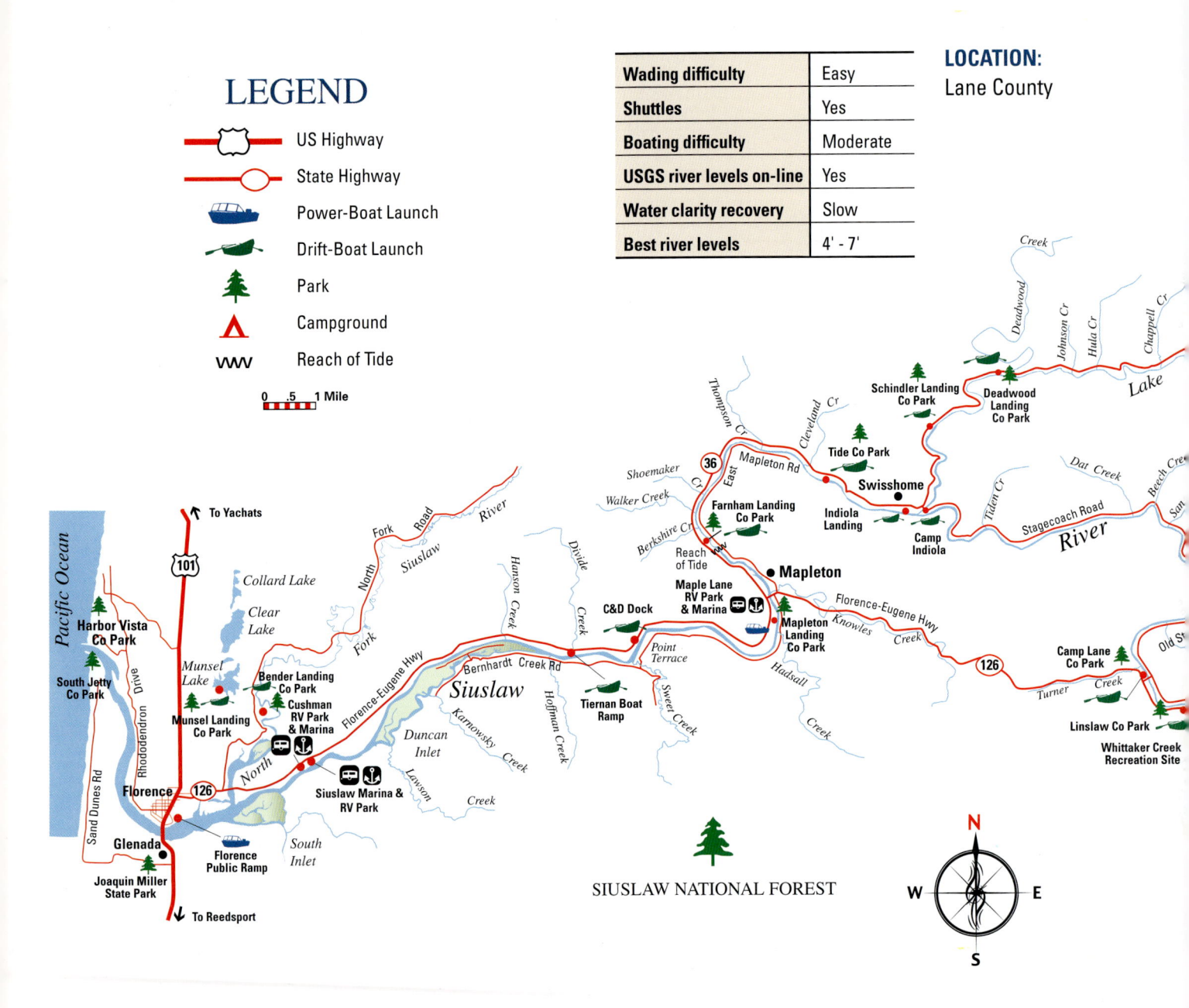

LEGEND

- US Highway
- State Highway
- Power-Boat Launch
- Drift-Boat Launch
- Park
- Campground
- Reach of Tide

0 .5 1 Mile

Wading difficulty	Easy
Shuttles	Yes
Boating difficulty	Moderate
USGS river levels on-line	Yes
Water clarity recovery	Slow
Best river levels	4' - 7'

LOCATION:
Lane County

34

SIUSLAW RIVER

BEST GEAR-FISHING TECHNIQUES & ESTIMATED HOOKUPS IN AN AVERAGE YEAR

	Jan	Feb	Mar	Apr	May	Jun	Jul	Aug	Sep	Oct	Nov	Dec
Winter Steelhead 1700	1,2 3,4 (Best)	1,2 3,4 (Good)	1,2 3,4 (Slow)								1,2 3,4 (Slow)	1,2 3,4 (Slow)
Fall Chinook (tide water) 2000								2,3,6 (Best)	2,3,6 (Best)	2,3,6 (Best)		
Fall Chinook (river) 2000									1,2,3 4,5,6 (Best)	1,2,3 4,5,6 (Best)	1,2,3 4,5,6 (Best)	1,2,3 4,5,6 (Best)
Coho 1500										1,2,3 4,5 (Best)	1,2,3 4,5 (Best)	
Ocean Salmon 15,000						6 (Good)	6 (Best)	6 (Best)	6 (Best)	6 (Good)		
Shad					2,6 (Slow)	2,6 (Best)						
Sea-Run Cutthroat		2 (Slow)	2 (Slow)	2 (Slow)				2 (Good)	2 (Best)	2 (Slow)	2 (Slow)	2 (Slow)

Legend: Best / Good / Slow

1. Drift fishing (from bank or boat, with or without bait)
2. Casting spinners, spoons, plugs
3. Float fishing (with jigs or bait)
4. Back-trolling (plugs or diver-and-bait)
5. Back-bouncing (boat)
6. Trolling (boat only)
7. Anchor fishing
8. Plunking
9. Jigging

BEST FLY-FISHING TECHNIQUES

	Jan	Feb	Mar	Apr	May	Jun	Jul	Aug	Sep	Oct	Nov	Dec
Winter Steelhead	4,6,7 (Best)	4,6,7 (Good)	4,6,7 (Slow)								4,6,7 (Slow)	4,6,7 (Slow)
Fall Chinook (Tidewater)								6,7,9 (Best)	6,7,9 (Best)	6,7,9 (Best)		
Fall Chinook (River)									4,6 7,9 (Best)	4,6 7,9 (Best)	4,6 7,9 (Best)	4,6 7,9 (Best)
Coho										3,4,7 8,9 (Best)	3,4,7 8,9 (Best)	
Shad					9 (Slow)	9 (Best)						
Sea-Run Cutthroat		2,6 8,9 (Slow)	2,6 8,9 (Slow)	2,6 8,9 (Slow)				2,6 8,9 (Good)	2,6 8,9 (Best)	2,6 8,9 (Slow)	2,6 8,9 (Slow)	2,6 8,9 (Slow)

1. Dry fly, dead-drift
2. Dry fly, swung
3. Wet fly, swung near surface
4. Wet fly, swung deep
5. Nymph(s), lightly weighted
6. Nymph(s), weighted with indicator
7. Deep drifted fly (with or without indicator)
8. Wet fly retrieved near surface
9. Deep swing with retrieve

SERVICES

CAMPING/PARKS
- **Port of Siuslaw Boat Ramp,** Florence, 97439, (541) 997-3040, www.portofsiuslaw.com
- **Siuslaw Marina & RV Park,** Florence, 97439, (541) 997-3254, www.facebook.com
- **Mapleton Landing County Park,** Eugene, 97408, (541) 682-2000, www.recreationparks.net/or/lane

ACCOMMODATIONS
- **Edwin K B & B,** Florence, 97439, (541) 997-8360, (800) 833-9465, www.bedandbreakfast.com
- **Blue Heron Inn,** Florence, 97439, (541) 997-4091, (800) 997-7780, www.blueheroninnflorence.com

TACKLE SHOPS
- **The Sportsman,** Florence, 97439, (541) 997-3336

VISITOR INFORMATION
- **City of Florence,** Florence, 97439, (541) 997-3437, www.ci.florence.or.us
- **Lane County Parks,** Eugene, 97408, (541) 682-2000, www.lanecounty.org/parks
- **Florence Area Chamber of Commerce,** Florence, 97439, (541) 997-3128, www.florencechamber.com

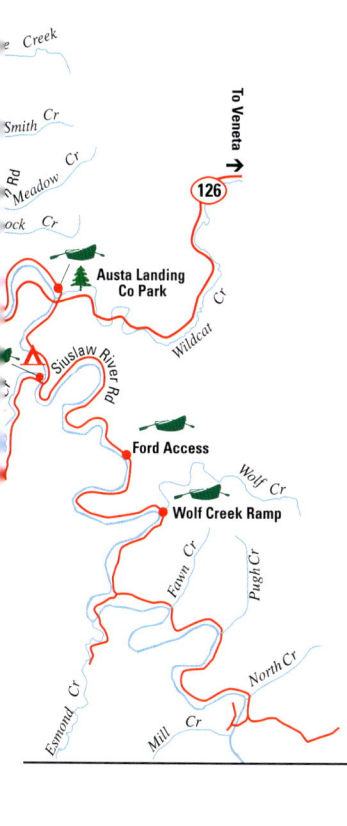

Oregon River Maps & Fishing Guide

Smith River

The Smith is one of the lesser-known steelhead rivers in Oregon, often confused with California's Smith River near the Oregon border. From its headwaters deep in the Siuslaw National Forest, the Smith flows over 75 miles through remote coastal rainforest to its mouth near the town of Gardiner.

The lower twenty miles of the Smith, from Gardiner up to Spencer Creek, is affected by ocean tides. This estuary is home to a wild run of striped bass. Stripers feed and spawn throughout the tidal reaches from March through October. The best striper fishing is in the upper ten miles of tidewater in spring and fall. During summer months, stripers migrate to Winchester Bay to feed on baitfish and other foods. Trolling plugs, spinners and flashers is the most common way to catch these wary fish. Casting plugs, spinners and spoons from a boat or from the bank is also effective.

Fall Chinook make a good showing in the Smith, accumulating in tidewater just below Spencer Creek from August through October, and moving into the upper river with the first fall rains. Fly-fishing from an anchored boat, float fishing with bait, and trolling spinners, plugs and bait are the best fishing methods in tidewater. Once the fish are in the upper river, any fishing method can be effective.

Winter steelhead run in the Smith from November through March. There are launches for drift boats, but most anglers prefer to access the Smith by foot, given the excellent bank access. River levels fluctuate widely during the rainy season, but the Smith clears quickly after a high-water event.

LOCATION:
Douglas County

Wading difficulty	Moderate
Shuttles	No
Boating difficulty	Easy
USGS river levels on-line	No
Water clarity recovery	Fast

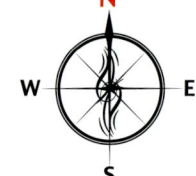

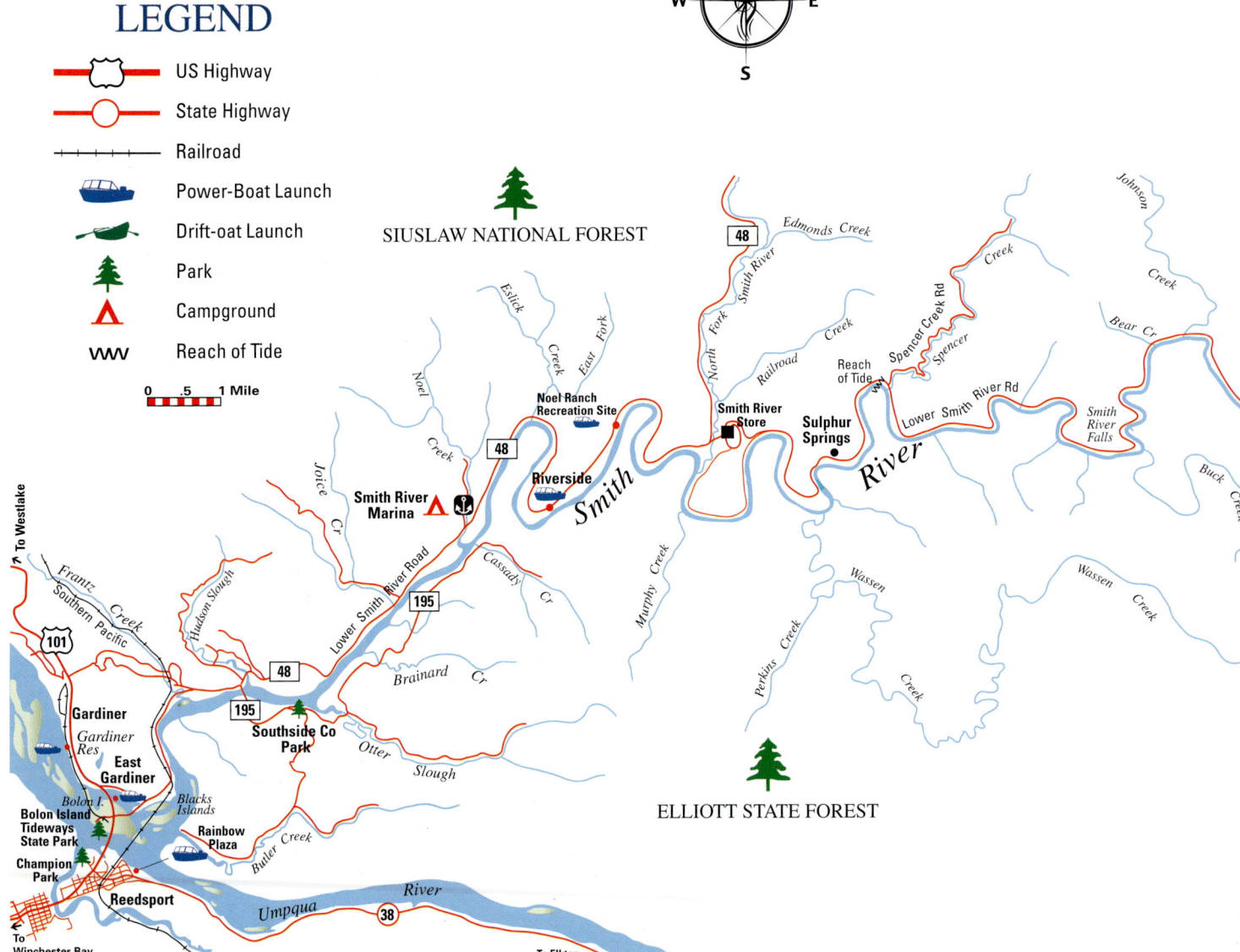

LEGEND

- US Highway
- State Highway
- Railroad
- Power-Boat Launch
- Drift-oat Launch
- Park
- Campground
- Reach of Tide

SMITH RIVER

BEST GEAR-FISHING TECHNIQUES & ESTIMATED HOOKUPS IN AN AVERAGE YEAR

Best / Good / Slow	Jan	Feb	Mar	Apr	May	Jun	Jul	Aug	Sep	Oct	Nov	Dec
Winter Steelhead 300	1,2 3,4	1,2 3,4	1,2 3,4								1,2 3,4	1,2 3,4
Fall Chinook 500								2,3,6	2,3,6	2,3,6	1,2 3,4,5	1,2 3,4,5
Coho 500									1,2 3,4	1,2 3,4	1,2 3,4	
Striped Bass				2,6	2,6	2,6	2,6		2,6	2,6		
Shad					2,9	2,9						
Sea-Run Cutthroat					2	2	2	2	2			

1. Drift fishing (from bank or boat, with or without bait)
2. Casting spinners, spoons, plugs
3. Float fishing (with jigs or bait)
4. Back-trolling (plugs or diver-and-bait)
5. Back-bouncing (boat)
6. Trolling (boat only)
7. Anchor fishing
8. Plunking
9. Jigging

BEST FLY-FISHING TECHNIQUES

Best / Good / Slow	Jan	Feb	Mar	Apr	May	Jun	Jul	Aug	Sep	Oct	Nov	Dec
Winter Steelhead	4,6,7	4,6,7	4,6,7								4,6,7	4,6,7
Fall Chinook								7,9	7,9	7,9	4,6 7,9	4,6 7,9
Coho									4,8,9	4,8,9	4,8,9	
Striped Bass				7,8,9	7,8,9	7,8,9	7,8,9		7,8,9	7,8,9		
Shad					8,9	8,9						
Sea-Run Cutthroat					1,2 6,8,9	1,2 6,8,9	1,2 6,8,9	1,2 6,8,9	1,2 6,8,9			

1. Dry fly, dead-drift
2. Dry fly, swung
3. Wet fly, swung near surface
4. Wet fly, swung deep
5. Nymph(s), lightly weighted
6. Nymph(s), weighted with indicator
7. Deep drifted fly (with or without indicator)
8. Wet fly retrieved near surface
9. Deep swing with retrieve

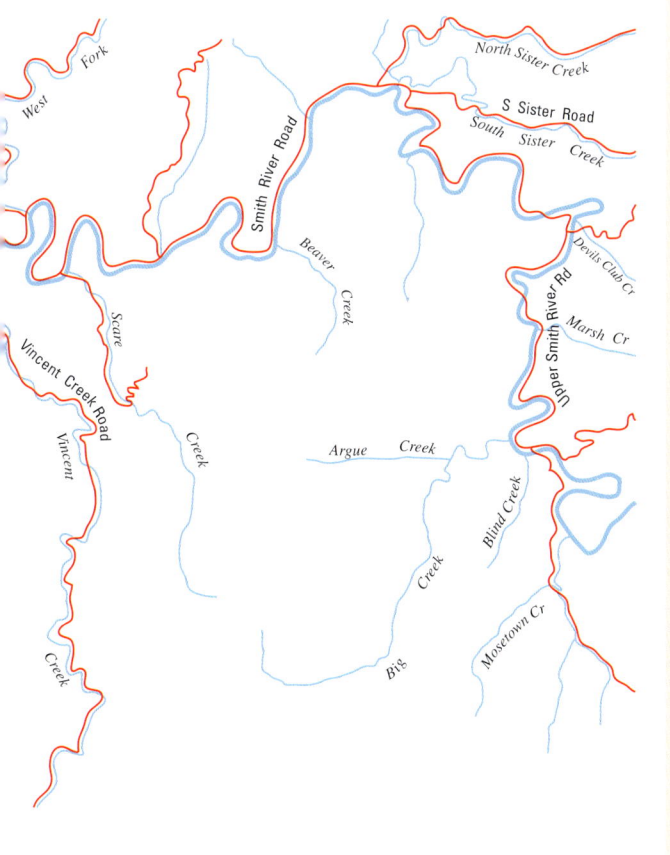

SERVICES

CAMPING/PARKS
- **Reedsport Rainbow Plaza Boat Ramp,** Reedsport, 97467, (541) 271-3603
- **Smith River Marina CG,** Reedsport, 97467, www.rvparkfinder.net

ACCOMMODATIONS
- **Daybreak Haven B&B,** Scottsburg, 97473, (541) 587-4205, www.daybreakhaven.com
- **Gardiner Guest House B&B,** Gardiner, 97441, (541) 543-0210, www.gardinerbedandbreakfast.com
- **Edwin K B&B,** Florence, 97439, (541) 997-8360, (800) 833-9465, www.bedandbreakfast.com
- **Blue Heron Inn,** Florence, 97439, (541) 997-4091, (800) 997-7780, www.blueheroninnflorence.com

TACKLE SHOPS
- **Turman Tackle,** Reedsport, 97467, (541) 271-0586
- **Salmon Harbor Tackle & Marine,** Winchester Bay, 97467, (541) 271-2010
- **Stockade Market & Tackle,** Winchester Bay, 97467, (541) 271-3800
- **Ringo's Lakeside Marina,** Lakeside, 97449, (541) 759-3312
- **Reedsport Outdoor Store,** Reedsport, 97467, (541) 271-2311

VISITOR INFORMATION
- **Oregon Dunes Recreation Area Visitor Center,** Reedsport, (541) 271-6000
- **Douglas County Parks,** (541) 957-7001, www.co.douglas.or.us
- **Douglas County Parks/Boat Ramps,** www.co.douglas.or.us/parks/boatramps.asp
- **Siuslaw National Forest,** Tidewater, 97390, (541) 750-7000, www.fs.usda.gov/siuslaw
- **Noel Ranch Recreation Site Boat Launch,** (541) 957-7001
- **Elliott State Forest,** www.oregon.gov/ODF
- **Reedsport/Winchester Bay Chamber of Commerce,** Reedsport, 97467, (541) 271-3495, www.reedsportcc.org

Oregon River Maps & FISHING GUIDE

Umpqua River, Lower

BEST GEAR-FISHING TECHNIQUES & ESTIMATED HOOKUPS IN AN AVERAGE YEAR

Best / Good / Slow	Jan	Feb	Mar	Apr	May	Jun	Jul	Aug	Sep	Oct	Nov	Dec
Winter Steelhead 4000	1,2 3,4	1,2 3,4	1,2 3,4							1,2 3,4	1,2 3,4	1,2 3,4
Summer Steelhead 1000			1,2 3,4	1,2 3,4	1,2 3,4	1,2 3,4	1,2 3,4	1,2 3,4	1,2 3,4			
Fall Chinook 3000							2,3,6	2,3,6	1,2,3 4,5,6	1,2,3 4,5,6	1,2,3 4,5,6	
Spring Chinook 2000				1,2,3,4,5	1,2,3 4,5	1,2,3 4,5	1,2,3 4,5					
Coho 1500									1,2,3 4,5	1,2,3 4,5	1,2,3 4,5	1,2,3 4,5
Sea-Run Cutthroat								2	2	2		
Smallmouth Bass					2,3	2,3	2,3	2,3	2,3	2,3		
Striped Bass	2,6	2,6	2,6	2,6	2,6	2,6	2,6	2,6	2,6	2,6	2,6	2,6
Sturgeon	8	8	8	8	8	8	8	8	8	8	8	8
Ocean Salmon 25,000						6,9	6,9	6,9	6,9			
Crabs												
Shad					2,5 7,9	2,5 7,9						

1. Drift fishing (from bank or boat, with or without bait)
2. Casting spinners, spoons, plugs
3. Float fishing (with jigs or bait)
4. Back-trolling (plugs or diver-and-bait)
5. Back-bouncing (boat)
6. Trolling (boat only)
7. Anchor fishing
8. Plunking
9. Jigging

LOCATION: Douglas County

Wading difficulty	Difficult
Shuttles	Yes
Boating difficulty	Moderate/Difficult
USGS river levels on-line	Yes
Water clarity recovery	Moderate/Slow

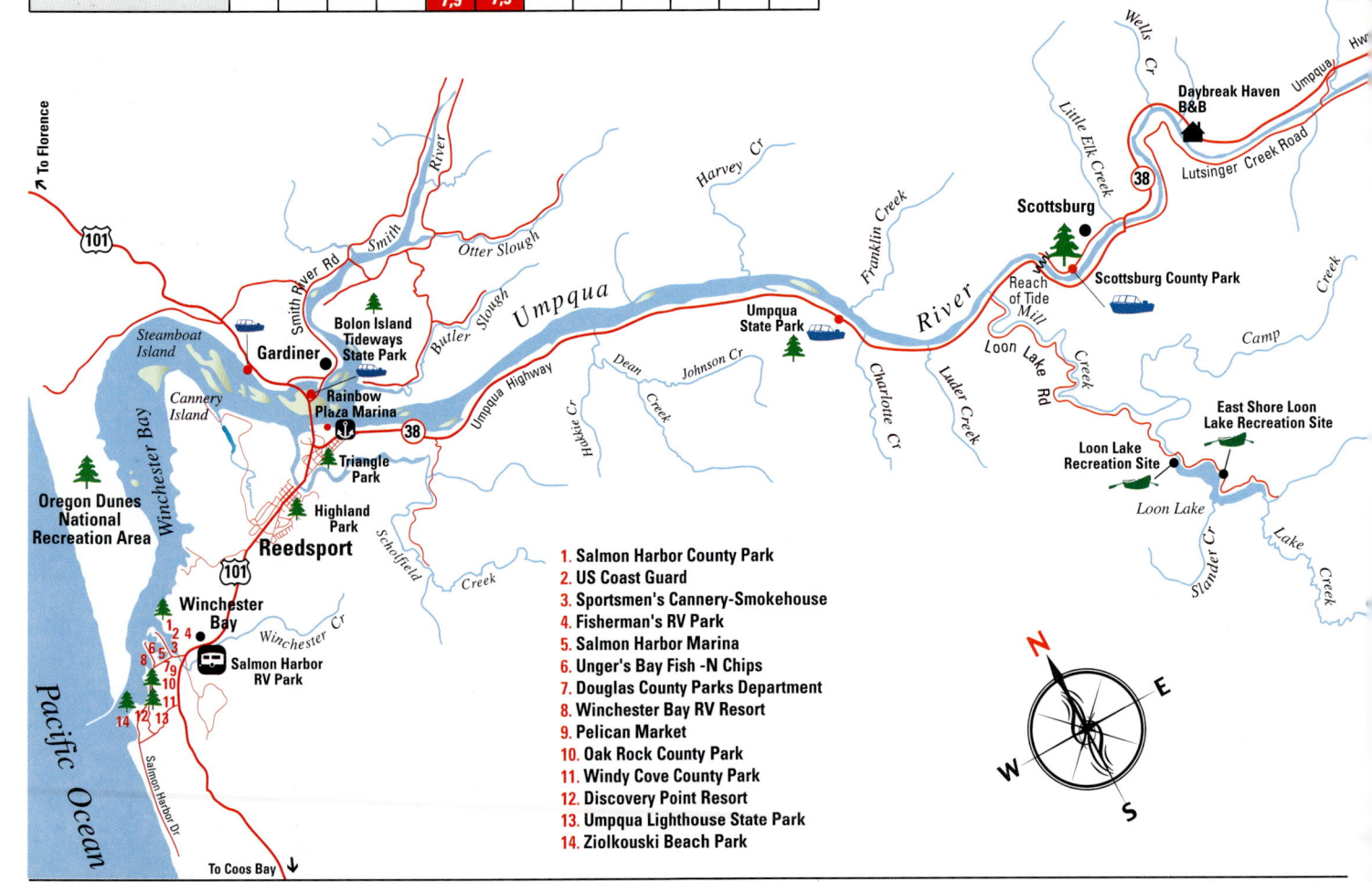

1. Salmon Harbor County Park
2. US Coast Guard
3. Sportsmen's Cannery-Smokehouse
4. Fisherman's RV Park
5. Salmon Harbor Marina
6. Unger's Bay Fish-N Chips
7. Douglas County Parks Department
8. Winchester Bay RV Resort
9. Pelican Market
10. Oak Rock County Park
11. Windy Cove County Park
12. Discovery Point Resort
13. Umpqua Lighthouse State Park
14. Ziolkouski Beach Park

38

UMPQUA RIVER, LOWER

Fishing Calendar

	Jan	Feb	Mar	Apr	May	Jun	Jul	Aug	Sep	Oct	Nov	Dec
Winter Steelhead	4,6,7	4,6,7	4,6,7							4,6,7	4,6,7	4,6,7
Summer Steelhead					2,4,6,7	2,4,6,7	2,4,6,7	2,4,6,7	2,4,6,7			
Fall Chinook							4,6,7,9	4,6,7,9	4,6,7,9	4,6,7,9	4,6,7,9	
Spring Chinook			3,7	3,7	3,7	3,7						
Coho								3,4,7,8,9	3,4,7,8,9	3,4,7,8,9	3,4,7,8,9	3,4,7,8,9
Sea-Run Cutthroat								2,6,8,9	2,6,8,9	2,6,8,9		
Smallmouth Bass					7,8,9	7,8,9	7,8,9	7,8,9	7,8,9	7,8,9		
Striped Bass	7,8,9	7,8,9	7,8,9	7,8,9	7,8,9	7,8,9	7,8,9	7,8,9	7,8,9	7,8,9	7,8,9	7,8,9
Shad					9	9						

Legend: Best / Good / Slow

BEST FLY-FISHING TECHNIQUES

1. Dry fly, dead-drift
2. Dry fly, swung
3. Wet fly, swung near surface
4. Wet fly, swung deep
5. Nymph(s), lightly weighted
6. Nymph(s), weighted with indicator
7. Deep drifted fly (with or without indicator)
8. Wet fly retrieved near surface
9. Deep swing with retrieve

SERVICES

CAMPING/PARKS
- **Winchester Bay RV Resort,** Winchester Bay, 97467, (541) 271-4636, www.winchesterbayrvresort.com
- **Fisherman's RV Park,** Winchester Bay, 97467, (541) 271-3536, www.fishermansrvpark.com
- **Reedsport Rainbow Plaza Marina,** Reedsport, 97467, (541) 271-3603
- **Loon Lake Recreation Sites (BLM),** (541) 756-0100, Reservations: www.recreation.gov
- **Sawyer's Rapids RV Resort,** Elkton, 97436, (541) 584-2226, www.sawyersrapids.com

ACCOMMODATIONS
- **Daybreak Haven B&B,** Scottsburg, 97473, (541) 587-4205, www.daybreakhaven.com
- **Gardiner Guest House B&B,** Gardiner, 97441, (541) 543-0210, www.gardinerbedandbreakfast.com

TACKLE SHOPS
- **Turman Tackle,** Reedsport, 97467, (541) 271-0586
- **Salmon Harbor Tackle & Marine,** Reedsport, 97467, (541) 271-2010
- **Stockade Market & Tackle,** Winchester Bay, 97467, (541) 271-3800
- **Ringo's Lakeside Marina,** Lakeside, 97449, (541) 759-3312
- **Reedsport Outdoor Store,** Reedsport, 97467, (541) 271-2311

VISITOR INFORMATION
- **Oregon Dunes Recreation Area Visitor Center,** Reedsport, (541) 271-6000
- **Douglas County Parks,** (541) 957-7001, www.co.douglas.or.us
- **Douglas County Parks/Boat Ramps,** www.co.douglas.or.us/parks/boatramps.asp
- **Elliott State Forest,** www.oregon.gov/ODF
- **Siuslaw National Forest,** Tidewater, 97390, (541) 750-7000, www.fs.usda.gov/siuslaw
- **Reedsport/Winchester Bay Chamber of Commerce,** Reedsport, 97467, (541) 271-3495, www.reedsportcc.org

LEGEND

- US Highway
- State Highway
- Power-Boat Launch
- Drift-Boat Launch
- Park
- Campground
- Reach of Tide

0 .5 1 2 Miles

Oregon River Maps & Fishing Guide

Umpqua River, Upper

From Winchester Bay to the upper reaches of the North and South forks (over 200 miles of river), the Umpqua offers the widest variety of world-class fishing opportunities of any river in the Northwest. The fishing possibilities are endless: white and green sturgeon, perch, striped bass, shad, spring and fall Chinook salmon, coho salmon, summer and winter steelhead, rainbow trout, brown trout, cutthroat trout and smallmouth bass. There is good crabbing and clamming in the lower reaches of Winchester Bay, and good ocean fishing for salmon and bottom fish offshore.

Chinook and coho salmon are the most sought after fish in the lower Umpqua. Spring Chinook arrive from April through August, fall Chinook and coho from August through September. Steelhead fishing is also very popular throughout the Umpqua basin. Summer steelhead start to arrive in late April, peak in June or July, and continue through October. Winter steelhead begin running in November and continue through April. During the summer months, the Umpqua's abundant smallmouth bass offer amazing action between the towns of Tyee and Elkton. The Umpqua also boasts Oregon's largest run of shad, which swarm the river from the forks down to Scottsburg in May and June.

The North Umpqua may be the most legendary steelhead river in the world. Thousands of summer and winter steelhead call the North Umpqua home. The upper half of the North Umpqua, from markers 700 feet upstream of Rock Creek to Soda Springs Dam, is managed as "fly fishing only." Summer steelhead run from May through October, winter steelhead from December through March. Below Rock Creek, boat fishing is preferred because of poor access, and conventional tackle and techniques are allowed.

The South Umpqua flows 100 miles to its confluence with the North Umpqua near Roseburg. Known as Oregon's most productive smallmouth bass fishery, the South Fork is also home to a respectable run of winter steelhead (from November through March), and hatchery rainbow trout.

LOCATION: Douglas County

Wading difficulty	Moderate-Dangerous
Shuttles	Yes
Boating difficulty	Difficult
USGS river levels on-line	Yes
Water clarity recovery	Moderate

1. Quintus Park
2. Stewart Park
3. River Front Park
4. Gaddis City Park
5. Laurelwood Park
6. Deer Creek Park
7. Templin Beach Park
8. Micelli Park
9. Umpqua Park
10. Green Oaks Co Park
11. Winston Dillard Co Park
12. Riverbend Park

An early season summer steelhead about to be released.

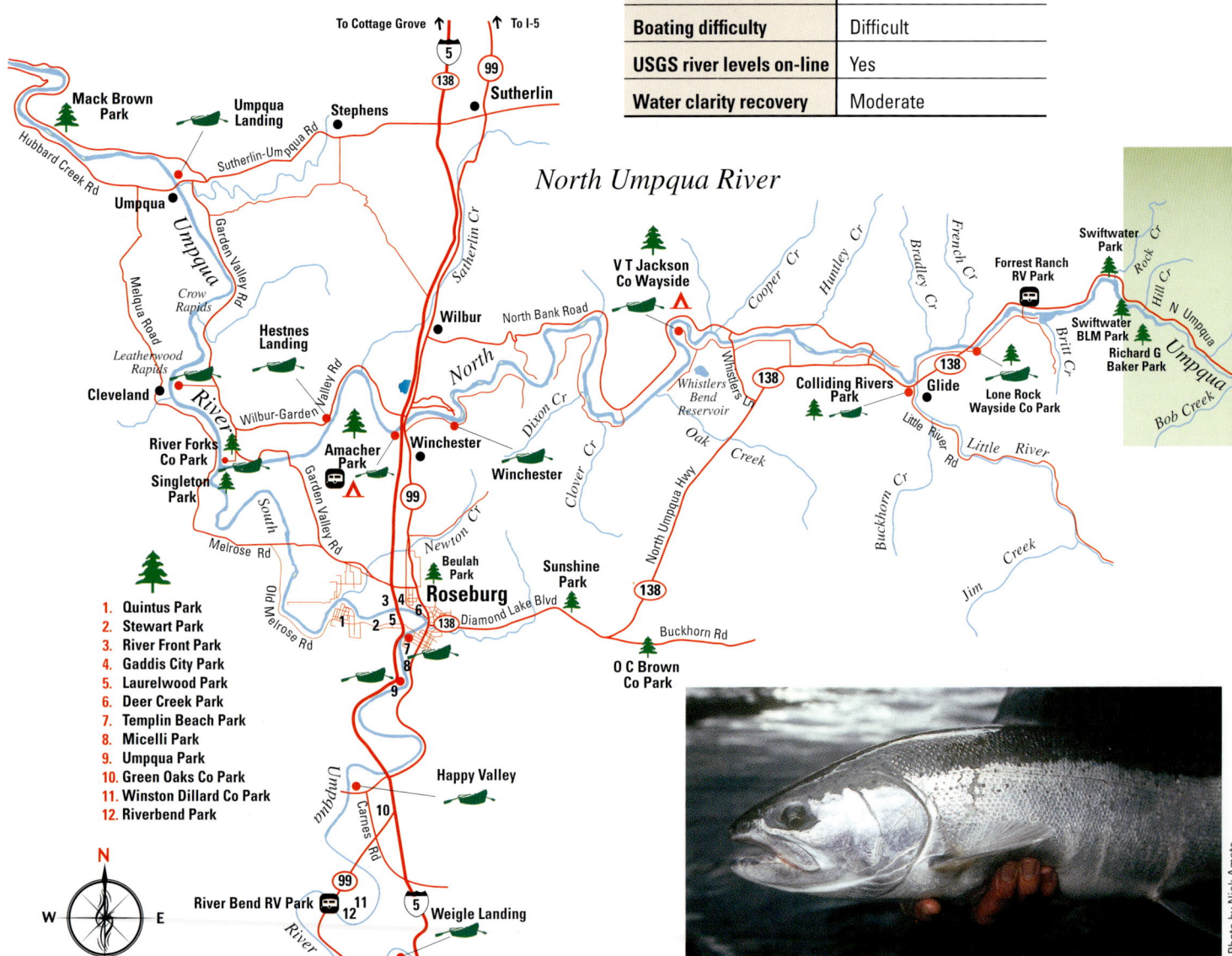

Photo by Nick Amato

40

UMPQUA RIVER, UPPER

BEST FLY-FISHING TECHNIQUES

	Jan	Feb	Mar	Apr	May	Jun	Jul	Aug	Sep	Oct	Nov	Dec
Winter Steelhead	4,6,7	4,6,7	4,6,7	4,6,7 / 4,6,7								4,6,7 / 4,6,7
Summer Steelhead					2,3 / 4,7	2,3 / 4,7	2,3 / 4,7	2,3 / 4,7	2,3 / 4,7	2,3 / 4,7		
Fall Chinook									4,6 / 7,9	4,6 / 7,9	4,6 / 7,9	4,6 / 7,9
Spring Chinook				3,7	3,7	3,7	3,7 / 3,7					
Coho									3,4,7 / 8,9	3,4,7 / 8,9	3,4,7 / 8,9	3,4,7 / 8,9
Smallmouth Bass				7,8,9	7,8,9	7,8,9	7,8,9	7,8,9	7,8,9 / 7,8,9	7,8,9		

Legend: Best / Good / Slow

1. Dry fly, dead-drift
2. Dry fly, swung
3. Wet fly, swung near surface
4. Wet fly, swung deep
5. Nymph(s), lightly weighted
6. Nymph(s), weighted with indicator
7. Deep drifted fly (with or without indicator)
8. Wet fly retrieved near surface
9. Deep swing with retrieve

BEST GEAR-FISHING TECHNIQUES & ESTIMATED HOOKUPS IN AN AVERAGE YEAR

	Jan	Feb	Mar	Apr	May	Jun	Jul	Aug	Sep	Oct	Nov	Dec
Winter Steelhead 2000	1,2 / 3,4	1,2 / 3,4	1,2 / 3,4	1,2 / 3,4								1,2 / 3,4
Summer Steelhead 4000					1,2 / 3,4	1,2 / 3,4	1,2 / 3,4	1,2 / 3,4	1,2 / 3,4	1,2 / 3,4		
Fall Chinook 70									1,2,3 / 4,5,6	1,2,3 / 4,5,6	1,2,3 / 4,5,6	1,2,3 / 4,5,6
Spring Chinook 1500				1,2,3 / 4,5	1,2,3 / 4,5	1,2,3 / 4,5	1,2,3 / 4,5					
Coho 350									1,2,3 / 4,5	1,2,3 / 4,5	1,2,3 / 4,5	1,2,3 / 4,5
Smallmouth Bass					2,3	2,3	2,3	2,3	2,3 / 2,3	2,3		

1. Drift fishing (from bank or boat, with or without bait)
2. Casting spinners, spoons, plugs
3. Float fishing (with jigs or bait)
4. Back-trolling (plugs or diver-and-bait)
5. Back-bouncing (boat)
6. Trolling (boat only)
7. Anchor fishing
8. Plunking
9. Jigging

This Area for Fly Fishing Only (to Conserve Wild Steelhead)

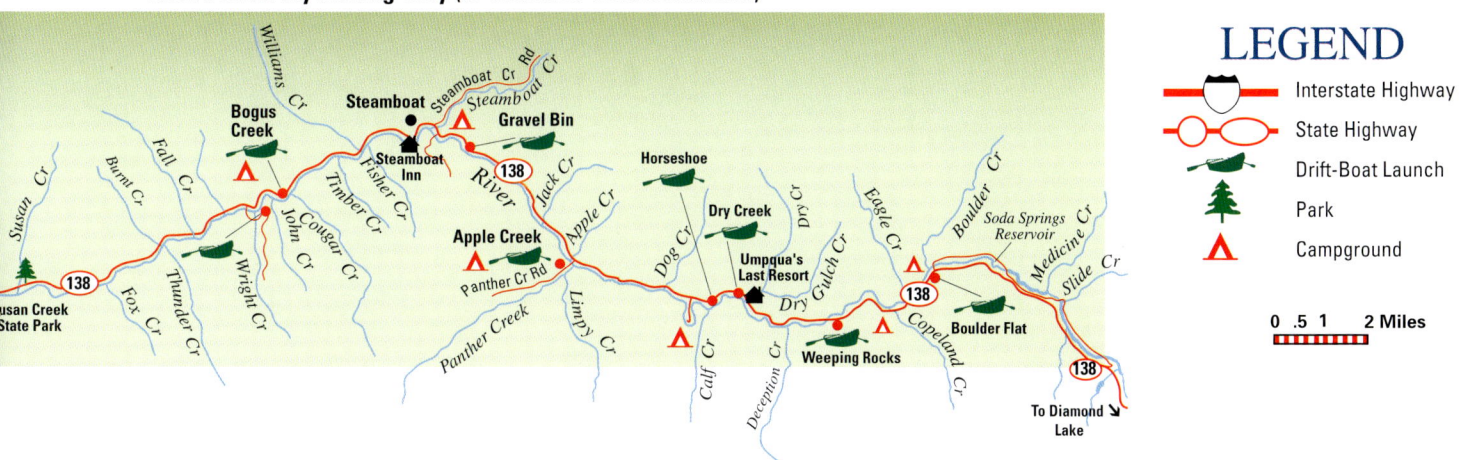

LEGEND
- Interstate Highway
- State Highway
- Drift-Boat Launch
- Park
- Campground

0 .5 1 2 Miles

SERVICES

CAMPING/PARKS
- **Amacher County RV Park and Campground,** Winchester, 97495, (541) 672-4901, www.co.douglas.or.us
- **Whistler's Bend County RV Park & Campground,** Roseburg, 97470, (541) 957-7001, www.co.douglas.or.us
- **Elk Haven RV Resort,** Idleyld Park, 97447, (541) 496-3090, (888) 552-0166, www.elkhavenrv.com
- **Umpqua's Last Resort, Wilderness RV Park & Campground,** Idleyld Park, 97447, (541) 498-2500, www.golastresort.com

ACCOMMODATIONS
- **C.H. Bailey House B&B,** Roseburg, 97470, (541) 672-1500, (877) 322-4539, www.chbaileyhouse.com
- **Delfino Vineyards B&B,** Roseburg, 97470, (541) 673-7575, outside Oregon: (855) 673-7575, www.delfinovineyards.com
- **Steamboat Inn,** Idleyld Park, 97447, (541) 498-2230, (800) 840-8825, www.thesteamboatinn.com

TACKLE SHOPS
- **Waldron's Outdoor Sports,** Roseburg, 97470, (541) 672-8992, www.waldronsoutdoor.com
- **Northwest Outdoors,** Roseburg, 97470, (541) 440-3042, www.merchantcircle.com

VISITOR INFORMATION
- **Oregon Dunes Recreation Area Visitor Center,** Reedsport, (541) 271-6000
- **Douglas County Parks,** (541) 957-7001, www.co.douglas.or.us
- **Douglas County Parks/Boat Ramps,** www.co.douglas.or.us/parks/boatramps.asp
- **Elliott State Forest,** www.oregon.gov/ODF
- **Siuslaw National Forest,** Tidewater, 97390, (541) 750-7000, www.fs.usda.gov/siuslaw
- **Roseburg Area Chamber of Commerce,** Roseburg, 97470, (541) 672-2648, www.roseburgareachamber.org

Oregon River Maps & Fishing Guide

Coos River & Bay

Coos Bay is one of the largest ports on the southern Oregon coast, at one time hosting a large fleet of commercial salmon fishing boats. Today the fishing fleet is relatively small, mostly targeting bottom fish instead of salmon. Fall Chinook and winter steelhead return in large enough numbers to support a good sport fishery in the upper bay and river. The lower bay and jetties are fished primarily for lingcod, rockfish and perch. There is good crabbing in the lower bay on an incoming tide most of the year.

Coos Bay is home to a good population of striped bass. Shad also make an excellent showing in May and June, running up the Coos and Millacoma.

Fall Chinook move into Coos Bay and tidewater of the Coos River in September and October. After the first good fall rains, the Chinook enter the river, accompanied by native coho salmon. While the salmon are still in the bay and tidewater stretches, anglers find best success trolling spinners, herring, or spinner/bait combinations. After the fall rains, anglers can catch salmon in the river using all manners of fishing styles.

Winter steelhead run in the Coos River system from November through March. The best steelheading is upstream of the Coos River in its main forks, the South Coos and the Millacoma. Drift-fishing with bait and casting spinners and spoons are the top producing methods for steelhead, although any method can be productive.

Shad are a popular summertime fishery in the Coos and its main tributaries. In May and June, thousands of shad from two to three pounds fill the river. Casting very small spinners, spoons and shad flies on light tackle is the preferred fishing method.

Resident and sea-run cutthroat are present in the estuary and river system, including the uppermost reaches of the South Coos and Millacoma. Spring and late summer are the best times for cutthroat. Fly-fishing with small streamers and dry flies is the most popular technique.

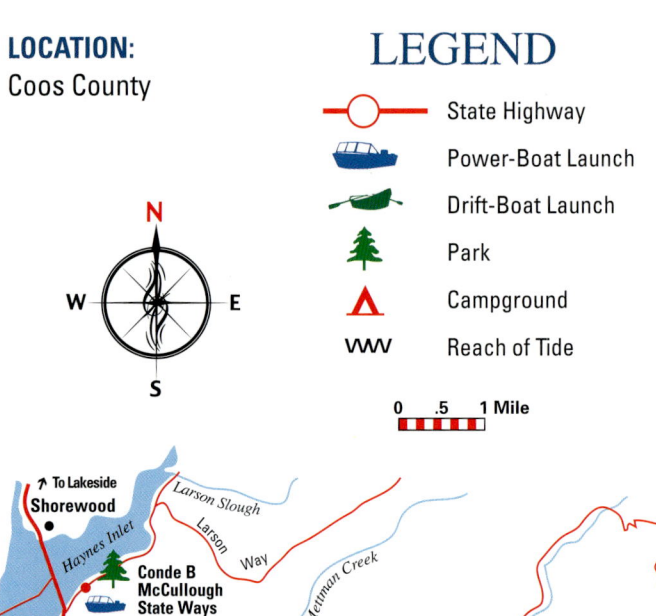

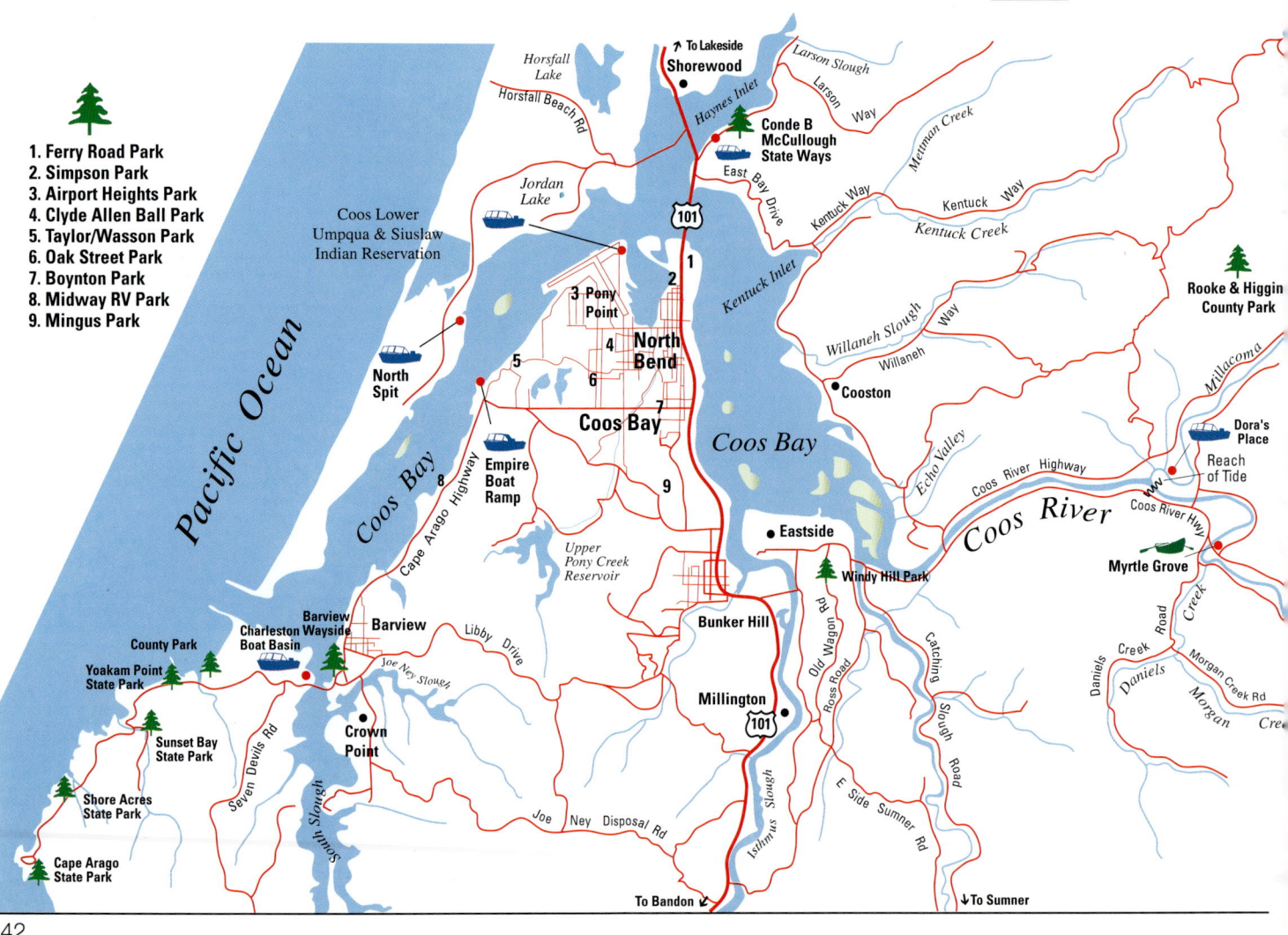

LOCATION:
Coos County

LEGEND
- State Highway
- Power-Boat Launch
- Drift-Boat Launch
- Park
- Campground
- Reach of Tide

0 .5 1 Mile

1. Ferry Road Park
2. Simpson Park
3. Airport Heights Park
4. Clyde Allen Ball Park
5. Taylor/Wasson Park
6. Oak Street Park
7. Boynton Park
8. Midway RV Park
9. Mingus Park

42

Coos River & Bay

BEST FLY-FISHING TECHNIQUES

	Jan	Feb	Mar	Apr	May	Jun	Jul	Aug	Sep	Oct	Nov	Dec
Winter Steelhead	4,6,7 (Best)	4,6,7 (Best)	4,6,7 (Good)								4,6,7 (Good)	4,6,7 (Good)
Spring Chinook				4,7,8 (Slow)	4,7,8 (Slow)	4,7,8 (Slow)						
Fall Chinook								6,7,9 (Good)	6,7,9 (Good)	4,6,7,9 (Best)	4,6,7,9 (Best)	
Coho										3,4,7,8,9 (Good)	3,4,7,8,9 (Good)	3,4,7,8,9 (Good)
Striped Bass			4,9 (Slow)	4,9 (Slow)	4,9 (Slow)				4,9 (Slow)	4,9 (Slow)		
Shad					4,9 (Good)	4,9 (Good)						
Cutthroat Trout		2,6,8,9 (Slow)	2,6,8,9 (Slow)	2,6,8,9 (Slow)	2,6,8,9 (Slow)			2,6,8,9 (Slow)	2,6,8,9 (Good)	2,6,8,9 (Good)	2,6,8,9 (Slow)	

1. Dry fly, dead-drift
2. Dry fly, swung
3. Wet fly, swung near surface
4. Wet fly, swung deep
5. Nymph(s), lightly weighted
6. Nymph(s), weighted with indicator
7. Deep drifted fly (with or without indicator)
8. Wet fly retrieved near surface
9. Deep swing with retrieve

BEST GEAR-FISHING TECHNIQUES & ESTIMATED HOOKUPS IN AN AVERAGE YEAR

	Jan	Feb	Mar	Apr	May	Jun	Jul	Aug	Sep	Oct	Nov	Dec
Winter Steelhead 750	1,2,3,4 (Best)	1,2,3,4 (Best)	1,2,3,4 (Good)								1,2,3,4 (Good)	1,2,3,4 (Good)
Spring Chinook 50				1,2,3,4,5 (Slow)	1,2,3,4,5 (Slow)	1,2,3,4,5 (Slow)						
Fall Chinook 1800								2,3,6 (Good)	2,3,6 (Good)	1,2,3,4,5,6 (Best)	1,2,3,4,5,6 (Good)	
Ocean Salmon 300							6 (Slow)	6 (Good)	6 (Good)			
Coho 100										1,2,3,4,5 (Good)	1,2,3,4,5 (Good)	1,2,3,4,5 (Good)
Striped Bass			2,6 (Slow)	2,6 (Slow)	2,6 (Slow)				2,6 (Slow)	2,6 (Slow)		
Shad					2,6 (Good)	2,6 (Good)						
Cutthroat Trout		2 (Slow)	2 (Slow)	2 (Slow)	2 (Slow)			2 (Slow)	2 (Slow)	2 (Slow)	2 (Slow)	

1. Drift fishing (from bank or boat, with or without bait)
2. Casting spinners, spoons, plugs
3. Float fishing (with jigs or bait)
4. Back-trolling (plugs or diver-and-bait)
5. Back-bouncing (boat)
6. Trolling (boat only)
7. Anchor fishing
8. Plunking
9. Jigging

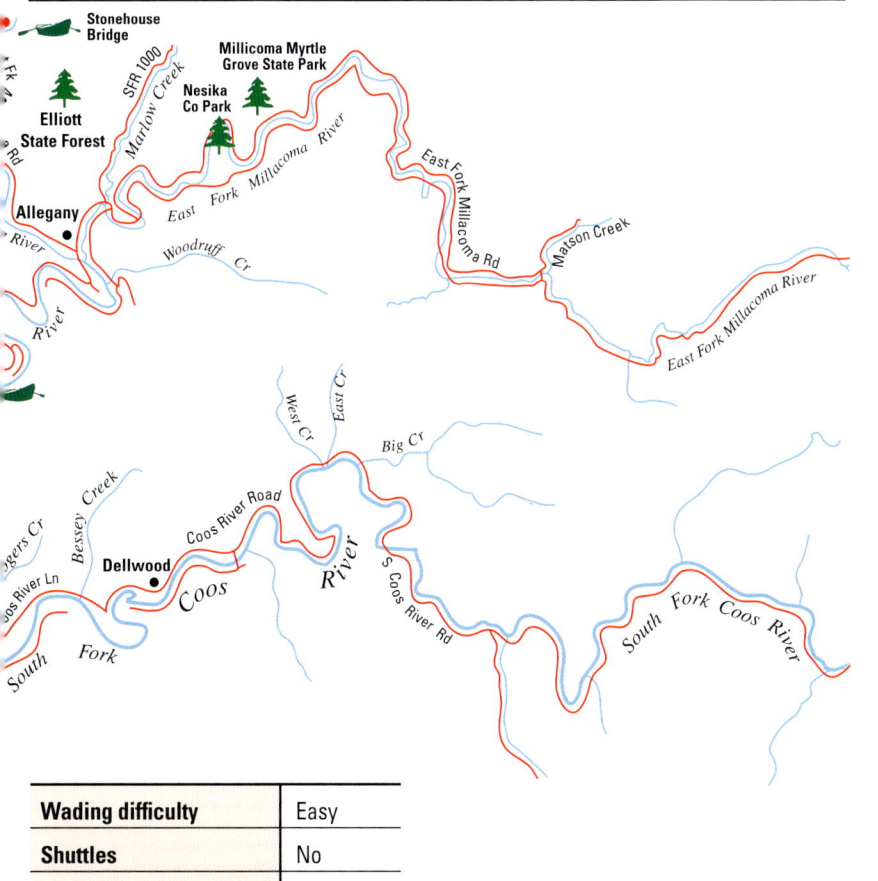

Wading difficulty	Easy
Shuttles	No
Boating difficulty	Easy
USGS river levels on-line	No
Water clarity recovery	Slow

SERVICES

CAMPING/PARKS
- **Midway RV Park,** Coos Bay, 97420, (541) 888-9300, www.rvparkfinder.net
- **Charleston Marina Complex,** Charleston, 97420, (541) 888-2548, www.charlestonmarina.com
- **Rooke & Higgins County Park,** Info: (541) 396-7759, Reserve: (541) 396-7755, www.co.coos.or.us
- **Sunset Bay State Park,** Info: (541) 888-4902, Reserve: (800) 452-5687, Reserve: www.reserveamerica.com

ACCOMMODATIONS
- **The Old Tower House B&B,** Coos Bay, 97420, (541) 888-6058, www.oldtowerhouse.com
- **Coos Bay Manor B&B,** Coos Bay, 97420, (800) 269-1224, www.coosbaymanor.com

TACKLE SHOPS
- **Englund Marine,** Coos Bay, 97420, (541) 888-6723, www.englundmarine.com
- **Bites on Bait & Tackle,** Coos Bay, 97420, (541) 888-4015
- **Basin Tackle Shop,** Coos Bay, 97420, (541) 888-3811

VISITOR INFORMATION
- **Coos County Parks,** Reserve: (541) 396-7755, www.co.coos.or.us
- **South Coast Oregon Directory City Guide,** www.scod.com
- **RV Park Finder,** www.rvparkfinder.net
- **Bay Area Chamber of Commerce,** Coos Bay, 97420, (541) 266-0868, www.oregonsbayarea.org

OREGON RIVER MAPS & FISHING GUIDE

Coquille River

The Coquille River is a productive mid-sized river, flowing over 50 miles from the densely forested coastal mountains to its small bay at the coastal town of Bandon. It is one of Oregon's best Chinook salmon and winter steelhead rivers, and it offers good fishing for sea-run and resident cutthroat trout. The Coquille also hosts a good run of healthy native coho salmon.

A tiny run of spring Chinook enter the Coquille from May through July, but the run is too small to produce good sport fishing. By September, fall Chinook begin to show, building in numbers through October, and continuing through November and into December. Before the fall rains, Chinook accumulate in the bay and tidewater. Anglers troll the bay and estuary with spinners,

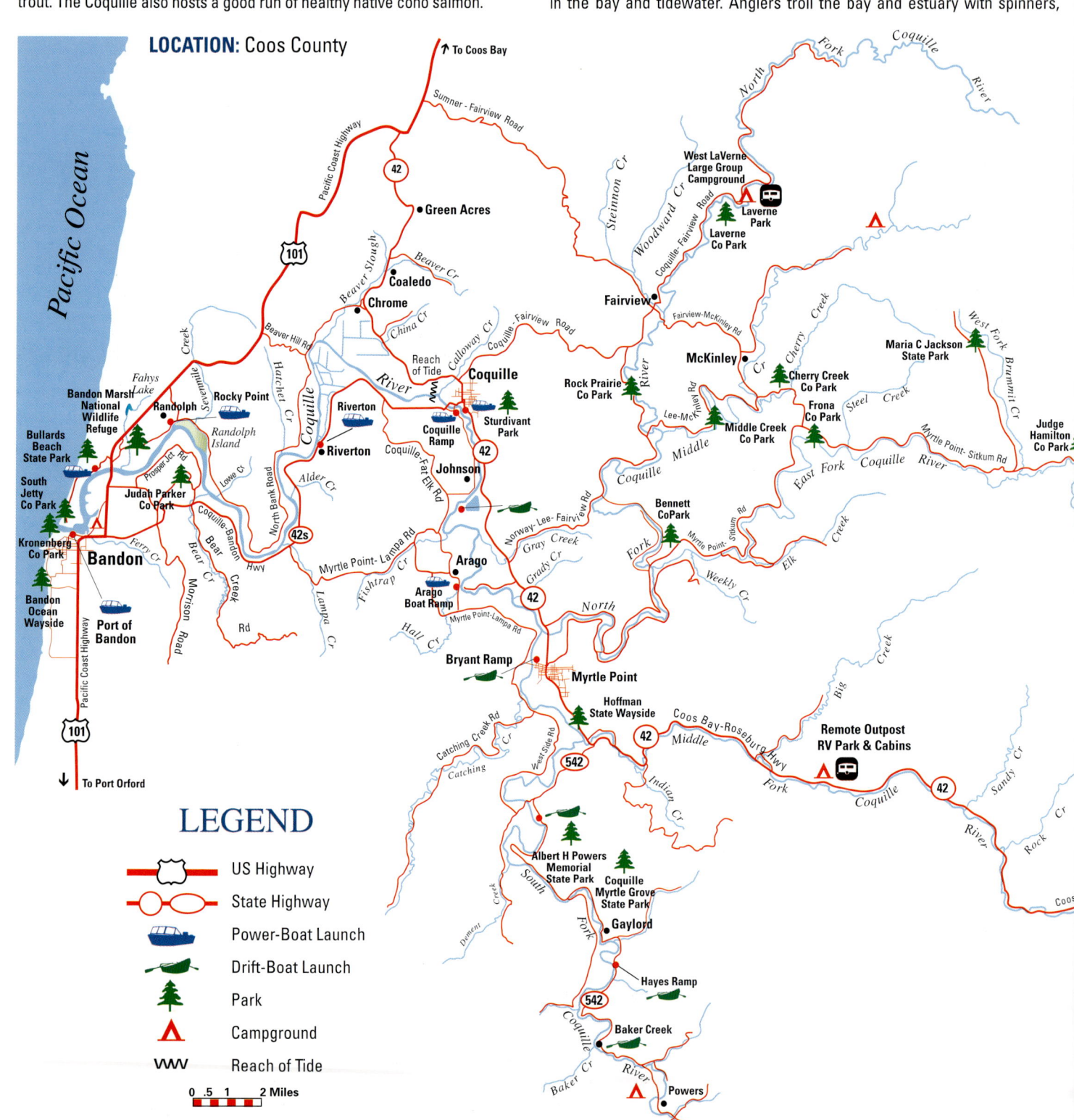

LOCATION: Coos County

LEGEND

- US Highway
- State Highway
- Power-Boat Launch
- Drift-Boat Launch
- Park
- Campground
- Reach of Tide

0 .5 1 2 Miles

COQUILLE RIVER

BEST FLY-FISHING TECHNIQUES

	Jan	Feb	Mar	Apr	May	Jun	Jul	Aug	Sep	Oct	Nov	Dec
Winter Steelhead	4,6,7	4,6,7	4,6,7	4,6,7							4,6,7	4,6,7
Fall Chinook									6,7,9	4,6 7,9	4,6 7,9	4,6 7,9
Spring Chinook					4,7,8	4,7,8						
Coho									3,4 7,8,9	3,4 7,8,9	3,4 7,8,9	
Sea-Run Cutthroat			2,6 8,9	2,6 8,9	2,6 8,9			2,6 8,9	2,6 8,9	2,6 8,9		

Legend: Best / Good / Slow

1. Dry fly, dead-drift
2. Dry fly, swung
3. Wet fly, swung near surface
4. Wet fly, swung deep
5. Nymph(s), lightly weighted
6. Nymph(s), weighted with indicator
7. Deep drifted fly (with or without indicator)
8. Wet fly retrieved near surface
9. Deep swing with retrieve

BEST GEAR-FISHING TECHNIQUES & ESTIMATED HOOKUPS IN AN AVERAGE YEAR

	Jan	Feb	Mar	Apr	May	Jun	Jul	Aug	Sep	Oct	Nov	Dec
Winter Steelhead 3000	1,2 3,4	1,2 3,4	1,2 3,4	1,2 3,4							1,2,3,4	1,2 3,4
Fall Chinook 3000									2,3,6	1,2,3 4,5,6	1,2,3 4,5,6	1,2,3 4,5,6
Spring Chinook 175					1,2,3 4,5	1,2,3 4,5						
Coho 300									1,2,3 4,5	1,2,3 4,5	1,2,3 4,5	
Sea-Run Cutthroat			2	2	2			2	2	2		

1. Drift fishing (from bank or boat, with or without bait)
2. Casting spinners, spoons, plugs
3. Float fishing (with jigs or bait)
4. Back-trolling (plugs or diver-and-bait)
5. Back-bouncing (boat)
6. Trolling (boat only)
7. Anchor fishing
8. Plunking
9. Jigging

Wading difficulty	Moderate
Shuttles	Yes
Boating difficulty	Moderate
USGS river levels on-line	No
Water clarity recovery	Moderate

herring, and spinner/bait combinations from September until the first heavy rains. Float fishing is also popular, especially near reach-of-tide, where the river enters the estuary.

Winter steelhead are caught throughout the Coquille system, especially on the South Fork, from late November through March. All methods of fishing are effective for steelhead, with drift fishing and casting spinners and spoons most effective.

Sea-run and resident cutthroat offer good trout fishing throughout the river. Trolling small plugs in tidewater during August and September is a popular way to catch sea-run cutthroat. Fly-fishing or casting small lures in the upper river and tributaries is good through summer and into the fall.

SERVICES

CAMPING/PARKS
- **Bullards Beach State Park,** Bandon, Info: (800) 551-6949, Reservations: (800) 452-5687, www.oregonstateparks.org
- **Bandon RV Park,** Bandon, 97411, (541) 347-4122, www.bandonrvpark.com
- **Sturdivant City Park,** Coquille, 97423, (541) 396-2115, www.cityofcoquille.org
- **Remote Outpost RV Park & Cabins,** Myrtle Point, 97458, (541) 572-5105
- **Powers County Park,** Powers, 97466, Reserve RV sites: (541) 439-2791, Cabins: (541) 396-7755, www.co.coos.or.us
- **River's Edge RV Park,** Coquille, 97423, (541) 396-6255

ACCOMMODATIONS
- **Lighthouse Bed & Breakfast,** Bandon, 97411, (541) 347-9316, www.lighthouselodging.com

TACKLE SHOPS
- **Port O' Call,** Bandon, 97411, (541) 347-2875
- **Coquille Liquor Store,** Coquille, 97423, (541) 396-4651
- **Englund Marine,** Coos Bay, 97420, (541) 888-6723, www.englundmarine.com

VISITOR INFORMATION
- **City of Coquille,** Coquille, 97423, (541) 396-2115, www.cityofcoquille.org
- **Coos County Parks, Info:** (541) 396-7759, **Reserve:** (541) 396-7755, www.co.coos.or.us
- **South Coast Oregon Directory City Guide,** www.scod.com
- **Bandon Chamber of Commerce,** Bandon, 97411, (541) 347-9616, www.bandon.com
- **Coquille Chamber of Commerce,** Coquille, 97423, (541) 396-3414, coquillechamber.net

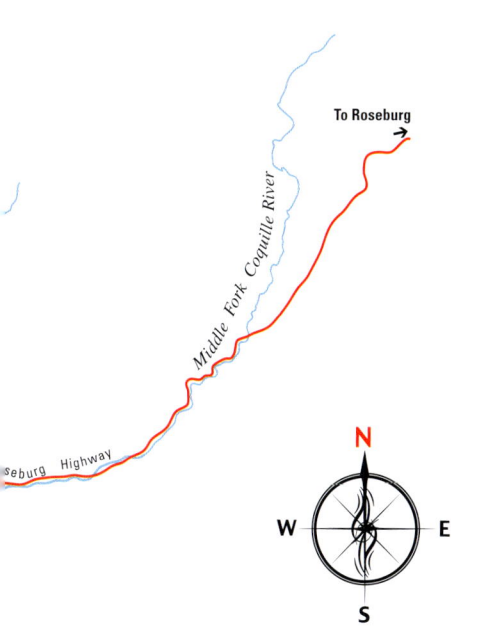

Oregon River Maps & Fishing Guide

Sixes River

A favorite south-coast salmon and steelhead river, the Sixes River flows about forty miles from its headwaters in the Siskiyou National Forest to its mouth, just north of Cape Blanco. It is open for fishing from the confluence of the South Fork down to the ocean—about 15 river-miles.

The Sixes is known to locals as an excellent sea-run cutthroat stream, but is best known for its salmon and steelhead fishing. Trout season is June through October, and fishing is good from tidewater up to the South Fork. Chinook salmon are the main attraction from October through December. Wild winter steelhead run strong from December through March.

The Sixes, like the Elk, is most popular as a late-season Chinook fishery. It is the preferred river for guides in November and December when the Elk is often crowded with boats. Drift boats are the best way to access the salmon and steelhead of the Sixes, although there is good bank access at several points upstream of Highway 101.

Port Orford is the nearest town, and offers good accommodations. Water clarity is slow to recover from a high-water event, which makes it a good bet when the Elk River is too low and clear.

LOCATION:
Coos, Curry Counties

Wading difficulty	Moderate
Shuttles	Yes
Boating difficulty	Moderate
USGS river levels on-line	No
Water clarity recovery	Moderate
Best river levels	When Elk R. is 3.5'-5.5'

SERVICES

CAMPING/PARKS
- **Edson Creek County Park,** Sixes, 97476, (541) 247-3386, www.blm.gov/or
- **Sixes River Recreation Site,** Port Orford, 97465, (541) 756-0100, www.blm.gov/or
- **Port Orford RV Village,** Port Orford, 97465, (541) 332-1041, www.portorfordrv.com
- **Madrona & 101 RV Park,** Port Orford, 97465, (541) 332-4025, (877) 722-5578, www.oregontravels.com
- **Cape Blanco State Park,** (800) 551-6949, (541) 332-2973, www.oregonstateparks.org
- **Bandon/Port Orford KOA Campground,** Langlois, 97450, (541) 348-2358, Reserve: (800) 562-3298, www.koa.com/campgrounds/bandon

ACCOMMODATIONS
- **WildSpring Guest Habitat,** Port Orford, 97465, (541) 332-0977, (866) 333-9453, email: info@wildspring.com, www.wildspring.com
- **The Compass Rose B&B,** Port Orford, 97465, (541) 551-0902, (541) 332-7076, doug@compassroseportorford.com, www.compassroseportorford.com

TACKLE SHOPS
- **Port-O-Call,** Bandon, 97411, (541) 347-2875, www.tonyscrabshack.com/port-o-call
- **Bandon Baits,** Bandon, 97411, (541) 347-3905, www.bandon.com
- **Rogue Outdoor Store,** Gold Beach, 97444, (541) 247-7142, www.facebook.com/rogueoutdoorstore
- **Griff's on the Dock,** Port Orford, 97465, (541) 332-8985

VISITOR INFORMATION
- **Curry County Parks,** Gold Beach, 97444, (541) 247-3386, www.co.curry.or.us
- **Siskiyou National Forest,** Medford, 97504, (541) 618-2200, www.fs.usda.gov/rogue-siskiyou
- **Coos Bay District BLM,** North Bend, 97459, (541) 756-0100, www.or.blm.gov/or
- **Port Orford and North Curry County Chamber of Commerce,** Port Orford, 97465, (541) 332-8055, www.portorfordchamber.com

SIXES RIVER

BEST FLY-FISHING TECHNIQUES

Best / Good / Slow	Jan	Feb	Mar	Apr	May	Jun	Jul	Aug	Sep	Oct	Nov	Dec
Winter Steelhead	3,4 6,7	3,4 6,7	3,4 6,7								3,4 6,7	3,4 6,7
Fall Chinook										4,6,9	4,6,9	4,6,9
Coho										4,9	4,9	
Sea-Run Cutthroat						2,3 8,9	2,3 8,9	2,3 8,9	2,3 8,9	2,3 8,9	2,3 8,9	

1. Dry fly, dead-drift
2. Dry fly, swung
3. Wet fly, swung near surface
4. Wet fly, swung deep
5. Nymph(s), lightly weighted
6. Nymph(s), weighted with indicator
7. Deep drifted fly (with or without indicator)
8. Wet fly retrieved near surface
9. Deep swing with retrieve

BEST GEAR-FISHING TECHNIQUES & ESTIMATED HOOKUPS IN AN AVERAGE YEAR

Best / Good / Slow	Jan	Feb	Mar	Apr	May	Jun	Jul	Aug	Sep	Oct	Nov	Dec
Winter Steelhead 200	1,2 3,4	1,2 3,4	1,2 3,4								1,2 3,4	1,2 3,4
Fall Chinook 1000										1,2,3 4,5	1,2,3 4,5	1,2,3 4,5
Coho 10										2	2	
Sea-Run Cutthroat						2	2	2	2	2	2	

1. Drift fishing (from bank or boat, with or without bait)
2. Casting spinners, spoons, plugs
3. Float fishing (with jigs or bait)
4. Back-trolling (plugs or diver-and-bait)
5. Back-bouncing (boat)
6. Trolling (boat only)
7. Anchor fishing
8. Plunking
9. Jigging

The Sixes is known for its big, late-season kings.

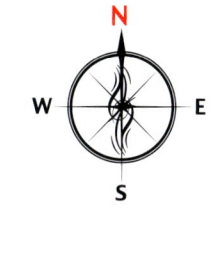

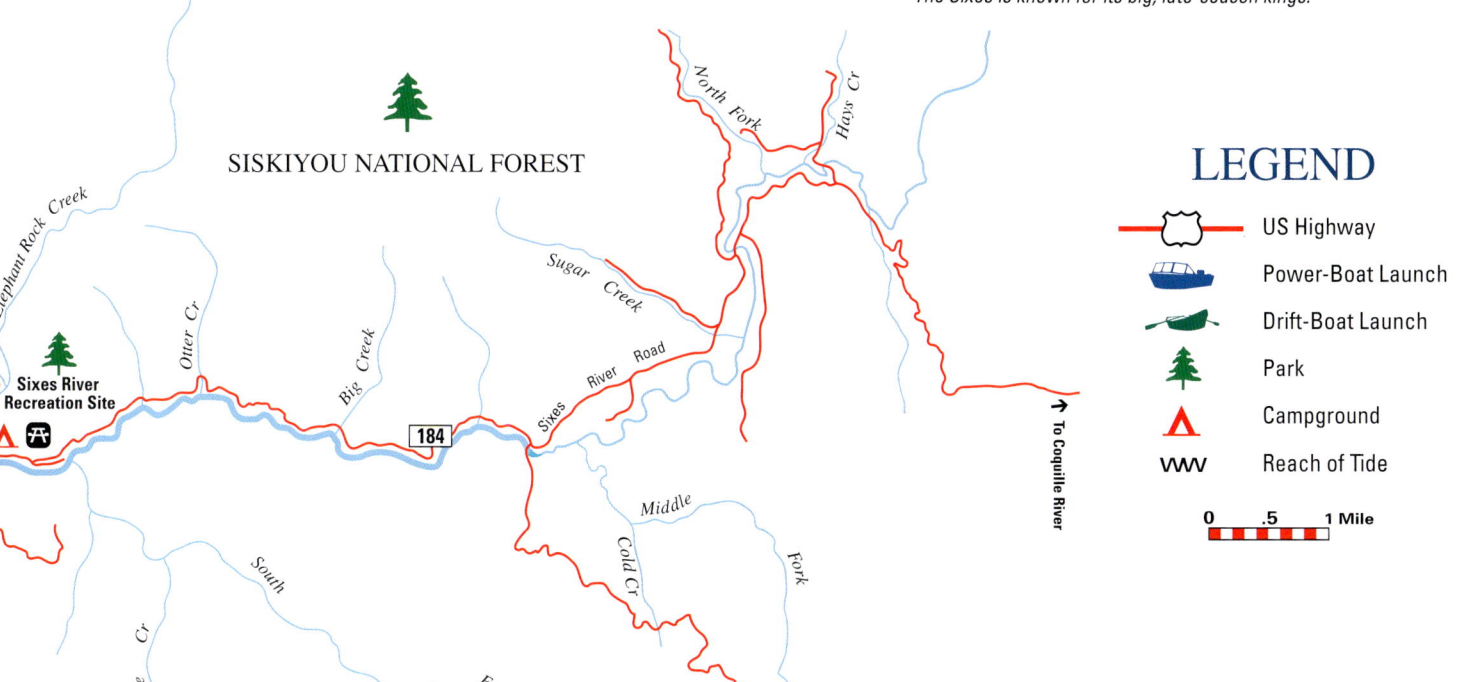

Photo by Nick Amato

LEGEND

- US Highway
- Power-Boat Launch
- Drift-Boat Launch
- Park
- Campground
- Reach of Tide

0 .5 1 Mile

47

OREGON RIVER MAPS & FISHING GUIDE

Elk River

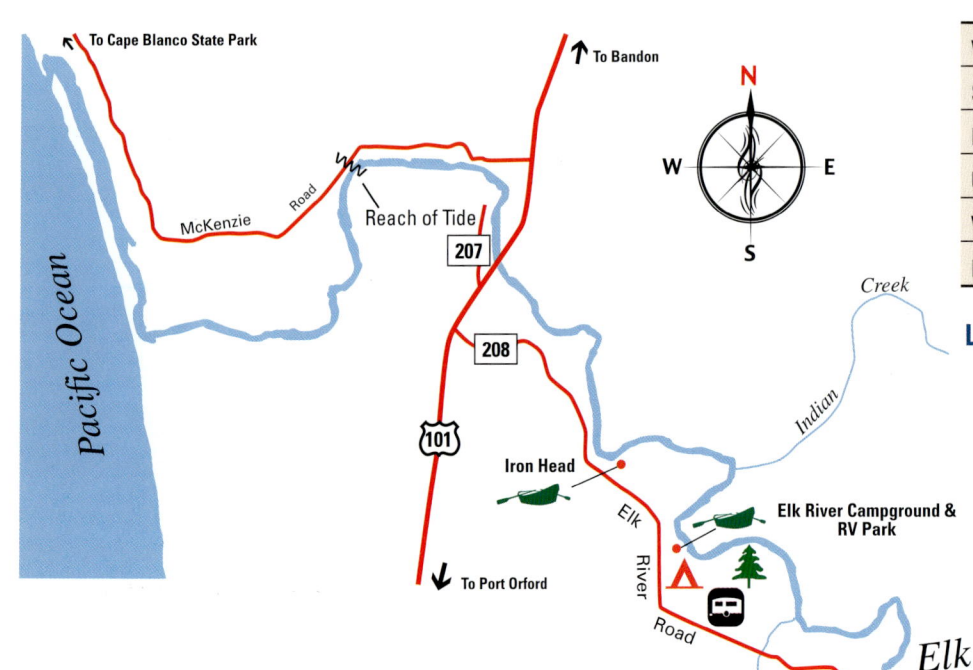

Wading difficulty	Moderate
Shuttles	Yes
Boating difficulty	Moderate
USGS river levels on-line	Call Elk River Hatchery
Water clarity recovery	Moderate
Best river levels	4'-6'

LOCATION: Curry County

Widely known as one of Oregon's best late-season Chinook salmon rivers, the Elk River flows from its sources at Salmon Mountain and the Grassy Knob Wilderness (Siskiyou National Forest) to its mouth, just a few miles north of Port Orford. It is a short river, just over 30 miles, with very little bank access, especially in the lower ten miles.

From late spring until the first big rains of autumn, the Elk River ends at a sandbar, cut off from the Pacific Ocean. Chinook salmon arrive along the ocean shore in late August, and continue to run through December. In years when the autumn rains arrive late, salmon may not be able to enter the river until November. During the late summer and fall, before the rains, there is a unique beach fishery at the mouth of the Elk. Once the rains come, angling pressure is focused between the upstream deadline at Bald Mountain Creek and Iron Head boat landing (the lowest boat launch on the Elk).

The Elk is also home to a respectable wild run of winter steelhead. These fish begin to arrive in December, but are most numerous from January through March. Drift boating is the best way to access the excellent salmon and steelhead fishing on the Elk. Only a few small public access areas are available for bank anglers. During the rest of the season (May 24 to October 31), the Elk is home to a good number of wild cutthroat trout.

Port Orford is the nearest town, and offers good accommodations and shuttles. The Elk is the first river in the area to clear after a rain—usually fishable within 24 to 48 hours after a blowout. For a current river report, call the Elk River Hatchery: (541) 332-7025.

This ocean-fresh salmon fell for a Venezuelan beauty!

Photo by Robert Russell

ELK RIVER

BEST FLY-FISHING TECHNIQUES

	Jan	Feb	Mar	Apr	May	Jun	Jul	Aug	Sep	Oct	Nov	Dec
Winter Steelhead	3,4,6,7	3,4,6,7	3,4,6,7									3,4,6,7
Fall Chinook										4,6,9	4,6,9	4,6,9
Coho										3,4,6,7,9	3,4,6,7,9	
Sea-Run Cutthroat						2,3,8,9	2,3,8,9	2,3,8,9	2,3,8,9	2,3,8,9	2,3,8,9	

Legend: Best / Good / Slow

1. Dry fly, dead-drift
2. Dry fly, swung
3. Wet fly, swung near surface
4. Wet fly, swung deep
5. Nymph(s), lightly weighted
6. Nymph(s), weighted with indicator
7. Deep drifted fly (with or without indicator)
8. Wet fly retrieved near surface
9. Deep swing with retrieve

BEST GEAR-FISHING TECHNIQUES & ESTIMATED HOOKUPS IN AN AVERAGE YEAR

	Jan	Feb	Mar	Apr	May	Jun	Jul	Aug	Sep	Oct	Nov	Dec
Winter Steelhead 400	1,2,3,4	1,2,3,4	1,2,3,4									1,2,3,4
Fall Chinook 2000	1,2,3,4,5									1,2,3,4,5	1,2,3,4,5	1,2,3,4,5
Coho 50										1,2,3,4,5	1,2,3,4,5	
Sea-Run Cutthroat						2	2	2	2	2	2	

1. Drift fishing (from bank or boat, with or without bait)
2. Casting spinners, spoons, plugs
3. Float fishing (with jigs or bait)
4. Back-trolling (plugs or diver-and-bait)
5. Back-bouncing (boat)
6. Trolling (boat only)
7. Anchor fishing
8. Plunking
9. Jigging

SERVICES

CAMPING/PARKS

- **Elk River Campground & RV Park,** Port Orford, 97465, (541) 332-2255, www.woodalls.com/campground
- **Port Orford RV Village,** Port Orford, 97465, (541) 332-1041, www.portorfordrv.com
- **Madrona & 101 RV Park,** Port Orford, 97465, (541) 332-4025, (877) 722-5578, www.oregontravels.com
- **Cape Blanco State Park,** (800) 551-6949, (541) 332-2973, www.oregonstateparks.org
- **Bandon/Port Orford KOA Kampground,** Langlois, 97450, (541) 348-2358, Reserve: (800) 562-3298, www.koa.com/campgrounds/bandon

ACCOMMODATIONS

- **WildSpring Guest Habitat,** Port Orford, 97465, (541) 332-0977, (866) 333-9453, email: info@wildspring.com, www.wildspring.com
- **The Compass Rose B&B,** Port Orford, 97465, (541) 551-0902, (541) 332-7076, email: doug@compassroseportorford.com, www.compassroseportorford.com

TACKLE SHOPS

- **Port-O-Call,** Bandon, 97411, (541) 347-2875, www.tonyscrabshack.com/port-o-call
- **Bandon Baits,** Bandon, 97411, (541) 347-3905, www.bandon.com
- **Rogue Outdoor Store,** Gold Beach, 97444, (541) 247-7142, www.facebook.com/rogueoutdoorstore

VISITOR INFORMATION

- **Curry County Parks,** Gold Beach, 97444, (541) 247-3386, www.co.curry.or.us
- **Siskiyou National Forest,** Medford, 97504, (541) 618-2200, www.fs.usda.gov/rogue-siskiyou
- **Coos Bay District BLM,** North Bend, 97459, (541) 756-0100, www.or.blm.gov/or
- **Southern Oregon Fishing:** Reports, News, Photos & More, www.southernoregonfishingreports.com
- **Port Orford and North Curry County Chamber of Commerce,** Port Orford, 97465, (541) 332-8055, www.portorfordchamber.com

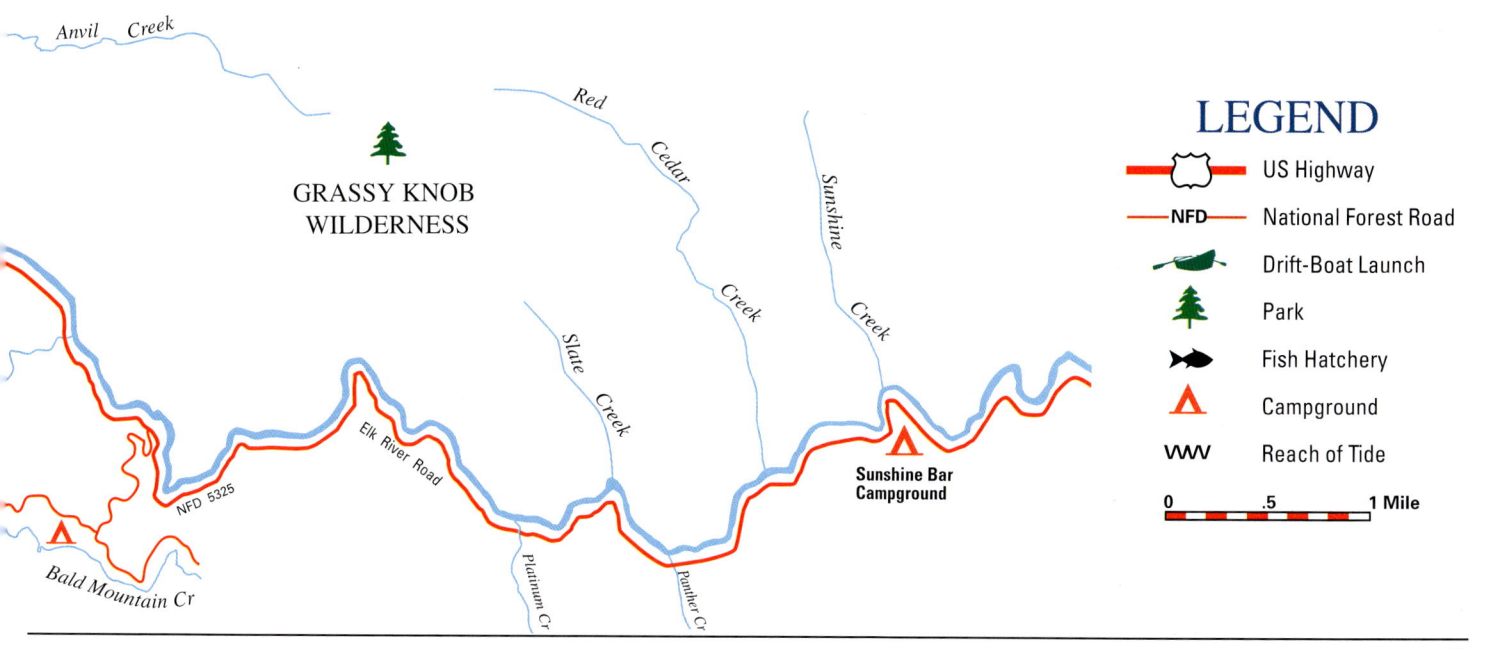

LEGEND

- US Highway
- NFD — National Forest Road
- Drift-Boat Launch
- Park
- Fish Hatchery
- Campground
- Reach of Tide

0 .5 1 Mile

Oregon River Maps & Fishing Guide

Rogue River, Lower

SERVICES

CAMPING/PARKS

- **Jot's Resort,** Gold Beach, 97444, (800) 367-5687, (541) 247-6676, www.jotsresort.com
- **Indian Creek RV Park,** Gold Beach, 97444, (541) 247-7704, www.indiancreekrv.com
- **Four Season's RV Resort,** Gold Beach, 97444, (541) 247-4503, www.fourseasonsrv.com
- **Huntly Park,** Gold Beach, 97444, (541) 247-9377, www.portofgoldbeach.com/HuntleyPark.htm
- **Lucky Lodge RV Park,** Gold Beach, 97444, (541) 247-7618,
- **Kimball Creek Bend RV Resort,** Gold Beach, 97444, (541) 247-7580, www.kimballcreek.com
- **Agness Rogue River RV Park,** Agness, 97406, (541) 247-2813, (866) 729-9043, www.rogueriverrvpark.com

ACCOMMODATIONS

- **Lucas Lodge,** Agness, 97406, (541) 247-7443, www.lucaslodgeoregon.com
- **Singing Springs Resort,** Agness, 97406, (541) 247-6162, (877) 330-3777, www.singingspringsresort.com
- **Tu Tu Tun Lodge,** Gold Beach, 97444, (541) 247-6664, (800) 864-6357, www.tututun.com

TACKLE SHOPS

- **Rogue Outdoor Store,** Gold Beach, 97444, (541) 247-7142, www.facebook.com/rogueoutdoorstore
- **Jot's Resort,** Gold Beach, 97444, (800) 367-5687, (541) 247-6676, www.jotsresort.com
- **Lex's Landing,** Gold Beach, 97444, (541) 247-0909, www.lexslanding.com

VISITOR INFORMATION

- **Rogue National Wild and Scenic River, Rogue River Float** Guide brochure: www.blm.gov/or/resources/recreation/rogue/files/FloatGuide04.pdf

The Rogue River is among the most renowned rivers in the West, known for its exceptional fishing for trout, steelhead and salmon. First popularized by western-writer Zane Grey in the 1930s, the Rogue attracts anglers from around the world. It produces some of the largest runs of salmon and steelhead anywhere on the Pacific Coast, and supports an excellent trout fishery within its upper reaches.

The Rogue River flows 155 miles from the Cascade Mountains to the Pacific. Thirty-eight improved boat launches offer excellent boating access, although boaters should be advised that there are hazardous rapids in most sections of the river. The Rogue is for experienced whitewater boaters only. Bank access

- **River Permits and Information, Smullin Visitor Center,** Merlin, 97532, (541) 479-3735, www.or.blm.gov/rogueriver
- **Rogue River-Siskiyou Forest,** Medford, 97504, (541) 618-2200, www.fs.usda.gov/rogue-siskiyou
- **Kalmiopsis Wilderness,** www.fs.usda.gov, Contact: Gold Beach Ranger District, Gold Beach, 97444, (541) 247-3600
- **Josephine County Parks,** Grants Pass, 97527, (541) 474-5285, www.co.josephine.or.us
- **Rogue River Guides Association,** www.rogueriverguides.com
- **Gold Beach Chamber of Commerce,** Gold Beach, 97444, (541) 247-0923, www.goldbeachchamber.com

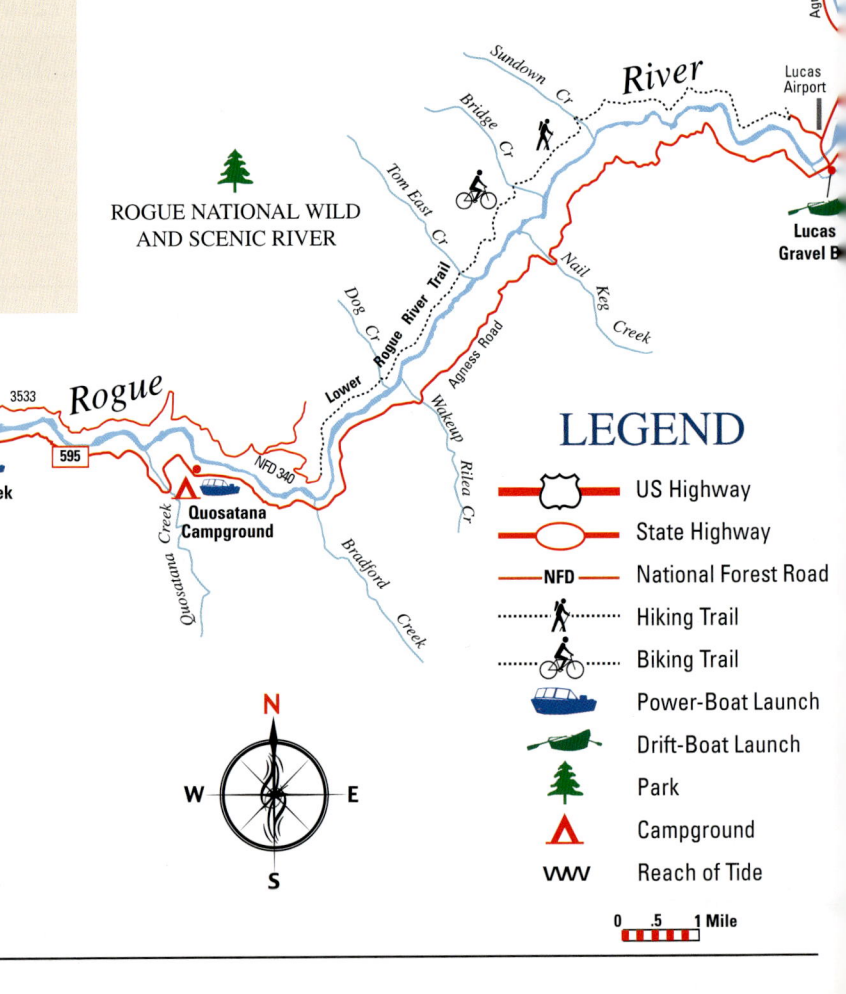

LEGEND

- US Highway
- State Highway
- NFD — National Forest Road
- Hiking Trail
- Biking Trail
- Power-Boat Launch
- Drift-Boat Launch
- Park
- Campground
- Reach of Tide

1. Jerry's Rogue Jets
2. Fishermen Direct Seafoods
3. Wild Coast Vacations
4. Hilltop House Gold Beach

ROGUE RIVER, LOWER

is spotty, but the many parks and boat landings are good places to bank-fish.

Rogue Bay is a popular estuary for salmon fishing. April and May are peak months for spring Chinook, August and September for fall Chinook and coho. Steelhead pass quickly through this section and are rarely caught below the reach-of-tide at the Clay Banks (River Mile 5, just downstream of Jim Hunt Creek).

The Lower Rogue, from Foster Bar to the bay, sees the bulk of the river's salmon-fishing pressure. From May through October, boaters ply this reach for ocean-fresh Chinook salmon. From August through October, coho salmon join the party, making for some world-class fishing. Steelhead are a common by-catch throughout the season. Winter steelhead are the main event from December through March.

The Wild Rogue is a 33-mile roadless wilderness stretching from the tiny village of Illahe upriver to Grave Creek. A hiking trail follows the north bank of the river, and many primitive campsites are nestled among the myrtle, oak and Douglas fir trees. Fishing for steelhead and salmon is excellent, and the waters are pristine. Bank angling is recommended, but experienced whitewater boaters can explore the entire section over several days of drifting and camping. Salmon fishing in May and June can be very good in this section, and there are always steelhead to be found.

LOCATION: Josephine County

Wading difficulty	Moderate-Difficult
Shuttles	Yes
Boating difficulty	Moderate-Difficult
USGS river levels on-line	Yes
Water clarity recovery	Moderate

BEST GEAR-FISHING TECHNIQUES & ESTIMATED HOOKUPS IN AN AVERAGE YEAR

Best / Good / Slow	Jan	Feb	Mar	Apr	May	Jun	Jul	Aug	Sep	Oct	Nov	Dec
Winter Steelhead 5,000	1,2,3,4	1,2,3,4	1,2,3,4								1,2,3,4	1,2,3,4
Summer Steelhead 10,000	1,2,3,4						1,2,3,4	1,2,3,4	1,2,3,4	1,2,3,4	1,2,3,4	1,2,3,4
Half-pounders 10,000	1,2,3,4	1,2,3,4						1,2,3,4	1,2,3,4	1,2,3,4	1,2,3,4	
Fall Chinook (Tidewater) 12,000							2,3,6	2,3,6	2,3,6	2,3,6		
Fall Chinook (River) 12,000								1,2,3 4,5	1,2,3 4,5	1,2,3 4,5	1,2,3 4,5	
Spring Chinook (Tidewater) 10,000					2,3,6	2,3,6	2,3,6					
Spring Chinook (River) 10,000						1,2,3 4,5	1,2,3 4,5	1,2,3,4,5				
Coho 1,000								1,2,3 4,5	1,2,3 4,5	1,2,3 4,5		

1. Drift fishing (from bank or boat, with or without bait)
2. Casting spinners, spoons, plugs
3. Float fishing (with jigs or bait)
4. Back-trolling (plugs or diver-and-bait)
5. Back-bouncing (boat)
6. Trolling (boat only)
7. Anchor fishing
8. Plunking
9. Jigging

BEST FLY-FISHING TECHNIQUES

Best / Good / Slow	Jan	Feb	Mar	Apr	May	Jun	Jul	Aug	Sep	Oct	Nov	Dec
Winter Steelhead	4,5,6,7	4,5,6,7	4,5,6,7								4,5,6,7	4,5,6,7
Summer Steelhead								2,3,4 5,6,7	2,3,4 5,6,7	2,3,4 5,6,7	2,3,4 5,6,7	2,3,4 5,6,7
Half-pounders	2,3,4 5,6,7	2,3,4 5,6,7					2,3,4,5,6,7	2,3,4 5,6,7	2,3,4 5,6,7	2,3,4 5,6,7		
Fall Chinook							4,6,7,8	4,6 7,8	4,6 7,8	4,6 7,8	4,6 7,8	
Spring Chinook				4,6 7,8	4,6 7,8	4,6 7,8	4,6 7,8	4,6,7,8				
Coho								4,7 9	4,7 9	4,7 9		

1. Dry fly, dead-drift
2. Dry fly, swung
3. Wet fly, swung near surface
4. Wet fly, swung deep
5. Nymph(s), lightly weighted
6. Nymph(s), weighted with indicator
7. Deep drifted fly (with or without indicator)
8. Wet fly retrieved near surface
9. Deep swing with retrieve

51

Oregon River Maps & Fishing Guide

Rogue River, Middle

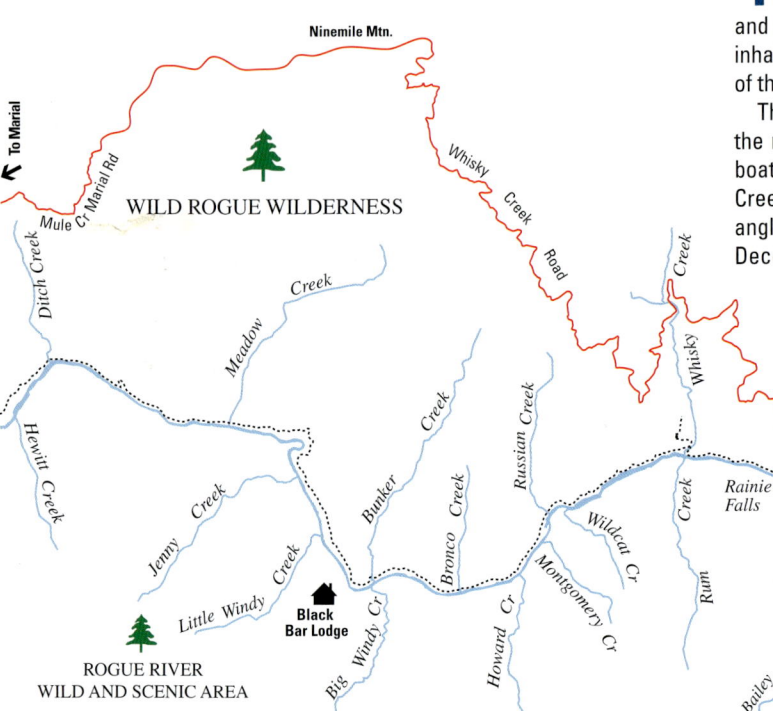

The middle and upper sections of the Rogue offer a wide variety of fishing opportunities, and are very accessible for boaters and bank anglers alike. Summer and winter steelhead, spring and fall Chinook salmon, and coho salmon all make strong runs through these sections. Rainbow trout inhabit the whole river, but are most concentrated in the uppermost stretch of the Rogue, known as the Holy Water.

The Lower Middle Rogue runs through the town of Grants Pass. It offers the most public access of any stretch, offering no less than 19 parks with boat launches. There is excellent fly-fishing water from Grants Pass to Hog Creek. Below Hog Creek, heavy raft and jet-boat traffic discourages some anglers, but the fishing can be excellent. Winter steelheading is best from December through March, spring Chinook run from May through July,

SERVICES

CAMPING/PARKS
- **Indian Mary Park,** Merlin, (541) 474-5285, www.josephine.or.us
- **Argo County Park,** Merlin, 97527, (541) 474-5285, www.co.josephine.or.us
- **Almeda County Park,** Merlin, 97527, (541) 474-5285, www.co.josephine.or.us
- **Bridgeview RV Resort,** Grants Pass, (541) 582-5980, www.bridgeviewrvresort.com
- **Cypress Grove RV Park,** Gold Hill, 97525, (541) 855-9000, (800) 758-0719, www.cypressgrovervpark.com

ACCOMMODATIONS
- **The Lodge at Riverside,** Grants Pass, (877) 955-0600, www.thelodgeatriverside.com
- **Doubletree Ranch,** Merlin, (541) 476-0120, www.doubletree-ranch.com
- **Riverhouse Camp Lodge,** Merlin, (541) 472-1052, www.riverhouseontherogue.com
- **Galice Resort,** Merlin, 97532, (541) 476-3818, www.galice.com
- **Restful Nest on the Rogue B&B,** Grants Pass, 97527, (541) 582-8259 or (541) 291-1216, www.restfulnestbandb.com
- **Lucas Lodge,** Agness, 97406, (541) 247-7443, www.lucaslodgeoregon.com
- **Singing Springs Resort,** Agness, 97406, (541) 247-6162, (877) 330-3777, www.singingspringsresort.com

TACKLE SHOPS
- **Bradbury's Gun-N-Tackle Bait Shop,** Grants Pass, 97527, (541) 479-1531
- **Backlash Tackle Shop,** Grants Pass, 97526, (541) 955-0312, www.backlashtacklegrantspass.com
- **Rogue Fly Shop,** Grants Pass, 97526, (541) 476-0552, www.rogueflyshop.com

VISITOR INFORMATION
- **Rogue National Wild and Scenic River, Rogue River Float Guide brochure,** www.blm.gov/or/resources/recreation/rogue/files/FloatGuide04.pdf
- **Rogue River-Siskiyou Forest,** Medford, 97504, (541) 618-2200, www.fs.usda.gov/rogue-siskiyou
- **Kalmiopsis Wilderness,** Contact: Gold Beach Ranger District, Gold Beach, 97444, (541) 247-3600
- **Josephine County Parks,** Grants Pass, 97527, (541) 474-5285, www.co.josephine.or.us
- **Rogue River Guides Association,** www.rogueriverguides.com
- **Grants Pass & Josephine County Chamber of Commerce,** Grants Pass, 97526, (541) 476-7717, (800) 547-5927, www.grantspasschamber.org

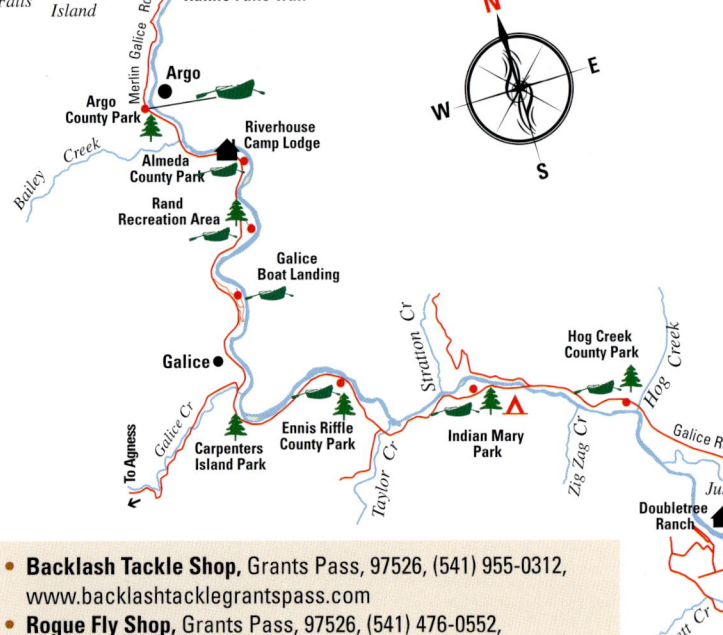

52

ROGUE RIVER, MIDDLE

summer steelhead swarm in this section from July through October, and fall Chinook and coho move in from September through November. Every day of the year offers the potential for great fishing.

The Upper Middle Rogue flows through the towns of Gold Hill and Rogue River. Steelhead and Chinook salmon are the dominant fish here. While fly-fishing is effective, big water and the proximity to rural towns makes conventional tackle the most popular. Bank access is limited in this section due to private property and difficult roads, but several municipal parks offer good fishing. Boating this stretch is best, but avoid the treacherous section between Gold Ray Dam and Gold Hill. Spring Chinook inhabit this section from May through August, summer steelhead from August through November.

The Upper Rogue is the most popular stretch for steelhead fly-fishing, although for much of the year conventional tackle is allowed (consult regulations). Thousands of summer-run steelhead converge in the upper river, a combination of "half-pounders" (small steelhead that have spent only one season feeding in the ocean) and full-sized steelhead (from four to fifteen pounds, and sometimes even bigger). To find steelhead in this section of the river, look for water that is two to six feet deep, walking speed. August through November is the prime steelhead season, and October is generally the best month. There is plenty of bank access in the upper river, and six boat launches. Drift-boaters should be sure to take out at Tou Velle State Park to avoid some dangerous rapids below.

The Holy Water is a classic tailwater trout fishery, planted by Oregon Fish & Wildlife (ODFW) with fingerling trout, and supporting some hefty holdovers. In the short half-mile section between Lost Creek Dam and the hatchery diversion, fly-anglers will find rainbow trout from 12 to 26 inches. The best fishing coincides with the best insect hatches (see chart), from April through October.

A beautiful Oregon native steelhead just before release.

Photo by Esther Poleo

LOCATION: Josephine & Jackson Counties

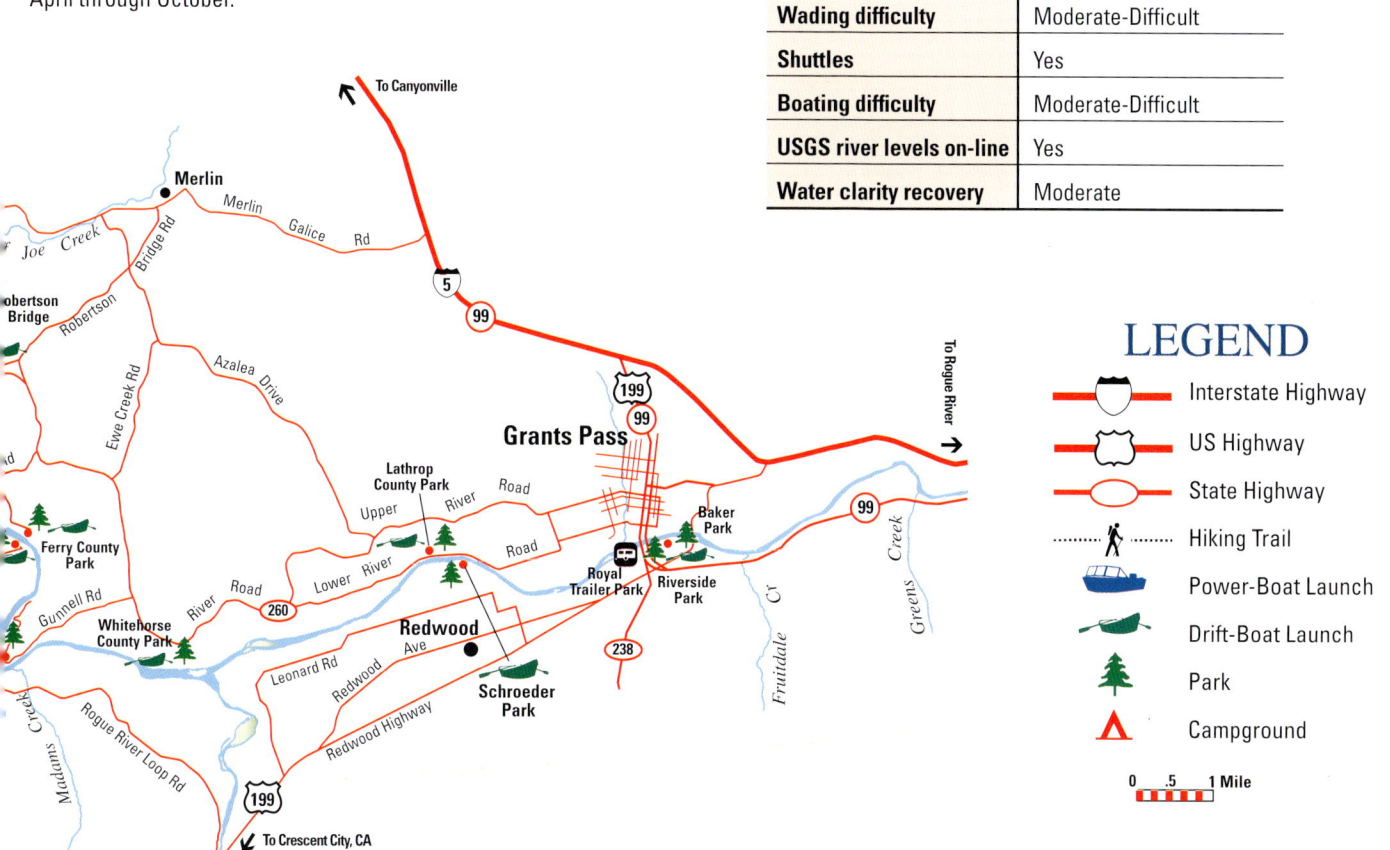

Wading difficulty	Moderate-Difficult
Shuttles	Yes
Boating difficulty	Moderate-Difficult
USGS river levels on-line	Yes
Water clarity recovery	Moderate

LEGEND

- Interstate Highway
- US Highway
- State Highway
- Hiking Trail
- Power-Boat Launch
- Drift-Boat Launch
- Park
- Campground

Oregon River Maps & Fishing Guide

Rogue River, Upper

SERVICES

CAMPING/PARKS
- **Bridgeview RV Resort,** Grants Pass, (541) 582-5980, www.bridgeviewrvresort.com
- **Cypress Grove RV Park,** Gold Hill, 97525, (541) 855-9000, (800) 758-0719, www.cypressgrovervpark.com
- **Fly Casters RV Park,** Shady Cove, 97539, (800) 806-4705, www.flycastersrv.com

ACCOMMODATIONS
- **Rogue River Lodge,** Trail, 97541, (541) 878-2555, www.therogueriverlodge.com
- **Rogue River Guest House,** Gold Hill, 97525, (541) 855-4485, (877) 764-8322, www.rogueriverguesthouse.com

TACKLE SHOPS
- **Rogue Steel,** Rogue River, 97537, (541) 761-7145, www.roguesteel.us
- **Rogue Rods,** White City, 97503, (541) 830-4141, (877) 352-7624, www.roguerods.com

VISITOR INFORMATION
- **Rogue National Wild and Scenic River, Rogue River Float Guide brochure:** www.blm.gov/or/resources/recreation/rogue/files/FloatGuide04.pdf
- **River Permits and Information, Smullin Visitor Center,** Merlin, 97532, (541) 479-3735, www.or.blm.gov/Rogueriver
- **Rogue River- Siskiyou Forest,** Medford, 97504, (541) 618-2200, www.fs.usda.gov/rogue-siskiyou
- **Kalmiopsis Wilderness, Contact: Gold Beach Ranger District,** Gold Beach, 97444, (541) 247-3600
- **Josephine County Parks,** Grants Pass, 97527, (541) 474-5285, www.co.josephine.or.us
- **Jackson County Parks,** Central Point, 97502, (541) 774-8183, www.co.jackson.or.us or www.jacksoncountyparks.com
- **Rogue River Guides Association,** www.rogueriverguides.com
- **Rogue River Chamber of Commerce,** Rogue River, 97537, (541) 582-0242, www.rogueriverchamber.com

BEST FLY-FISHING TECHNIQUES

	Jan	Feb	Mar	Apr	May	Jun	Jul	Aug	Sep	Oct	Nov	Dec
Winter Steelhead	4,5 6,7	4,5 6,7	4,5 6,7	4,5 6,7							4,5 6,7	4,5 6,7
Summer Steelhead	2,3,4 5,6,7							2,3,4 5,6,7	2,3,4 5,6,7	2,3,4 5,6,7	2,3,4 5,6,7	2,3,4 5,6,7
Half-pounders	2,3,4 5,6,7	2,3,4 5,6,7							2,3,4 5,6,7	2,3,4 5,6,7	2,3,4 5,6,7	2,3,4 5,6,7
Fall Chinook								4,6 7,8	4,6 7,8	4,6 7,8	4,6 7,8	4,6 7,8
Spring Chinook					4,6 7,8	4,6 7,8	4,6 7,8	4,6 7,8	4,6 7,8			
Coho									4,7 9	4,7 9		
Rainbow Trout	1,3 5,6	1,3 5,6	1,3 5,6	1,3 5,6	1,3 5,6	1,3 5,6	1,3 5,6	1,3 5,6	1,3 5,6	1,3 5,6	1,3 5,6	1,3 5,6

Legend: Best / Good / Slow

1. Dry fly, dead-drift
2. Dry fly, swung
3. Wet fly, swung near surface
4. Wet fly, swung deep
5. Nymph(s), lightly weighted
6. Nymph(s), weighted with indicator
7. Deep drifted fly (with or without indicator)
8. Wet fly retrieved near surface
9. Deep swing with retrieve

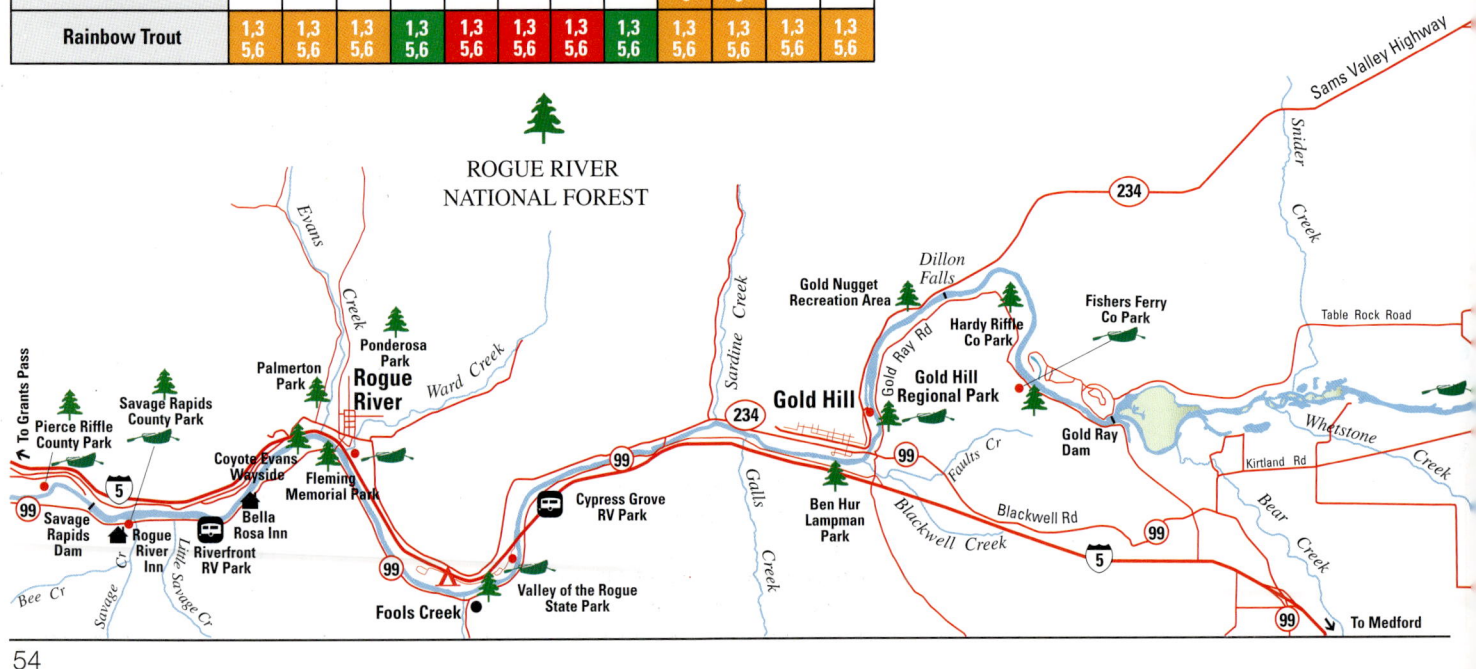

ROGUE RIVER, UPPER

LOCATION: Josephine & Jackson Counties

Wading difficulty	Moderate-Difficult
Shuttles	Yes
Boating difficulty	Moderate-Difficult
USGS river levels on-line	Yes
Water clarity recovery	Moderate

LEGEND

- Interstate Highway
- US Highway
- State Highway
- Hiking Trail
- Power-Boat Launch
- Drift-Boat Launch
- Park
- Campground

0 .5 1 Mile

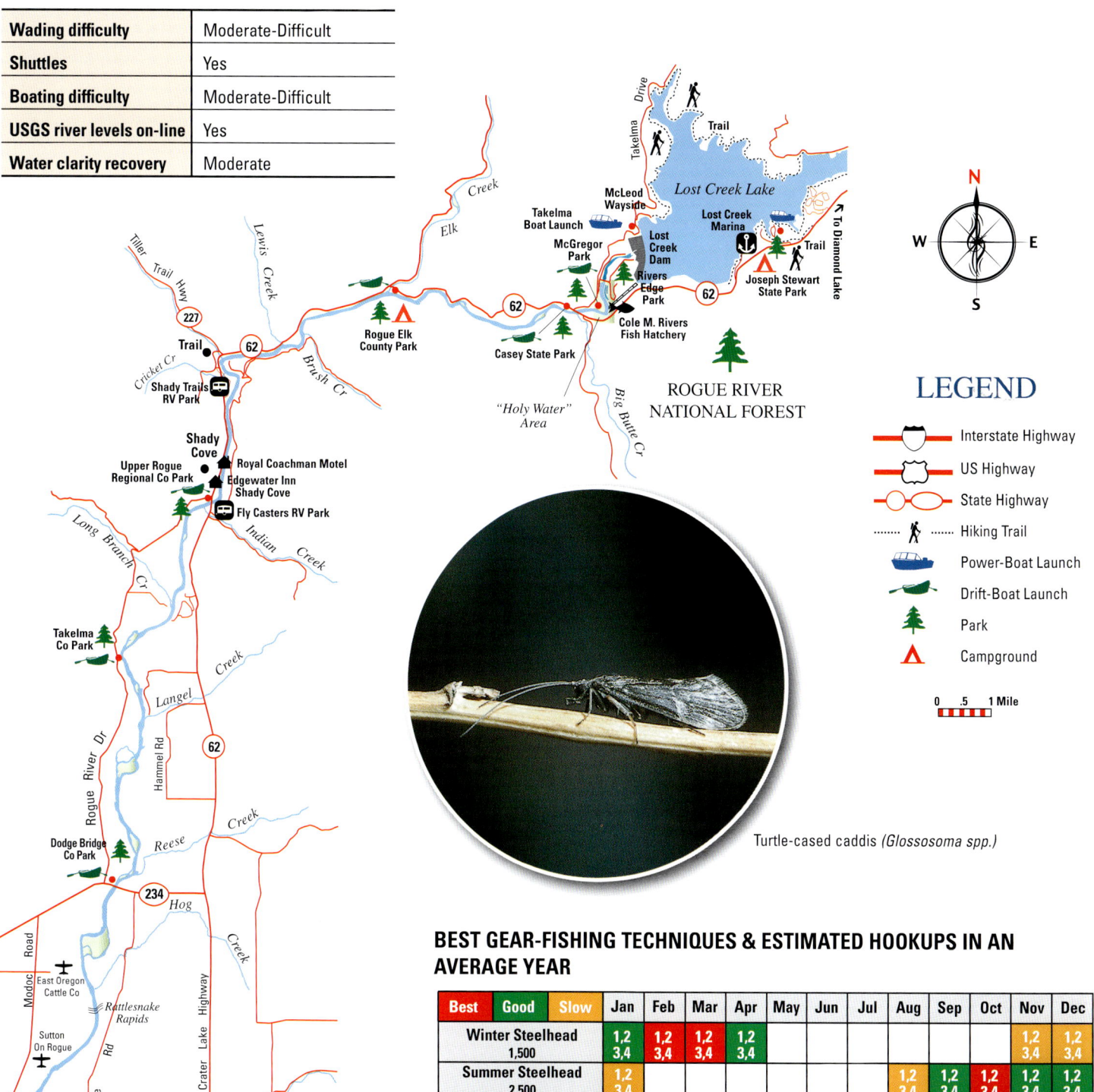

Turtle-cased caddis (*Glossosoma spp.*)

BEST GEAR-FISHING TECHNIQUES & ESTIMATED HOOKUPS IN AN AVERAGE YEAR

Best / Good / Slow	Jan	Feb	Mar	Apr	May	Jun	Jul	Aug	Sep	Oct	Nov	Dec
Winter Steelhead 1,500	1,2 3,4	1,2 3,4	1,2 3,4	1,2 3,4							1,2 3,4	1,2 3,4
Summer Steelhead 2,500	1,2 3,4							1,2 3,4	1,2 3,4	1,2 3,4	1,2 3,4	1,2 3,4
Half-Pounders 2,000	1,2 3,4	1,2 3,4							1,2 3,4	1,2 3,4	1,2 3,4	1,2 3,4
Fall Chinook 500								1,2 3,4,5	1,2 3,4,5	1,2 3,4,5	1,2 3,4,5	1,2 3,4,5
Spring Chinook 5,000					1,2 3,4,5	1,2 3,4,5	1,2 3,4,5	1,2 3,4,5	1,2 3,4,5			
Coho 100									1,2 3,4,5	1,2 3,4,5		
Rainbow Trout	2	2	2	2	2	2	2	2	2	2	2	2

1. Drift fishing (from bank or boat, with or without bait)
2. Casting spinners, spoons, plugs
3. Float fishing (with jigs or bait)
4. Back-trolling (plugs or diver- and-bait)
5. Back-bouncing (boat)
6. Trolling (boat only)
7. Anchor fishing
8. Plunking
9. Jigging

55

OREGON RIVER MAPS & FISHING GUIDE

Chetco River

The Chetco River is located in the southwest corner of Oregon, only a few miles north of the California border. The Chetco is famous for its superb salmon and steelhead fishing, especially with California anglers. Originating in the high mountains of the Siskiyou National Forest, the Chetco's uppermost reaches are protected within the Kalmiopsis Wilderness (a popular destination for hikers and backpackers). From there, the river flows southwest for 50 miles to its mouth at the town of Brookings. For most of its length, the Chetco offers excellent bank and drift-boat access. Where it meets the ocean, it enters Chetco Cove (sometimes called Chetco Bay), one of the West Coast's friendliest small-craft ports.

Throughout the year, resident and sea-run cutthroat inhabit every reach of the river, but salmon and steelhead are the main attraction for anglers. Salmon fishing begins in Chetco Cove in late July or August. Chinook salmon feed voraciously on anchovies and other baitfish in the protected waters of the cove. Trolling herring, anchovies and spinners is the most popular style of fishing.

By September, a good number of Chinook begin to hold in the tidewater reaches of the river, as well as the first few deep pools above the reach-of-tide. Until the fall rains arrive, salmon accumulate in this section of the river, where fly-fishing from anchored boats is a preferred fishing method. Float fishing and casting lures are also popular. Once the rains of autumn arrive (in October or November), the salmon move into the greater river, and anglers can catch them with virtually all fishing techniques.

Winter steelhead move into the Chetco from November to the end of March, and provide excellent sport. Because of exceptional public access, the Chetco is conducive to all styles of angling, from the bank or from a drift boat. Motorized boats are banned above reach-of-tide.

BEST FLY-FISHING TECHNIQUES

	Jan	Feb	Mar	Apr	May	Jun	Jul	Aug	Sep	Oct	Nov	Dec
Winter Steelhead	4,6,7	4,6,7	4,6,7								4,6,7	4,6,7
Fall Chinook (tidewater)									6,7,9	6,7,9	6,7,9	
Fall Chinook (river)										4,6 7,9	4,6 7,9	4,6 7,9
Spring Chinook				4,6 7,9	4,6 7,9	4,6 7,9						
Sea-Run Cutthroat						2,3 8,9	2,3 8,9	2,3 8,9	2,3 8,9	2,3 8,9		
Coho									8,9	8,9	8,9	

(Best / Good / Slow)

1. Dry fly, dead-drift
2. Dry fly, swung
3. Wet fly, swung near surface
4. Wet fly, swung deep
5. Nymph(s), lightly weighted
6. Nymph(s), weighted with indicator
7. Deep drifted fly (with or without indicator)
8. Wet fly retrieved near surface
9. Deep swing with retrieve

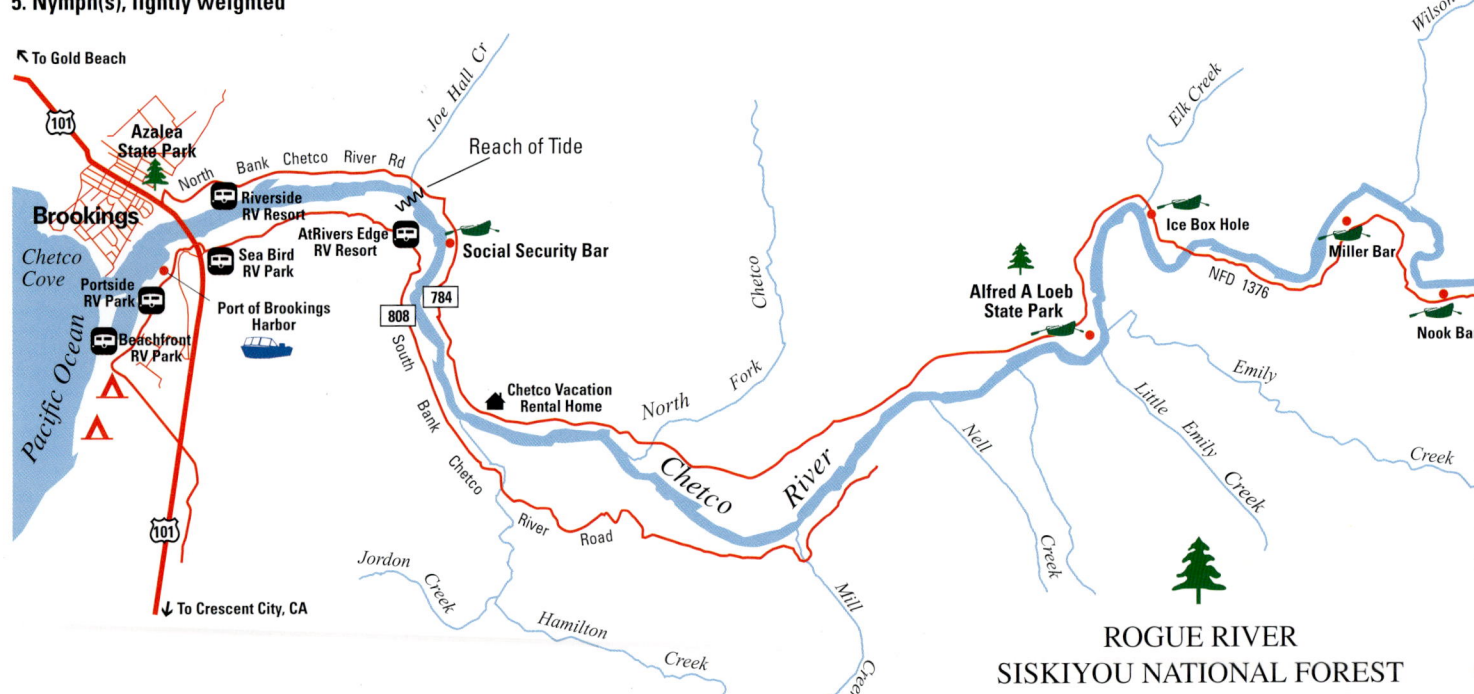

LEGEND

- US Highway
- NFD — National Forest Road
- Power-Boat Launch
- Drift-Boat Launch
- Park
- Campground
- Reach of Tide

0 — .5 — 1 Mile

ROGUE RIVER SISKIYOU NATIONAL FOREST

CHETCO RIVER

BEST GEAR-FISHING TECHNIQUES & ESTIMATED HOOKUPS IN AN AVERAGE YEAR

	Jan	Feb	Mar	Apr	May	Jun	Jul	Aug	Sep	Oct	Nov	Dec
Winter Steelhead 1500	1,2,3,4 Best	1,2,3,4 Best	1,2,3,4 Good								1,2,3,4 Slow	1,2,3,4 Best
Fall Chinook (tidewater) 1000									2,3,6 Best	2,3,6 Best	2,3,6 Good	
Fall Chinook (river) 1500										1,2,3,4,5 Best	1,2,3,4,5 Best	1,2,3,4,5 Good
Spring Chinook 50				1,2,3,4,5 Slow	1,2,3,4,5 Slow	1,2,3,4,5 Slow						
Ocean Salmon 16,000							6 Good	6 Best	6 Best	6 Best	6 Best	6 Slow
Coho									1,2,3,4 Best	1,2,3,4 Best	1,2,3,4 Slow	
Sea-Run Cutthroat						2 Slow	2 Slow	2 Slow	2 Slow	2 Slow	2 Slow	
Perch		1,8 Best	1,8 Best	1,8 Good								
Crabs	Best	Good	Good	Good	Good	Good	Good	Good	Good	Good	Good	Best

Legend: Best / Good / Slow

1. Drift fishing (from bank or boat, with or without bait)
2. Casting spinners, spoons, plugs
3. Float fishing (with jigs or bait)
4. Back-trolling (plugs or diver-and-bait)
5. Back-bouncing (boat)
6. Trolling (boat only)
7. Anchor fishing
8. Plunking
9. Jigging

LOCATION: Curry County

Wading difficulty	Easy-Moderate
Shuttles	Yes
Boating difficulty	Moderate
USGS river levels on-line	No
Water clarity recovery	Moderate
Best river levels	2.5 - 4'

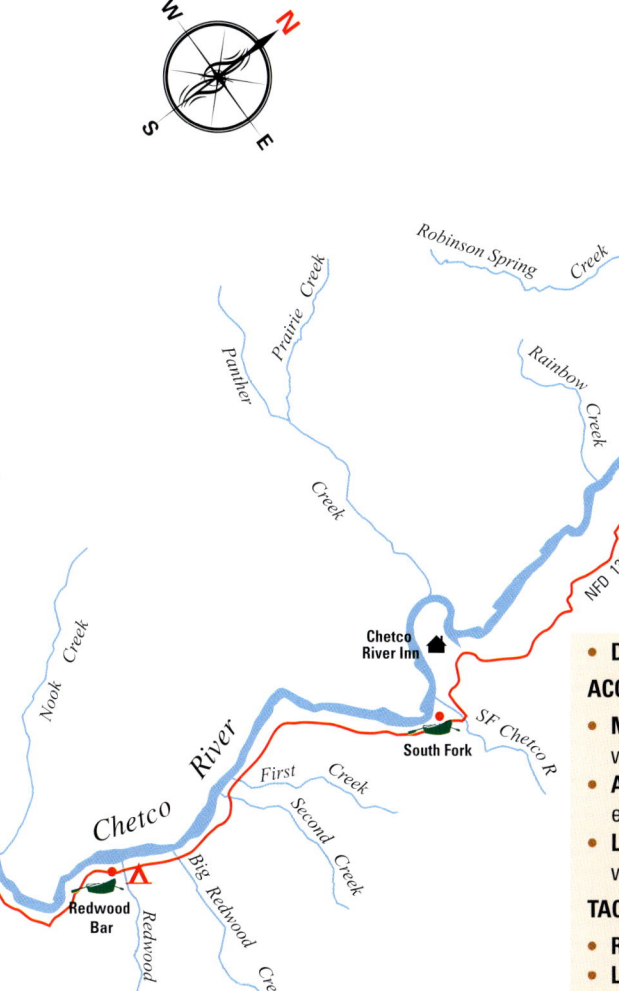

SERVICES

CAMPING/PARKS

- **Riverside RV Resort,** Brookings, 97415, (541) 469-4799, **email:** chetcocharlie@riverside-rv.com, www.riverside-rv.com
- **AtRivers Edge RV Resort,** Brookings, 97415, (541) 469-3356, www.atriversedge.com
- **Alfred A. Loeb Campground,** Brookings, 97415, info: (800) 551-6949, reservations: (800) 452-5687, www.oregonstateparks.org
- **Harris Beach Campground & RV,** Brookings, 97415, info: (800) 551-6949, reservations: (800) 452-5687, www.oregonstateparks.org
- **Driftwood RV Park,** Brookings-Harbor, 97415, 541-469-9089, www.driftwoodrvpark.com

ACCOMMODATIONS

- **Mt. Emily Ranch B&B,** Brookings, 97415, (541) 469-3983, email: carol@mtemilyranch.com, www.mtemilyranch.com
- **A Country Retreat B&B,** Brookings, (800) 856-8604, (541) 661-3773, email: info@countryretreatbnb.com, www.countryretreatbnb.com
- **Lowden's Beachfront B&B,** Brookings, 97415, (541) 469-7045, (800) 453-4768, www.beachfrontbb.com

TACKLE SHOPS

- **Riverside Market,** Brookings, 97415, (541) 469-4496, www.chetcokayaks.com
- **Lunker Fish Trips Bait & Tackle,** Crescent City, CA 95531, (707) 458-4704, (800) 248-4704, www.lunkerfishtrips.com
- **Four M Tackle,** Brookings, 97415, (541) 469-6951

VISITOR INFORMATION

- **Curry County Parks,** Gold Beach, 97444, (541) 247-3386, www.co.curry.or.us
- **Siskiyou National Forest,** Grants Pass, 97526, (541) 618-2200, www.fs.usda.gov/rogue-siskiyou
- **Coos Bay District BLM,** North Bend, 97459, (541) 756-0100, hooww.or.blm.gov/coosbay
- **Southern Oregon Fishing:** Reports, News, Photos & More, www.southernoregonfishingreports.com
- **Brookings-Harbor Chamber of Commerce,** Brookings, 97415, (541) 469-3181, (800) 535-9469, www.brookingsharborchamber.com

Willamette River, Lower

The lower Willamette River, from Willamette Falls downstream to the Columbia River, is among Oregon's most popular fisheries. Spring Chinook are the main attraction, running from March through June. Early in the salmon season, from March through April, much of the fishing pressure is concentrated from downtown Portland to the Columbia. As the season progresses, anglers move upriver to the area near Willamette Falls. Most anglers troll herring, spinners or plugs from power boats. Anchor fishing is also very popular. In a few places, good bank fishing can be found, primarily around Meldrum Bar, just downstream of the Clackamas confluence. Summer steelhead, which run at the same time, are commonly caught by salmon anglers.

Shad return to the lower Willamette in droves from May through June. This exciting fishery attracts a crowd of anglers from Willamette Falls to the mouth of the Clackamas. Shad anglers use light tackle and very small spinners, spoons or flies.

White sturgeon are present year-round in the deepest holes throughout the Willamette. Plunking sand shrimp or whole smelt is the best sturgeon fishing method.

Coho salmon make an impressive showing in September and October, but are notoriously difficult to catch. Casting spinners and trolling plugs are the best methods.

BEST FLY-FISHING TECHNIQUES

Best / Good / Slow	Jan	Feb	Mar	Apr	May	Jun	Jul	Aug	Sep	Oct	Nov	Dec
Spring Chinook		9	9	9	9	9	9					
			9		9	9						
Smallmouth Bass				8,9	8,9	8,9	8,9	8,9	8,9	8,9		
Shad					9	9						

1. Dry fly, dead-drift
2. Dry fly, swung
3. Wet fly, swung near surface
4. Wet fly, swung deep
5. Nymph(s), lightly weighted
6. Nymph(s), weighted with indicator
7. Deep drifted fly (with or without indicator)
8. Wet fly retrieved near surface
9. Deep swing with retrieve

BEST GEAR-FISHING TECHNIQUES & ESTIMATED HOOKUPS IN AN AVERAGE YEAR

Best / Good / Slow	Jan	Feb	Mar	Apr	May	Jun	Jul	Aug	Sep	Oct	Nov	Dec
Fall Chinook — 100									4,5 6,7	4,5 6,7		
Spring Chinook — 10,000		4,5,6 7,8	4,5,6 7,8	4,5,6 7,8	4,5,6 7,8	4,5,6 7,8	4,5,6,7,8					
Coho — 100								4,5 6,7	4,5 6,7	4,5 6,7		
Summer Steelhead — 500			4,5,6 7,8	4,5,6 7,8	4,5,6 7,8	4,5,6 7,8	4,5,6 7,8	4,5,6 7,8	4,5,6 7,8			
Winter Steelhead — 1000	4,5,6 7,8	4,5,6 7,8	4,5,6 7,8								4,5,6 7,8	4,5,6 7,8
Sturgeon	7,8	7,8	7,8	7,8	7,8	7,8	7,8	7,8	7,8	7,8	7,8	7,8
Smallmouth Bass					2	2	2	2	2	2		
Shad					2,5,7	2,5,7						

1. Drift fishing (from bank or boat, with or without bait)
2. Casting spinners, spoons, plugs
3. Float fishing (with jigs or bait)
4. Back-trolling (plugs or diver-and-bait)
5. Back-bouncing (boat)
6. Trolling (boat only)
7. Anchor fishing
8. Plunking
9. Jigging

SERVICES

CAMPING/PARKS

- **Scappoose RV Park,** Scappoose, 97056, (503) 543-3225, reservations: (503) 366-3984, www.co.columbia.or.us
- **Reeder Beach Resort,** Portland, 97231, (503) 621-3970, www.reederbeach.com
- **Jantzen Beach RV Park,** Portland, 97217, (503) 289-7626, www.jantzenbeachrv.com
- **Clackamette Park,** Oregon City, 97045, (503) 496-1201, www.orcity.org/parksandrecreation

ACCOMMODATIONS

- **Nob Hill Riverview B&B,** St. Helens, 97051, (503) 396-5555, email: stay@nobhillbb.com, www.nobhillbb.com
- **Bellaterra B&B,** Portland, 97239, (503) 332-8125, email: bellaterrabnb@gmail.com, www.bellaterrabnb.com
- **Sandes of Time,** Portland, 97267, (503) 654-8813, stay@sandesoftime.com, www.sandesoftime.com
- **Clackamas River House,** Oregon City, 97045, (503) 502-8478, email: contact@clackamasriverhouse.com, www.clackamasriverhouse.com

TACKLE SHOPS

- **Fisherman's Marine,** Oregon City, 97045, (503) 557-3313; Portland, 97217, (503) 283-0044; Tigard, 97223, (503) 549-5066, www.fishermans-marine.com
- **Great American Tackle Shop,** Clackamas, 97015, (503) 650-2662
- **BC Angling Post,** Gladstone, 97027, (503) 655-4161

WILLAMETTE RIVER, LOWER

LOCATION: Columbia, Multnomah & Clackamas Counties

Wading difficulty	N/A
Shuttles	No
Boating difficulty	Easy
USGS river levels on-line	Yes
Water clarity recovery	Slow

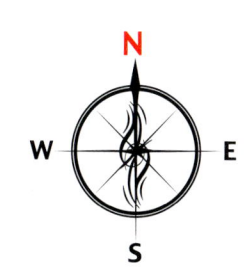

LEGEND

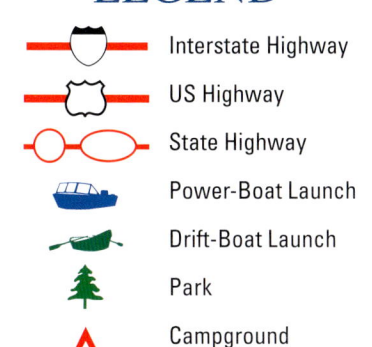

- Interstate Highway
- US Highway
- State Highway
- Power-Boat Launch
- Drift-Boat Launch
- Park
- Campground

0 .5 1 2 Miles

VISITOR INFORMATION

- **Oregon Fishing Reports,** (503) 377-9696, www.theguidesforecast.com
- **Clackamas County Parks** (boat ramps), reservations: (503) 742-4414, email: parksreservations@co.clackamas.or.us, www.clackamas.us/parks
- **Multnomah County Parks,** (503) 797-1700, www.oregonmetro.gov
- **Columbia County Parks,** St. Helens, 97051, (503) 397-2353, reservations: (503) 366-3984, email: parksdept@co.columbia.or.us, www.co.columbia.or.us
- **South Columbia County Chamber of Commerce,** St Helens, 97051, (503) 397-0685, www.sccchamber.org
- **Portland Business Alliance,** Portland, 97201, (503) 224-8684, www.portlandalliance.com
- **Lake Oswego Oregon Chamber of Commerce,** Lake Oswego, 97034, (503) 636-3634, www.lake-oswego.com
- **North Clackamas County Chamber of Commerce,** Milwaukie, 97222, (503) 654-7777, yourchamber.com
- **Oregon City Chamber of Commerce,** Oregon City, 97045, (503) 656-1619, www.oregoncity.org

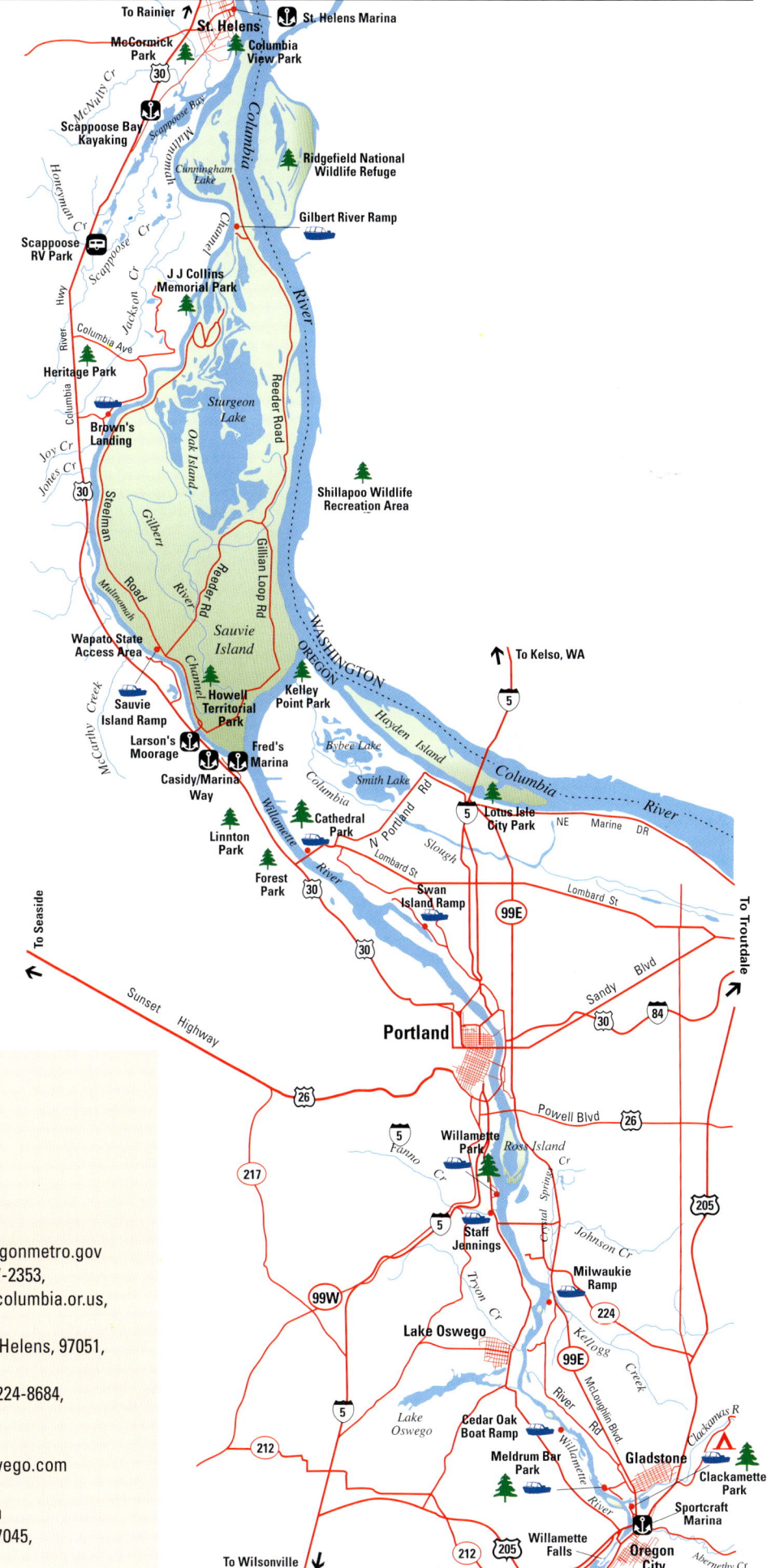

59

Sandy River

The Sandy is one of Oregon's most celebrated steelhead and salmon rivers, hosting strong runs of winter and summer steelhead, spring and fall Chinook, and fall coho salmon. It flows just over fifty miles from the glaciers of Mount Hood to its confluence with the Columbia River at Troutdale. Most of the river is designated as "Wild and Scenic" by the federal government, helping to preserve its natural beauty for future generations.

Winter steelhead attract the most attention from Sandy River anglers. Traditionally, winter steelheading begins on Thanksgiving, when the first fish arrive. The hatchery run peaks in December and January, and is limited to the water below Marmot Dam (hatchery fish are stopped here to protect the spawning of wild steelhead above). Wild steelhead are present from December through April, peaking in February and March. The Sandy's wild steelhead are impressive, averaging ten pounds and reaching over twenty pounds. Drift fishing and casting lures are the most popular fishing methods. There is also a strong tradition of fly-fishing on the Sandy, especially within Oxbow Regional Park, where fishing from a boat is prohibited.

Spring Chinook are another popular fish on the Sandy, beginning in April and lasting through July. In May and June when the salmon run peaks, boaters have the advantage, back-bouncing bait in the deep holes, or back-trolling plugs where there is good current and depth. By mid-June, bank anglers search out the deep holding pools from Oxbow Park upstream to Revenue Bridge. Float-fishing the deep holes with small egg clusters and shrimp can be very productive.

Fall Chinook and coho salmon show up in September and October. The river is typically low this time of year, and anglers focus on the lowest portion of the river. Very few boats run the Sandy at this time due to low water. Bank anglers use a variety of methods to catch fall fish, but casting spinners is usually most productive. Coho are primarily of hatchery origin, reared at the Sandy River Hatchery on Cedar Creek (near the town of Sandy).

Summer steelhead, once a major fishery on the Sandy, are not as numerous as in the past. In an attempt to help preserve native winter steelhead, Oregon Department of Fish & Wildlife (ODFW) has cut back the number of juvenile summer steelhead released in the Sandy. The fish are stopped at Marmot Dam, eliminating an historic summer steelhead fishery in the Salmon River (a major mid-river tributary). The remaining fishery begins in April and lasts into October, with May and June the peak months.

LOCATION: Clackamas and Multnomah Counties

Wading difficulty	Moderate
Shuttles	Yes
Boating difficulty	Moderate-Difficult
USGS river levels on-line	Yes
Water clarity recovery	Moderate
Best river levels	8.5' to 11'

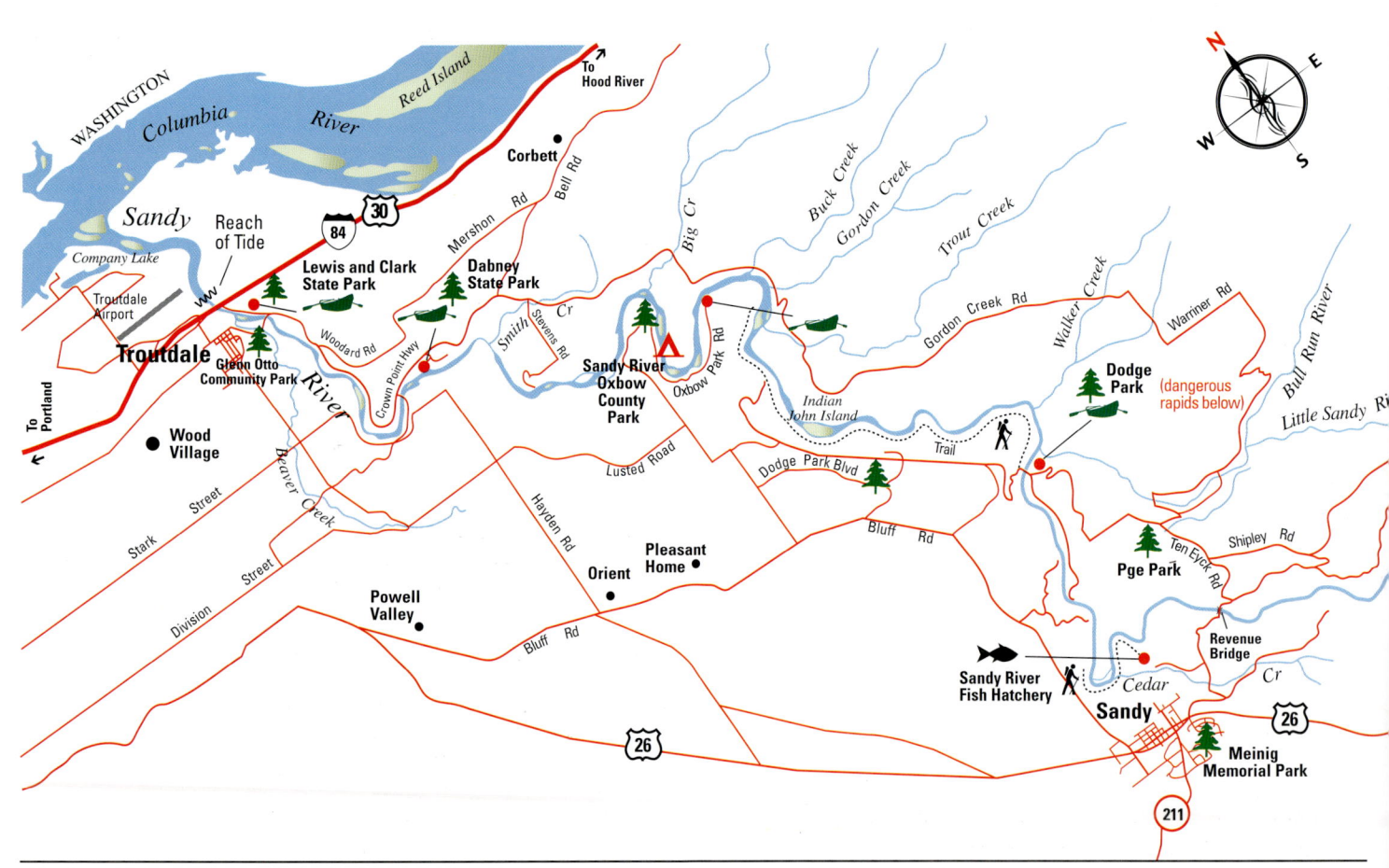

SANDY RIVER

BEST GEAR-FISHING TECHNIQUES & ESTIMATED HOOKUPS IN AN AVERAGE YEAR

	Jan	Feb	Mar	Apr	May	Jun	Jul	Aug	Sep	Oct	Nov	Dec
Winter Steelhead 4000	1,2 3,4	1,2 3,4	1,2 3,4	1,2 3,4							1,2,3,4	1,2 3,4
Summer Steelhead 1000				1,2,3,4	1,2 3,4	1,2 3,4	1,2 3,4	1,2 3,4	1,2 3,4	1,2 3,4		
Spring Chinook 1800				1,2,3,4,5	1,2,3 4,5	1,2,3 4,5	1,2,3 4,5	1,2,3 4,5				
Fall Chinook 500									1,2,3 4,5,6	1,2,3 4,5,6	1,2,3 4,5,6	
Coho 500									1,2,3 4,5,6	1,2,3 4,5	1,2,3 4,5	

Legend: Best (red), Good (green), Slow (orange)

1. Drift fishing (from bank or boat, with or without bait)
2. Casting spinners, spoons, plugs
3. Float fishing (with jigs or bait)
4. Back-trolling (plugs or diver-and-bait)
5. Back-bouncing (boat)
6. Trolling (boat only)
7. Anchor fishing
8. Plunking
9. Jigging

BEST FLY-FISHING TECHNIQUES

	Jan	Feb	Mar	Apr	May	Jun	Jul	Aug	Sep	Oct	Nov	Dec
Winter Steelhead	4,6,7	4,6,7	4,6,7	4,6,7							4,6,7	4,6,7
Summer Steelhead					2,3,4 5,6,7	2,3,4 5,6,7	2,3,4 5,6,7	2,3,4 5,6,7	2,3,4 5,6,7	2,3,4 5,6,7		
Spring Chinook				4,6,7,9	4,6 7,9	4,6 7,9	4,6 7,9	4,6 7,9				
Fall Chinook									4,6 7,9	4,6 7,9	4,6 7,9	
Coho									3,4 7,8	3,4 7,8	3,4 7,8	

1. Dry fly, dead-drift
2. Dry fly, swung
3. Wet fly, swung near surface
4. Wet fly, swung deep
5. Nymph(s), lightly weighted
6. Nymph(s), weighted with indicator
7. Deep drifted fly (with or without indicator)
8. Wet fly retrieved near surface
9. Deep swing with retrieve

SERVICES

CAMPING/PARKS
- **Mt. Hood Village RV Resort & Campground,** Welches, 97067, (503) 622-4011, www.mthoodvillage.com
- **Sandy Riverfront RV Resort,** Troutdale, 97060, (503) 665-6722, email: info@sandyrv.com, www.sandyrv.com
- **Sandy River Oxbow County Park,** (503) 797-1850, www.oregonmetro.gov
- **Dodge Park,** Sandy, 97055, (503) 823-7404, www.portlandoregon.gov

ACCOMMODATIONS
- **Sandy Salmon B&B Lodge,** Sandy, 97055, (503) 622-6699, www.sandysalmon.com
- **The Resort at the Mountain,** Welches, 97067, (503) 622-3101, reservations: (877) 439-6774, www.theresort.com
- **Brightwood Guest House B&B,** Brightwood, 97011, (503) 314-1107, email: brightwoodbnb@hotmail.com, www.mounthoodbnb.com

TACKLE SHOPS
- **Jacks Snack N Tackle,** Troutdale, 97060, (503) 665-2257, www.jackssnackandtackle.com
- **The Fly Fishing Shop,** Welches, 97067, (503) 622-4607, (800) 266-3971, email: flyfish@flyfishusa.com, www.flyfishusa.com

VISITOR INFORMATION
- **Mt. Hood National Forest,** Sandy, 97055, (503) 668-1700, www.fs.usda.gov/mthood
- **Oregon Fishing Reports,** www.theguidesforecast.com
- **Oregon Metro Parks,** (503) 797-1700, www.oregonmetro.gov
- **Sandy Area Chamber of Commerce,** Sandy, 97055, (503) 668-4006, www.sandyoregonchamber.org
- **West Columbia Gorge Chamber of Commerce,** Troutdale, 97060, (503) 669-7473, www.westcolumbiagorgechamber.com

LEGEND

- Interstate Highway
- US Highway
- State Highway
- Hiking Trail
- Drift-Boat Launch
- Park
- Campground
- Fish Hatchery
- Reach of Tide

0 .5 1 Mile

Clackamas River

The Clackamas River is one of the largest rivers in the Willamette Valley, descending over 80 miles from the High Cascades to its junction with the Willamette River at Oregon City. It is an historic river, representing the final leg of the Oregon Trail for early Willamette Valley pioneers. The Clackamas once supported one of the largest wild runs of spring salmon, before dams, and industry caused their near-extinction. Today, the Clackamas is in recovery. Spring Chinook, winter steelhead, summer steelhead, and coho salmon again run strong in the river, sustained by vigorous hatchery programs. A modest number of resident rainbow trout occur throughout the river, commonly exhibiting cutthroat trout features due to natural hybridizing with the migratory Willamette cutthroat.

The modern Clackamas is still known for its exceptional spring salmon fishing. Every spring, from May through July, thousands of hatchery-reared Chinook salmon enter the Clackamas, pursued by an army of anglers. Fishing for spring Chinook is best from mid-May to mid-June. By July, Clackamas kings become more difficult to catch, and the boating also becomes more challenging because of lower water levels.

Winter and summer steelhead both return to the Clackamas. Winter steelhead run from December through mid-April, summer steelhead from April through October. Most steelhead in the Clackamas are of hatchery origin, although there is a recovering native run of winter steelhead. There are fishable numbers of steelhead year-round in the lower Clackamas River, (below River Mill Dam). All methods of fishing are effective, with drift fishing and casting spinners most popular.

Coho salmon return to the Clackamas every fall, beginning in early September and continuing through October. Most coho in the Clackamas are reared in the Eagle Creek Hatchery, and consequently, most run up Eagle Creek. Before the first heavy rains of autumn, coho accumulate in the Clackamas near the mouth of Eagle Creek. Though they have a reputation for being difficult to catch, there are times when spinners and attractor flies can lure them to strike.

Cutthroat and rainbow trout inhabit the entire Clackamas, from meandering beaver ponds high in the Cascades, to the lowest miles of river where salmon and steelhead are dominant. Beautiful resident cutthroat occur in the mountain reaches.

LOCATION: Clackamas County

Wading difficulty	Moderate
Shuttles	Yes
Boating difficulty	Moderate-Dangerous
USGS river levels on-line	Yes, at Estacada
Water clarity recovery	Moderate
Best river levels	10' - 13' feet

CLACKAMAS RIVER

BEST GEAR-FISHING TECHNIQUES & ESTIMATED HOOKUPS IN AN AVERAGE YEAR

	Jan	Feb	Mar	Apr	May	Jun	Jul	Aug	Sep	Oct	Nov	Dec
Winter Steelhead 2000	1,2 3,4	1,2 3,4	1,2 3,4	1,2 3,4							1,2,3,4	1,2 3,4
Summer Steelhead 2000			1,2,3,4	1,2 3,4	1,2 3,4	1,2 3,4	1,2 3,4	1,2 3,4	1,2 3,4	1,2 3,4	1,2 3,4	
Spring Chinook 4000		1,2,3,4,5	1,2,3 4,5	1,2,3 4,5	1,2,3 4,5	1,2,3 4,5	1,2,3 4,5	1,2,3 4,5				
Fall Chinook 200									4,6 7,9	4,6 7,9		
Coho 1500									1,2,3 4,5	1,2,3 4,5	1,2,3 4,5	
Rainbow Trout				2	2	2	2	2	2	2		

Legend: Best (red), Good (green), Slow (orange)

1. Drift fishing (from bank or boat, with or without bait)
2. Casting spinners, spoons, plugs
3. Float fishing (with jigs or bait)
4. Back-trolling (plugs or diver-and-bait)
5. Back-bouncing (boat)
6. Trolling (boat only)
7. Anchor fishing
8. Plunking
9. Jigging

BEST FLY-FISHING TECHNIQUES

	Jan	Feb	Mar	Apr	May	Jun	Jul	Aug	Sep	Oct	Nov	Dec
Winter Steelhead	4,6,7	4,6,7	4,6,7	4,6,7 4,6,7							4,7,6	4,7,6
Summer Steelhead			2,3,4 5,6,7	2,3,4 5,6,7	2,3,4 5,6,7	2,3,4 5,6,7	2,3,4 5,6,7	2,3,4 5,6,7	2,3,4 5,6,7	2,3,4 5,6,7	2,3,4 5,6,7	
Spring Chinook		4,6,7,9	4,6 7,9	4,6 7,9	4,6 7,9	4,6 7,9	4,6 7,9	4,6 7,9				
Fall Chinook									4,6 7,9	4,6 7,9		
Coho									3,4 7,8	3,4 7,8	3,4 7,8	
Rainbow Trout				1,2,3 4,5,6	1,2,3 4,5,6	1,2,3 4,5,6	1,2,3 4,5,6	1,2,3 4,5,6	1,2,3 4,5,6	1,2,3 4,5,6		

1. Dry fly, dead-drift
2. Dry fly, swung
3. Wet fly, swung near surface
4. Wet fly, swung deep
5. Nymph(s), lightly weighted
6. Nymph(s), weighted with indicator
7. Deep drifted fly (with or without indicator)
8. Wet fly retrieved near surface
9. Deep swing with retrieve

SERVICES

CAMPING/PARKS
- **Clackamette Park**, Oregon City, 97045, (503) 496-1201, www.orcity.org
- **Barton Park Camping & RV**, Boring, 97009, Barton Park Ranger Office, (503) 637-3015, reserve: 503-742-4414, www.clackamas.us
- **Milo McIver State Park**, Estacada, 97023, (503) 630-7150, www.oregonstateparks.org

ACCOMMODATIONS
- **Clackamas River House**, Oregon City, 97045, (503) 502-8478, email: contact@clackamasriverhouse.com, www.clackamasriverhouse.com
- **Sandes of Time**, Portland, 97267, (503) 654-8813, stay@sandesoftime.com, www.sandesoftime.com

TACKLE SHOPS
- **Fisherman's Marine**, Oregon City, 97045, (503) 557-3313; Portland, 97217, (503) 283-0044; Tigard, 97223, (503) 549-5066, www.fishermans-marine.com
- **Great American Tackle Shop**, Clackamas, 97015, (503) 650-2662
- **BC Angling Post**, Gladstone, 97027, (503) 655-4161

VISITOR INFORMATION
- **Clackamas County Parks** (boat ramps), reservations: (503) 742-4414, email: parksreservations@co.clackamas.or.us, www.clackamas.us/parks
- **Oregon Fishing Reports**, (503) 377-9696, www.theguidesforecast.com
- **Oregon City Parks**, Oregon City, 97045, (503) 496-1201, www.orcity.org
- **North Clackamas County Chamber of Commerce**, Milwaukie, 97222, (503) 654-7777, www.yourchamber.com
- **Oregon City Chamber of Commerce**, Oregon City, 97045, (503) 656-1619, www.oregoncity.org

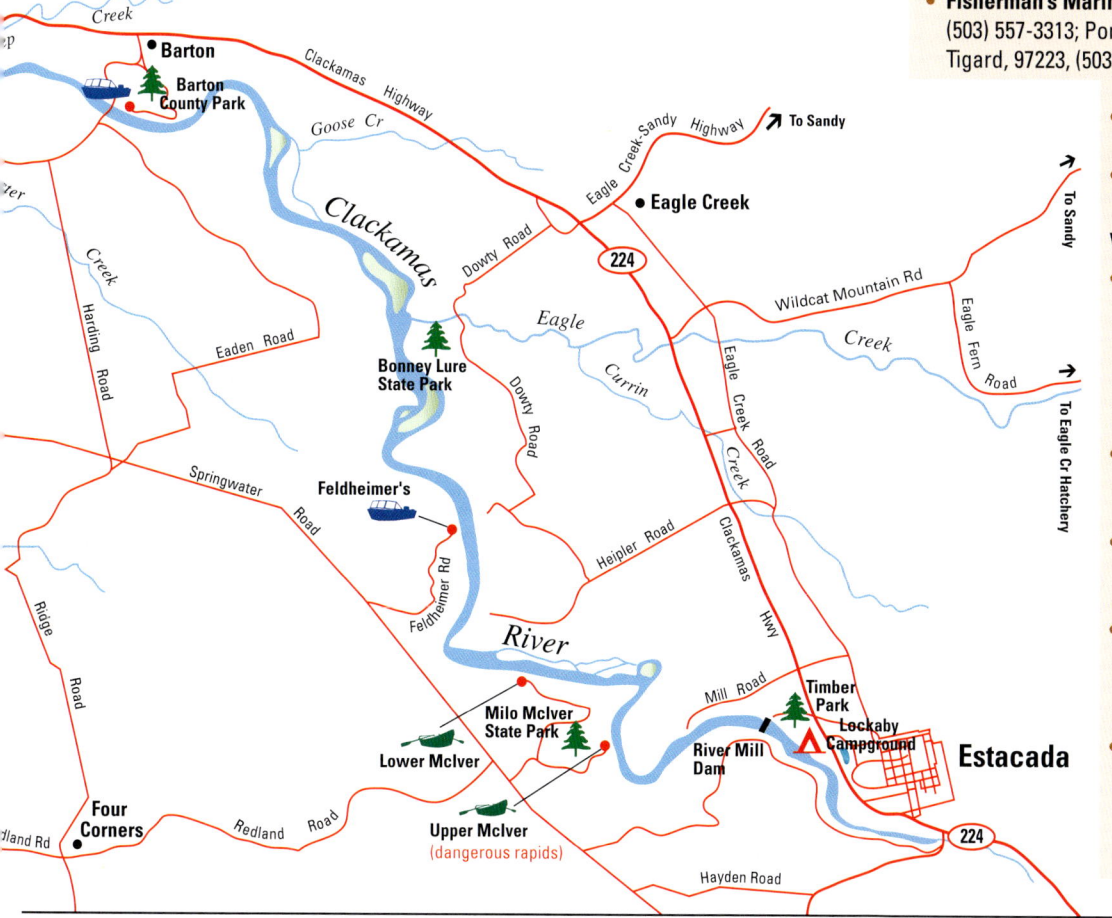

Molalla River

The Molalla is one of the smaller Willamette River tributaries, known primarily as a winter and spring steelhead fishery. It also receives a modest run of spring Chinook, and can offer good trout fishing in its upper reaches. The lower miles are drift-boat accessible, with very little bank access. The upper reaches are paralleled by a forest road, and offer good bank access.

Molalla steelhead run from December through April, peaking late in the season, from early March through April. Historically, hatchery steelhead were planted in the Molalla, but since 1998, Oregon has managed the river for wild steelhead only. The occasional stray hatchery steelhead does make its way into the Molalla, and fin-clipped steelhead may be kept. Drift fishing and casting spinners are the most common methods used on the Molalla. Fly-fishing is also popular, especially from the Meadowbrook Bridge (Hwy 211) downstream to the town of Canby.

Spring Chinook arrive in late April and run through early June. Most Chinook stay low in the river, from the town of Liberal to the Willamette River confluence. Through the warm months of summer, salmon hold in the river's deep pools. Back-bouncing or float-fishing with bait are the best fishing methods for Molalla salmon.

Trout fishing can be good in the upper Molalla, although most rainbows are actually juvenile steelhead. The uppermost reaches, within the Table Rock Wilderness, are home to beautiful resident cutthroat trout. Fly-fishing is the preferred method for catching Molalla trout, and all trout should be released unharmed.

BEST GEAR-FISHING TECHNIQUES & ESTIMATED HOOKUPS IN AN AVERAGE YEAR

Best	Good	Slow	Jan	Feb	Mar	Apr	May	Jun	Jul	Aug	Sep	Oct	Nov	Dec
Winter Steelhead 150			1,2 3,4	1,2 3,4	1,2 3,4	1,2 3,4								1,2 3,4
Spring Chinook 100							1,2 3,4,5	1,2 3,4,5	1,2 3,4,5					

1. Drift fishing (from bank or boat, with or without bait)
2. Casting spinners, spoons, plugs
3. Float fishing (with jigs or bait)
4. Back-trolling (plugs or diver-and-bait)
5. Back-bouncing (boat)
6. Trolling (boat only)
7. Anchor fishing
8. Plunking
9. Jigging

BEST FLY-FISHING TECHNIQUES

Best	Good	Slow	Jan	Feb	Mar	Apr	May	Jun	Jul	Aug	Sep	Oct	Nov	Dec
Winter Steelhead			4,6,7	4,6,7	4,6,7	4,6,7								4,6 7,9
Spring Chinook							4,6 7,9	4,6 7,9	4,6 7,9					

1. Dry fly, dead-drift
2. Dry fly, swung
3. Wet fly, swung near surface
4. Wet fly, swung deep
5. Nymph(s), lightly weighted
6. Nymph(s), weighted with indicator
7. Deep drifted fly (with or without indicator)
8. Wet fly retrieved near surface
9. Deep swing with retrieve

SERVICES

CAMPING/PARKS
- **Riverside RV Park,** Canby, 97013, (503) 263-3000, (800) 425-2250, www.riversiderv.net
- **Camp Dakota,** Scotts Mills, 97375, (503) 873-7432, email: info@campdakota.com, www.campdakota.com

ACCOMMODATIONS
- **Prairie House Inn,** Molalla, 97038, (503) 829-8245, email: prairiehouseinn@gmail.com, www.theprairiehouseinn.com
- **Feller House B&B,** Aurora, 97002, (503) 678-0268, email: fellerhouse@centurytel.net, www.thefellerhouse.com

TACKLE SHOPS
- **W W Grigg Rods,** Canby, 97013, (971) 678-5552, email: wwgrigg@aol.com, www.wwgrigg.com
- **Fisherman's Marine,** Oregon City, 97045, (503) 557-3313; Portland, 97217, (503) 283-0044; Tigard, 97223, (503) 549-5066, www.fishermans-marine.com
- **Great American Tackle Shop,** Clackamas, 97015, (503) 650-2662
- **BC Angling Post,** Gladstone, 97027, (503) 655-4161

VISITOR INFORMATION
- **Clackamas County Parks** (boat ramps), reservations: (503) 742-4414, email: parksreservations@co.clackamas.or.us, www.clackamas.us/parks
- **Oregon Fishing Reports,** (503) 377-9696, www.theguidesforecast.com
- **Canby City Parks,** Canby, 97013, (503) 266-4021, www.ci.canby.or.us
- **Molalla Area Chamber of Commerce,** Molalla, 97038, (503) 829-6941, www.molallachamber.com
- **Canby Area Chamber of Commerce,** Canby, 97013, (503) 266-4600, www.canbyareachamber.org

MOLALLA RIVER

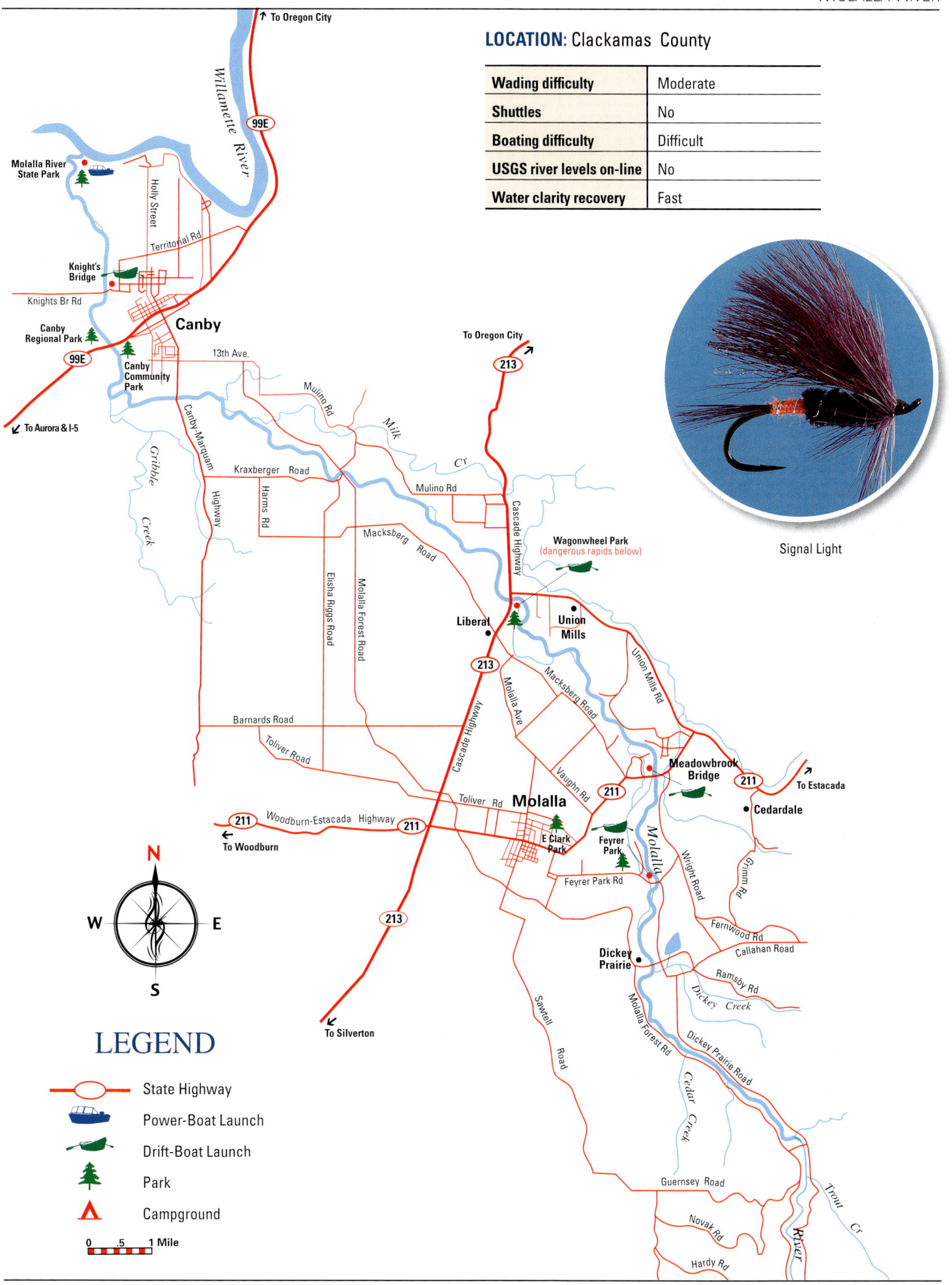

LOCATION: Clackamas County

Wading difficulty	Moderate
Shuttles	No
Boating difficulty	Difficult
USGS river levels on-line	No
Water clarity recovery	Fast

Signal Light

LEGEND

- State Highway
- Power-Boat Launch
- Drift-Boat Launch
- Park
- Campground

0 .5 1 Mile

65

Santiam River, North

The North Santiam River is a major tributary to the Willamette River, and one of two main forks draining a large swath of the Cascade Range. The North Fork is the largest and fastest of the forks, and offers excellent fishing for winter and summer steelhead, as well as spring Chinook salmon and rainbow trout.

Steelhead are the main attraction for Santiam anglers. Wild winter steelhead appear in late December and run well into April. Summer steelhead are not native, but a substantial hatchery program sustains an excellent summer fishery. The North Santiam gets some wild summer steelhead, presumably the result of "naturalization" of the hatchery strain. Summer steelhead first appear in April, and run through October. May and June are the best months for fresh summer steelhead. After the long hot summer, Santiam steelhead become aggressive again in September and October.

Spring Chinook enter the North Santiam in May and continue through July. Jet-boaters fish the main Santiam River, from the Willamette River up to the north and south forks. Late May through mid-June is the peak, and the river can get fairly crowded. By mid-June many salmon have moved into the deeper holes above the forks. Casting lures in the faster water or float fishing with bait in the deep, slow pools, are preferred bank-fishing methods. From a boat, back-bouncing bait or back-trolling plugs is preferred.

Trout in the North Santiam are mainly in the upper river, from its sources in the Cascades to Stayton. A few native cutthroat and resident rainbows are hidden throughout the river. Detroit Lake is a very popular reservoir for trout anglers, as are the two main feeder streams, Breitenbush River and the North Santiam. April through September are the best months for trout fishing.

BEST GEAR-FISHING TECHNIQUES & ESTIMATED HOOKUPS IN AN AVERAGE YEAR

	Jan	Feb	Mar	Apr	May	Jun	Jul	Aug	Sep	Oct	Nov	Dec
Winter Steelhead 1000	1,2 3,4	1,2 3,4	1,2 3,4	1,2 3,4								1,2 3,4
Summer Steelhead 3000					1,2 3,4	1,2 3,4	1,2 3,4	1,2 3,4	1,2 3,4	1,2 3,4	1,2 3,4	1,2 3,4
Spring Chinook 2000					1,2,3 4,5	1,2,3 4,5	1,2,3 4,5	1,2,3 4,5				
Rainbow Trout				2	2	2	2	2	2	2		
Cutthroat Trout			2	2	2	2	2	2	2	2		

1. Drift fishing (from bank or boat, with or without bait)
2. Casting spinners, spoons, plugs
3. Float fishing (with jigs or bait)
4. Back-trolling (plugs or diver-and-bait)
5. Back-bouncing (boat)
6. Trolling (boat only)
7. Anchor fishing
8. Plunking
9. Jigging

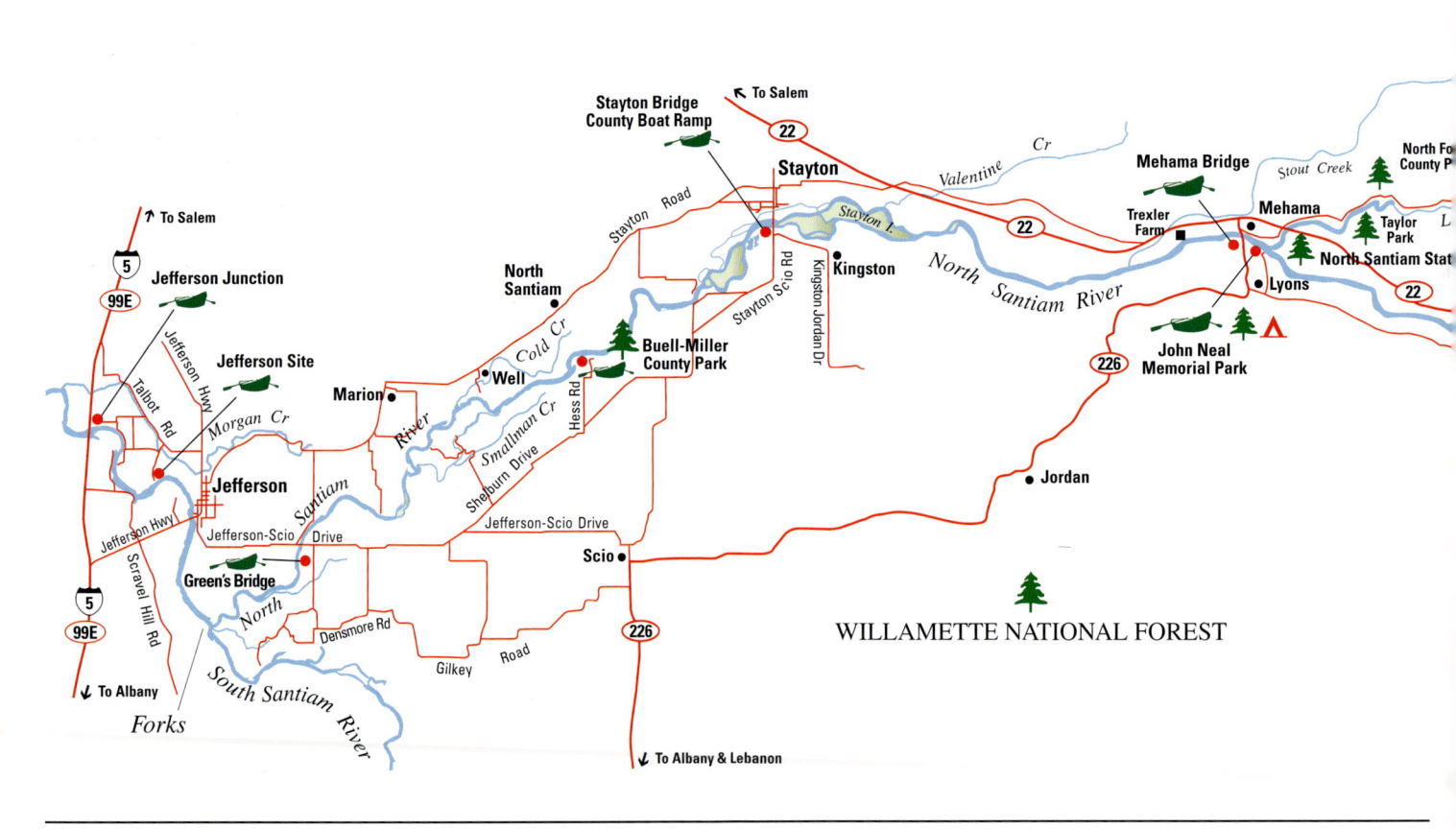

SANTIAM RIVER, NORTH

BEST FLY-FISHING TECHNIQUES

	Jan	Feb	Mar	Apr	May	Jun	Jul	Aug	Sep	Oct	Nov	Dec
Winter Steelhead	4,6,7	4,6,7	4,6,7	4,6,7								4,6,7
Summer Steelhead					2,3,4 5,6,7	2,3,4 5,6,7	2,3,4 5,6,7	2,3,4 5,6,7	2,3,4 5,6,7	2,3,4 5,6,7	2,3,4 5,6,7	2,3,4 5,6,7
Spring Chinook					4,6 7,9	4,6 7,9	4,6 7,9	4,6 7,9				
Rainbow Trout				1,3 5,6	1,3 5,6	1,3 5,6	1,3 5,6	1,3 5,6	1,3 5,6	1,3 5,6		
Cutthroat Trout			1,3 5,6,8	1,3 5,6,8	1,3 5,6,8	1,3 5,6,8	1,3 5,6,8	1,3 5,6,8	1,3 5,6,8	1,3 5,6,8		

Legend: Best / Good / Slow

1. Dry fly, dead-drift
2. Dry fly, swung
3. Wet fly, swung near surface
4. Wet fly, swung deep
5. Nymph(s), lightly weighted
6. Nymph(s), weighted with indicator
7. Deep drifted fly (with or without indicator)
8. Wet fly retrieved near surface
9. Deep swing with retrieve

SERVICES

CAMPING/PARKS
- **Kane's Marina,** Detroit, 97342, (503) 854-3362, www.kanesmarina.com
- **Salem Campground & RVs,** Salem, 97317, (503) 581-6736, (800) 826-9605, www.salemrv.com
- **John Neal Memorial Park,** Lyons, 97358, (541) 967-3917, www.linnparks.com
- **Detroit Lake State Recreation Area,** Reserve: (800) 452-5687, Info: (800) 551-6949, www.oregonstateparks.org
- **Fisherman's Bend Recreation Site,** Mill City, 97360, (503) 897-2406, www.blm.gov/or

ACCOMMODATIONS
- **The Lodge at Detroit Lake,** Detroit, 97342, (503) 854-3344, lodgeatdetroitlake.com
- **Gardner House B&B,** Stayton, 97383, (503) 769-5478, email: host@gardnerhousebnb.com, www.gardnerhousebnb.com
- **Bird & Hat Inn,** Stayton, 97383, (503) 769-7817, www.birdandhatinn.com
- **The Elkhorn Valley B&B,** Lyons, 97358, (503) 897-3033 (800) 707-3033, www.elkhornvalleyinn.com

TACKLE SHOPS
- **Flies By Ilene,** Salem, 97302, (503) 566-7351
- **Dick's Sporting Goods,** Salem, 97301, (503) 363-4860, www.dickssportinggoods.com
- **Creekside Fly Fishing,** Salem, 97301, (503) 588-1768, www.creeksideflyfishing.com

VISITOR INFORMATION
- **Willamette National Forest,** Springfield, 97477, (541) 225-6300, www.fs.usda.gov/willamette
- **Linn County Parks,** Reservations: (541) 967-3917, www.linnparks.com
- **Oregon Fishing Reports,** (503) 377-9696, www.theguidesforecast.com
- **Jefferson Area Chamber of Commerce,** Jefferson, 97352, (541) 974-0717, email: info@jeffersonareachamber.com, www.jeffersonareachamber.com
- **Stayton/Sublimity Chamber of Commerce,** Stayton, 97383, (503) 769-3464, www.staytonsublimitychamber.org

LOCATION: Linn County

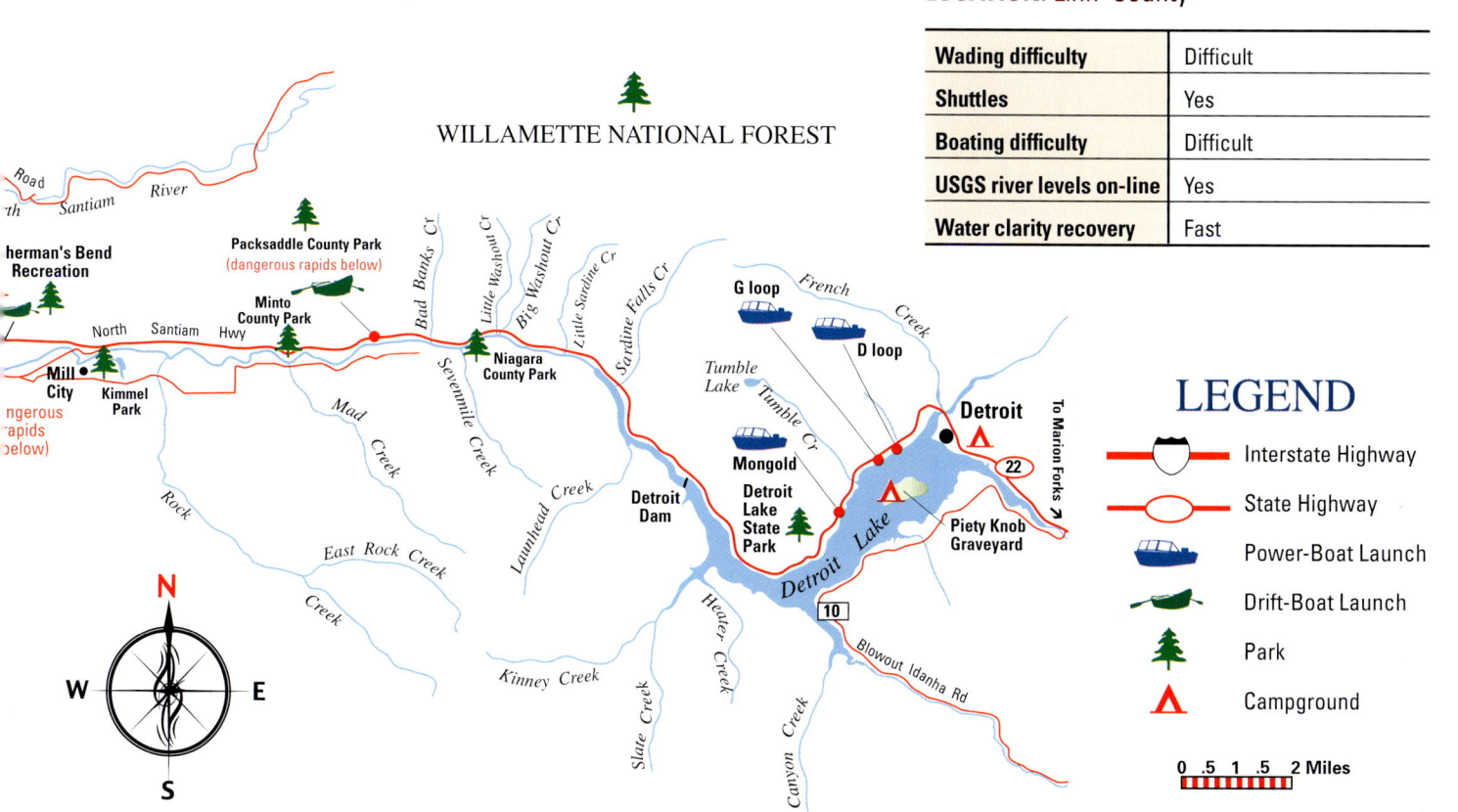

Wading difficulty	Difficult
Shuttles	Yes
Boating difficulty	Difficult
USGS river levels on-line	Yes
Water clarity recovery	Fast

Santiam River, South

The South Santiam, the smaller of the two forks, is best known for its hatchery-raised summer steelhead and spring Chinook salmon. Steelhead and salmon migration ends at Foster Dam, resulting in heavy concentrations of fish and anglers near the dam. For its size, the South Santiam receives a tremendous number of hatchery fish, making it the most popular destination for locals.

Wild and hatchery winter steelhead run in the South Santiam from December through March, peaking in February and March. Summer steelhead arrive in April and run through October, peaking in June and July. Bank fishing is best from Foster Dam to Sweet Home, with drift-fishing and float-jig combinations most productive. Below Sweet Home, drift boating offers the best access.

Spring Chinook enter the South Santiam in large numbers from late April through July, some moving straight to Foster Dam, others accumulating in the deep holes between Foster Dam and Sanderson's Bridge (fee launch). In May and June, back-bouncing bait, back-trolling plugs, and casting spinners are the most popular fishing methods. By July and August, float fishing with eggs and shrimp in the deep holes is most productive.

Trout fishing can be excellent in the South and Middle Santiams above the dams. A substantial number of wild rainbow and cutthroat are present here. Fly-fishing, or spin-casting small lures are the best techniques. The best fishing coincides with spring and summer insect hatches (see Hatch Chart, page 6). Santiam trout fishing is best from early May through September.

BEST GEAR-FISHING TECHNIQUES & ESTIMATED HOOKUPS IN AN AVERAGE YEAR

	Jan	Feb	Mar	Apr	May	Jun	Jul	Aug	Sep	Oct	Nov	Dec
Winter Steelhead 800	1,2 3,4	1,2 3,4	1,2 3,4	1,2 3,4								1,2 3,4
Summer Steelhead 4000					1,2 3,4	1,2 3,4	1,2 3,4	1,2 3,4	1,2 3,4	1,2 3,4		
Spring Chinook 2500					1,2,3 4,5	1,2,3 4,5	1,2,3 4,5	1,2,3 4,5				

Legend: Best / Good / Slow

1. Drift fishing (from bank or boat, with or without bait)
2. Casting spinners, spoons, plugs
3. Float fishing (with jigs or bait)
4. Back-trolling (plugs or diver-and-bait)
5. Back-bouncing (boat)
6. Trolling (boat only)
7. Anchor fishing
8. Plunking
9. Jigging

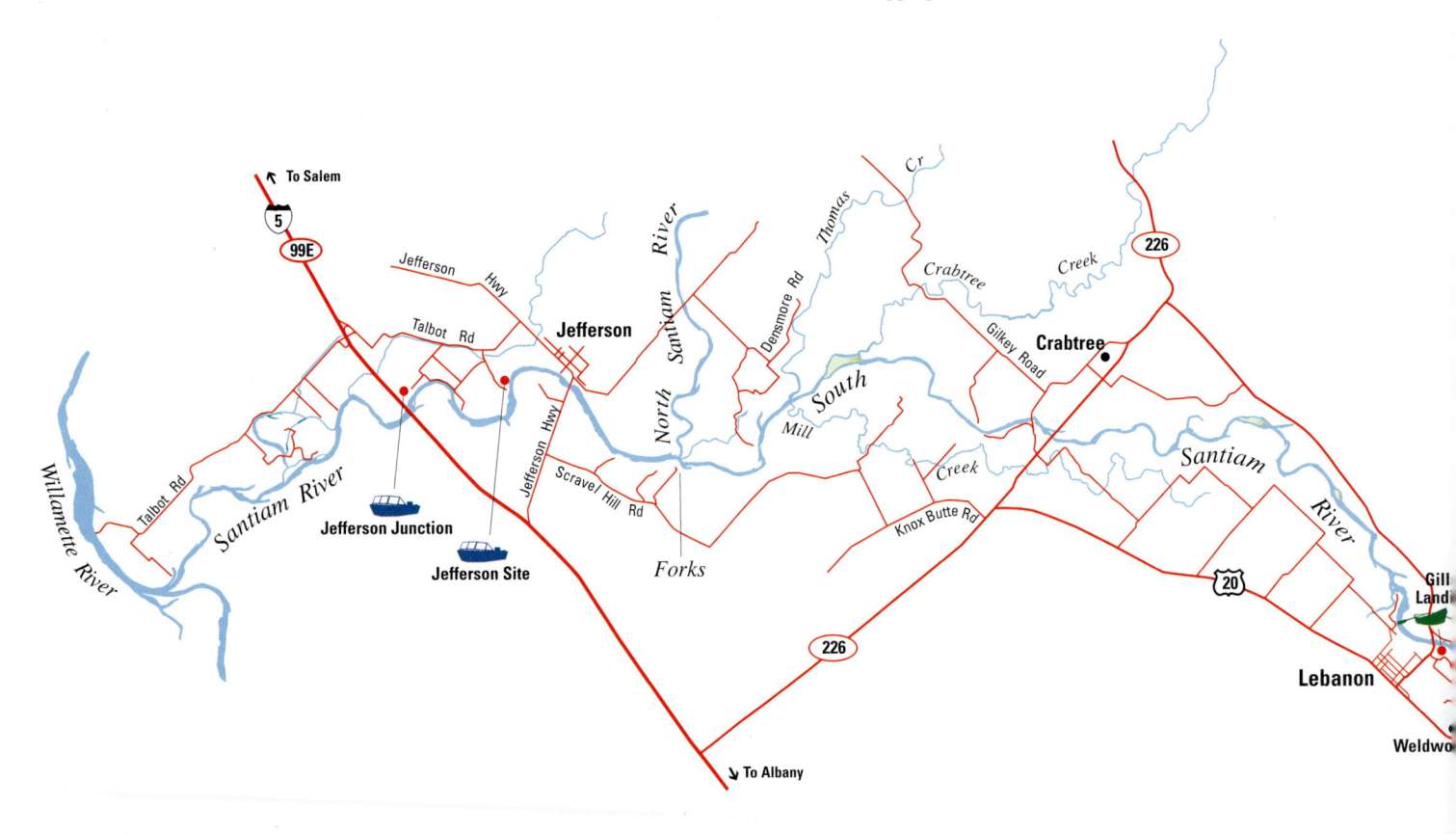

SANTIAM RIVER, SOUTH

BEST FLY-FISHING TECHNIQUES

	Jan	Feb	Mar	Apr	May	Jun	Jul	Aug	Sep	Oct	Nov	Dec
Winter Steelhead	4,6,7	4,6,7	4,6,7	4,6,7								4,6,7
Summer Steelhead					2,3,4 5,6,7	2,3,4 5,6,7	2,3,4 5,6,7	2,3,4 5,6,7	2,3,4 5,6,7	2,3,4 5,6,7		
Spring Chinook					4,6 7,9	4,6 7,9	4,6 7,9	4,6 7,9				

Legend: Best (red), Good (green), Slow (orange)

1. Dry fly, dead-drift
2. Dry fly, swung
3. Wet fly, swung near surface
4. Wet fly, swung deep
5. Nymph(s), lightly weighted
6. Nymph(s), weighted with indicator
7. Deep drifted fly (with or without indicator)
8. Wet fly retrieved near surface
9. Deep swing with retrieve

SERVICES

CAMPING/PARKS
- **River Bend County Park,** Reservations: (541) 967-3917, www.linnparks.com
- **Gills Landing RV City Park,** Lebanon, 97355, (541) 258-4917, www.ci.lebanon.or.us

ACCOMMODATIONS
- **The Century House B&B,** Lebanon, 97355, (542) 259-5592, www.the-centuryhouse.com
- **The Brownsville House B&B,** Brownsville, 97327, (541) 466-3043, email: thebrownsvillehouse@gmail.com, www.thebrownsvillehouse.com

TACKLE SHOPS
- **Flies By Ilene,** Salem, 97302, (503) 566-7351
- **Dick's Sporting Goods,** Salem, OR 97301, (503) 363-4860, www.dickssportinggoods.com
- **Creekside Fly Fishing,** Salem, 97301, (503) 588-1768, www.creeksideflyfishing.com

VISITOR INFORMATION
- **Willamette National Forest,** Springfield, 97477, (541) 225-6300, www.fs.usda.gov/willamette
- **Linn County Parks,** Reservations: (541) 967-3917, www.linnparks.com
- **Oregon Fishing Reports,** (503) 377-9696, www.theguidesforecast.com
- **Jefferson Area Chamber of Commerce,** Jefferson, 97352, (541) 974-0717, email: info@jeffersonareachamber.com, www.jeffersonareachamber.com

LOCATION: Linn County

Wading difficulty	Easy
Shuttles	Yes
Boating difficulty	Moderate
USGS river levels on-line	Yes
Water clarity recovery	Fast

The South Santiam is brimming with spring salmon in May and June.

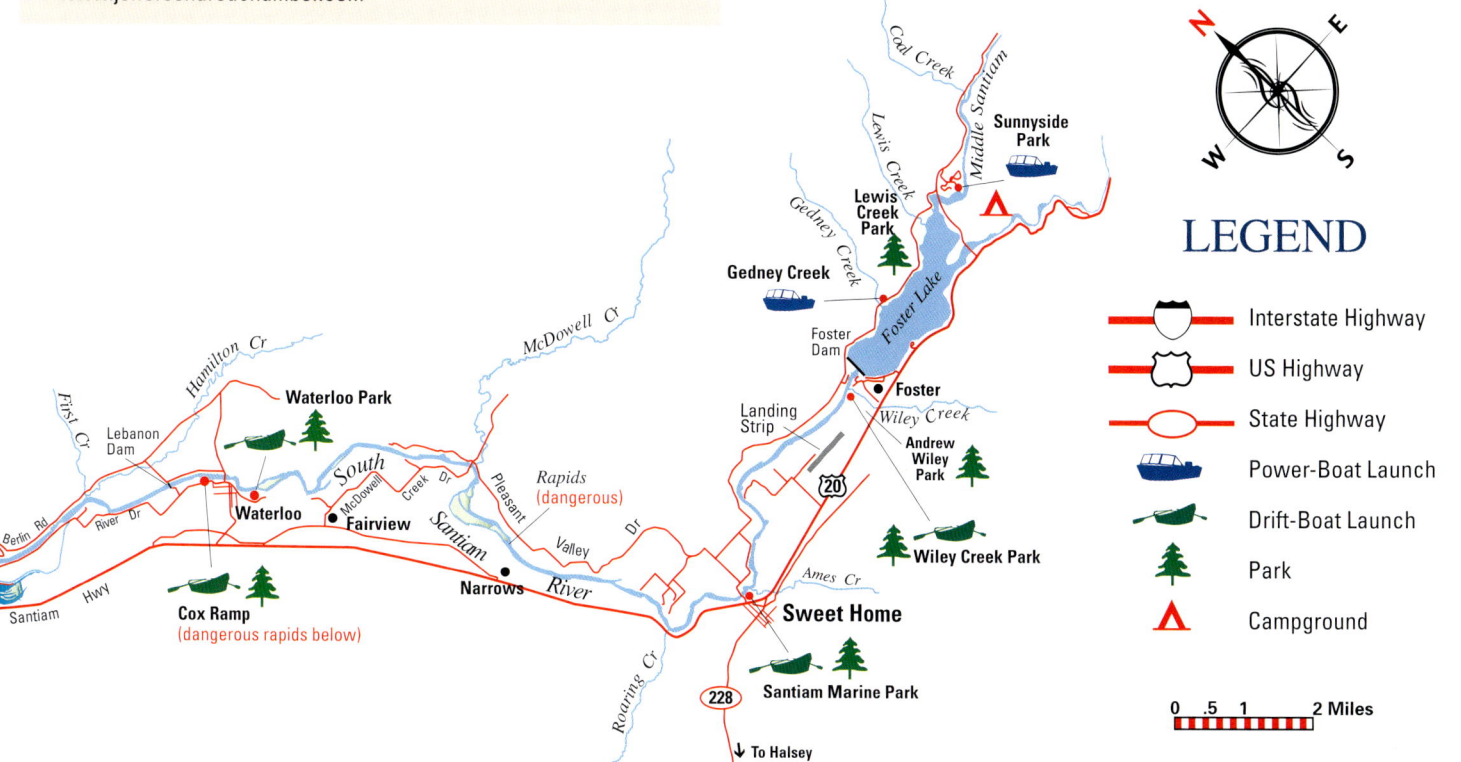

Photo by Nick Amato

LEGEND
- Interstate Highway
- US Highway
- State Highway
- Power-Boat Launch
- Drift-Boat Launch
- Park
- Campground

69

OREGON RIVER MAPS & FISHING GUIDE

McKenzie River, Lower

The McKenzie River is one of the main tributaries to the upper Willamette River, flowing almost 100 miles from its source at Clear Lake in the High Cascades, to its confluence with the Willamette River near Eugene. It is most famous for its rainbow and cutthroat trout fishing, but it is also known for its excellent runs of spring Chinook and summer steelhead. To Northwest anglers, the McKenzie is also renowned as the birthplace of the McKenzie river dory, today's most popular river-boat design.

Trout fishing is good throughout the McKenzie, but the best water is in the upper river, above Leaburg Dam (see the Upper McKenzie map on page 72).

Summer steelhead run from late April through October. Most McKenzie anglers target these sea-run rainbows at or near Leaburg Dam, but trout anglers are often pleasantly surprised when what appears to be a rising trout proves to be an acrobatic steelhead.

Spring salmon arrive in May and continue to run through July. Casting spinners and spoons is the most popular fishing method for salmon and steelhead. They can also be enticed by large attractor-type flies (see steelhead and salmon flies, page 7).

A typical fat rainbow trout from the lower McKenzie.

Photo by Nick Amato

SERVICES

CAMPING/PARKS
- **Armitage Park Campground,** Eugene 97408, (541) 682-2000, www.eugenecascadescoast.org

ACCOMMODATIONS
- **McKenzie Orchards B&B,** Springfield, 97478, (541) 515-8153, www.mkobb.com

TACKLE SHOPS
- **Mazama Sporting Goods,** Eugene, 97402, (541) 357-4419, www.mazamasportinggoods.com
- **The Caddis Fly Angling Shop,** Eugene, 97401, (541) 342-7005, www.caddisflyshop.com
- **Cabela's,** Springfield, 97477, (541) 349-5760, www.cabelas.com
- **Oregon Rod Reel and Tackle,** Eugene, 97408, (541) 683-4965, www.oregonrrt.com
- **Home Waters Fly Fishing,** Eugene, 97401, (541) 342-6691

VISITOR INFORMATION
- **Lane County Parks,** Eugene, 97408, (541) 682-2000, www.lanecounty.org
- **Springfield Parks,** (541) 736-4104, www.willamalane.org
- **Willamette National Forest,** Springfield, 97477, (541) 225-6300, www.fs.usda.gov/willamette
- **Springfield Chamber of Commerce,** Springfield, 97477, (541) 746-1651, (866) 346-1651, www.springfield-chamber.org

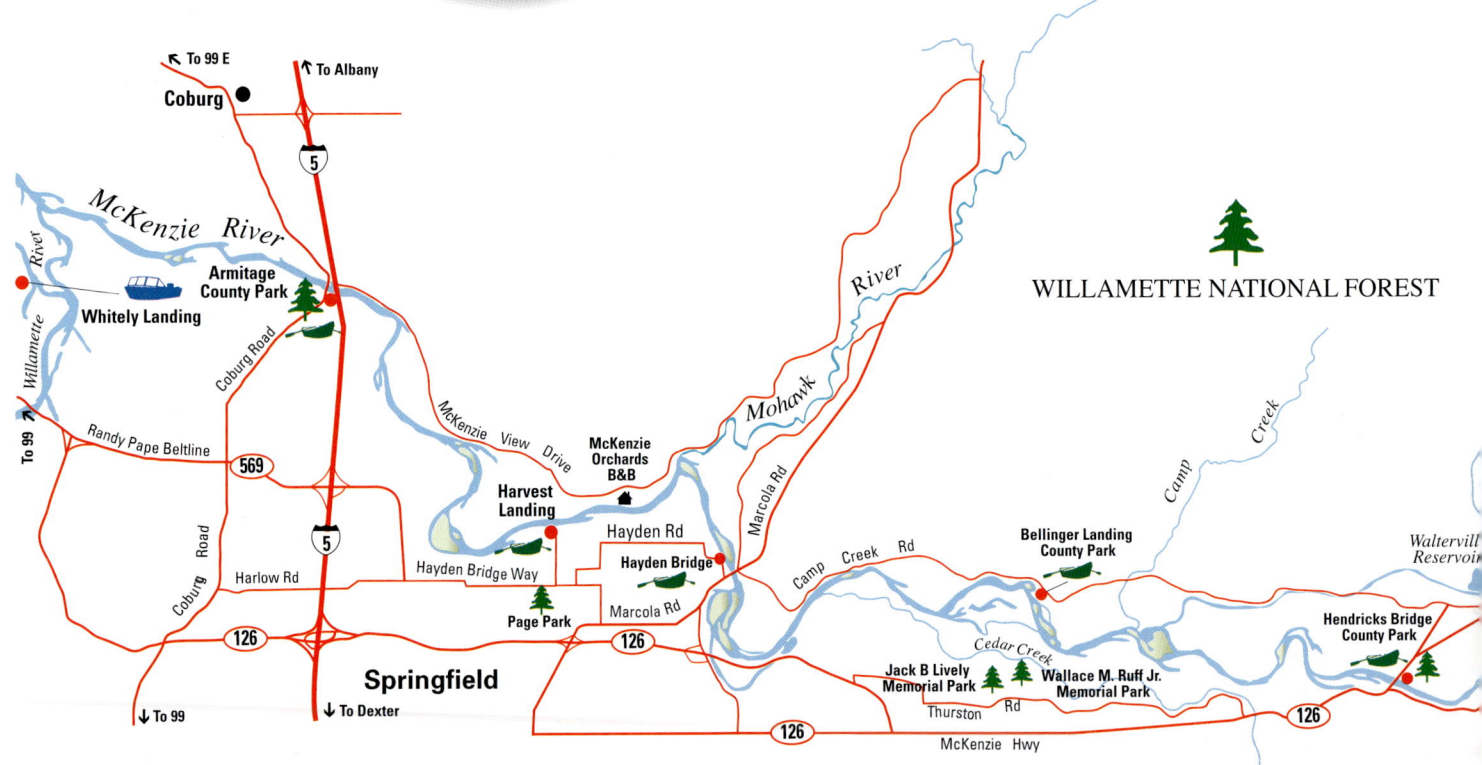

McKENZIE RIVER, LOWER

BEST FLY-FISHING TECHNIQUES

	Jan	Feb	Mar	Apr	May	Jun	Jul	Aug	Sep	Oct	Nov	Dec
Summer Steelhead 2000				2,3,4 5,6,7	2,3,4 5,6,7	2,3,4 5,6,7	2,3,4 5,6,7	2,3,4 5,6,7	2,3,4 5,6,7	2,3,4 5,6,7		
Spring Chinook 1000					4,6 7,9	4,6 7,9	4,6 7,9					
Rainbow Trout		1,2,3 5,6,8	1,2,3 5,6,8	1,2,3 5,6,8	1,2,3 5,6,8	1,2,3 5,6,8	1,2,3 5,6,8	1,2,3 5,6,8	1,2,3 5,6,8	1,2,3 5,6,8	1,2,3 5,6,8	
Cutthroat		1,2,3 5,6,8	1,2,3 5,6,8	1,2,3 5,6,8	1,2,3 5,6,8	1,2,3 5,6,8	1,2,3 5,6,8	1,2,3 5,6,8	1,2,3 5,6,8	1,2,3 5,6,8	1,2,3 5,6,8	

Legend: Best / Good / Slow

1. Dry fly, dead-drift
2. Dry fly, swung
3. Wet fly, swung near surface
4. Wet fly, swung deep
5. Nymph(s), lightly weighted
6. Nymph(s), weighted with indicator
7. Deep drifted fly (with or without indicator)
8. Wet fly retrieved near surface
9. Deep swing with retrieve

BEST GEAR-FISHING TECHNIQUES & ESTIMATED HOOKUPS IN AN AVERAGE YEAR

	Jan	Feb	Mar	Apr	May	Jun	Jul	Aug	Sep	Oct	Nov	Dec
Summer Steelhead 2000				1,2 3,4	1,2 3,4	1,2 3,4	1,2 3,4	1,2 3,4	1,2 3,4	1,2 3,4		
Spring Chinook 1000					1,2,3 4,5	1,2,3 4,5	1,2,3 4,5					
Rainbow Trout		2	2	2	2	2	2	2	2	2	2	
Cutthroat		2	2	2	2	2	2	2	2	2	2	

Legend: Best / Good / Slow

1. Drift fishing (from bank or boat, with or without bait)
2. Casting spinners, spoons, plugs
3. Float fishing (with jigs or bait)
4. Back-trolling (plugs or diver-and-bait)
5. Back-bouncing (boat)
6. Trolling (boat only)
7. Anchor fishing
8. Plunking
9. Jigging

LOCATION: Lane County

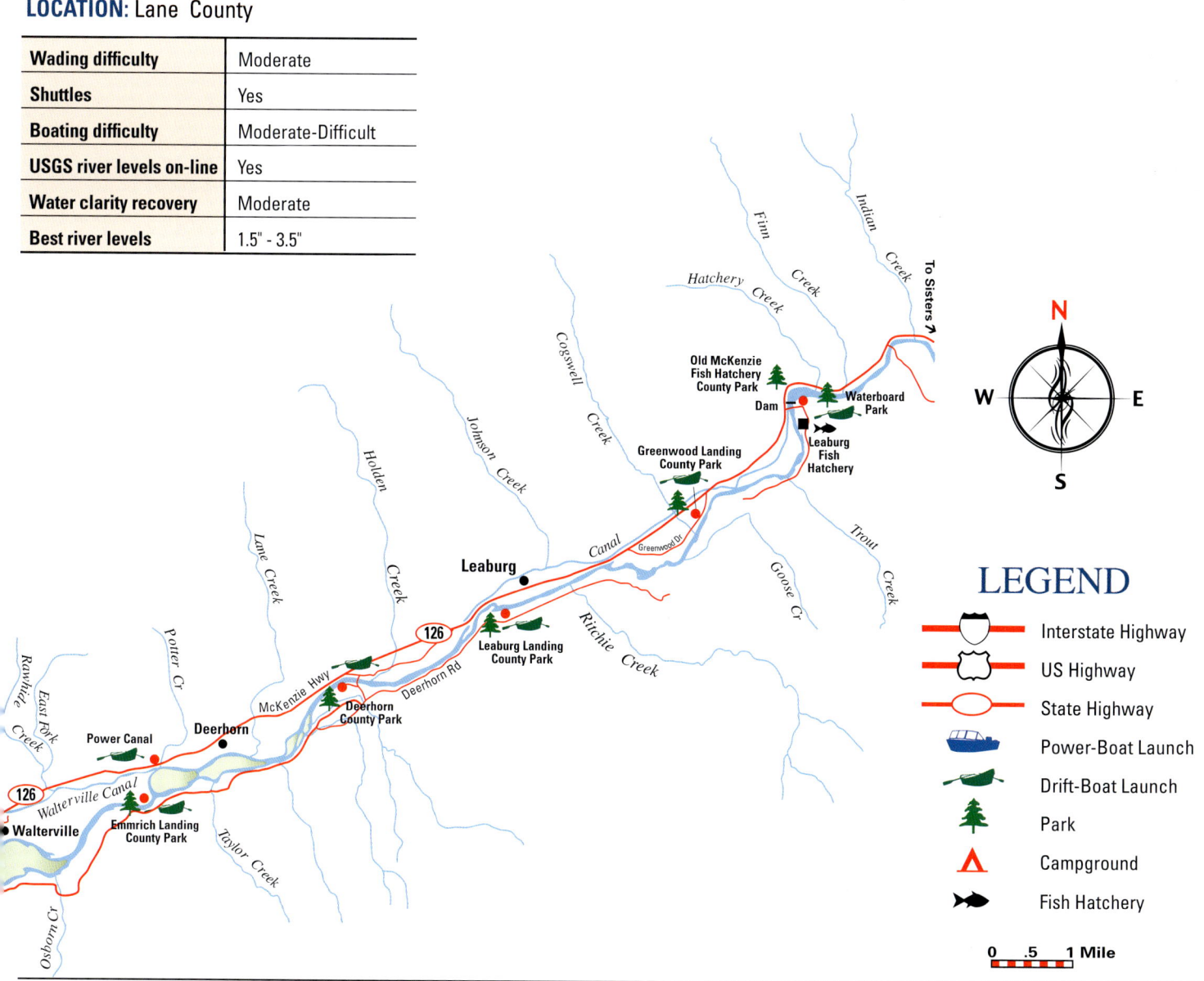

Wading difficulty	Moderate
Shuttles	Yes
Boating difficulty	Moderate-Difficult
USGS river levels on-line	Yes
Water clarity recovery	Moderate
Best river levels	1.5" - 3.5"

LEGEND

- Interstate Highway
- US Highway
- State Highway
- Power-Boat Launch
- Drift-Boat Launch
- Park
- Campground
- Fish Hatchery

0 .5 1 Mile

71

McKenzie River, Upper

Fly-fishing for resident rainbow trout and migratory cutthroat trout is a time-honored tradition on the McKenzie. The best fly-fishing occurs in April and May, coinciding with the March Brown and Green Caddis hatches. The wild behavior of the McKenzie's Green Caddis drives the trout to distraction, and makes them vulnerable to skated dry flies. The rest of the year, McKenzie trout are more wary, and catching the larger fish requires more skill (see Hatch Chart, page 6).

The McKenzie is very popular with boaters, offering over 25 public landings from the upper reaches to its confluence with the Willamette. There is only one hazardous section for boaters, Marten Rapids, just downstream of Ben & Kay Doris State Park.

SERVICES

CAMPING/PARKS

- **Patio RV Park,** Blue River, 97413, (541) 822-3596, www.patiorv.com
- **Mona Campground,** Blue River Ranger District, Blue River, 97413, (541) 603-8564; reservations available May-mid September
- **Delta Campground,** Blue River, 97413, (541) 603-8564, www.reserveamerica.com
- **McKenzie Bridge Campground,** (541) 603-8564
- **Paradise In Oregon Campground,** Blue River, 97413, (801) 226-3564, www.reserveamerica.com
- **Limberlost Campground,** (877) 444-6777, www.recreation.gov
- **Olallie Campground,** McKenzie Bridge, 97413, (541) 603-8564, www.reserveamerica.com
- **Trail Bridge Campground,** McKenzie Bridge, 97413, (541) 225-6300, www.reserveamerica.com

ACCOMMODATIONS

- **Caddis Fly Resort,** McKenzie Bridge, 97413, (541) 822-3556, www.caddisflyresort.com
- **Inn at the Bridge,** McKenzie Bridge, 97413, (541) 743-2012, www.mckenzie-river-cabins.com
- **Cedarwood Lodge,** McKenzie Bridge, (541) 822-3351, www.cedarwoodlodge.com
- **Loloma Lodge,** McKenzie Bridge, 97413, (541) 822-6231, www.lolomalodge.com
- **McKenzie Orchards B&B,** Springfield, 97478, (541) 515-8153, www.mkobb.com
- **McKenzie River Mountain Resort,** Road 2620, Blue River, 97413, (541) 822-6272, www.mckenzierivermountainresort.com
- **Eagle Rock Lodge,** McKenzie Highway Vida, 97488, (541) 822-3630, www.eaglerocklodge.com
- **McKenzie River Inn,** McKenzie Highway Vida, 97488, (541) 822-6260, www.mckenzieriverinn.com
- **Holiday Farm Resort,** Blue River, 97413, (541) 822-3725, www.holidayfarmresort.com

LOCATION: Lane County

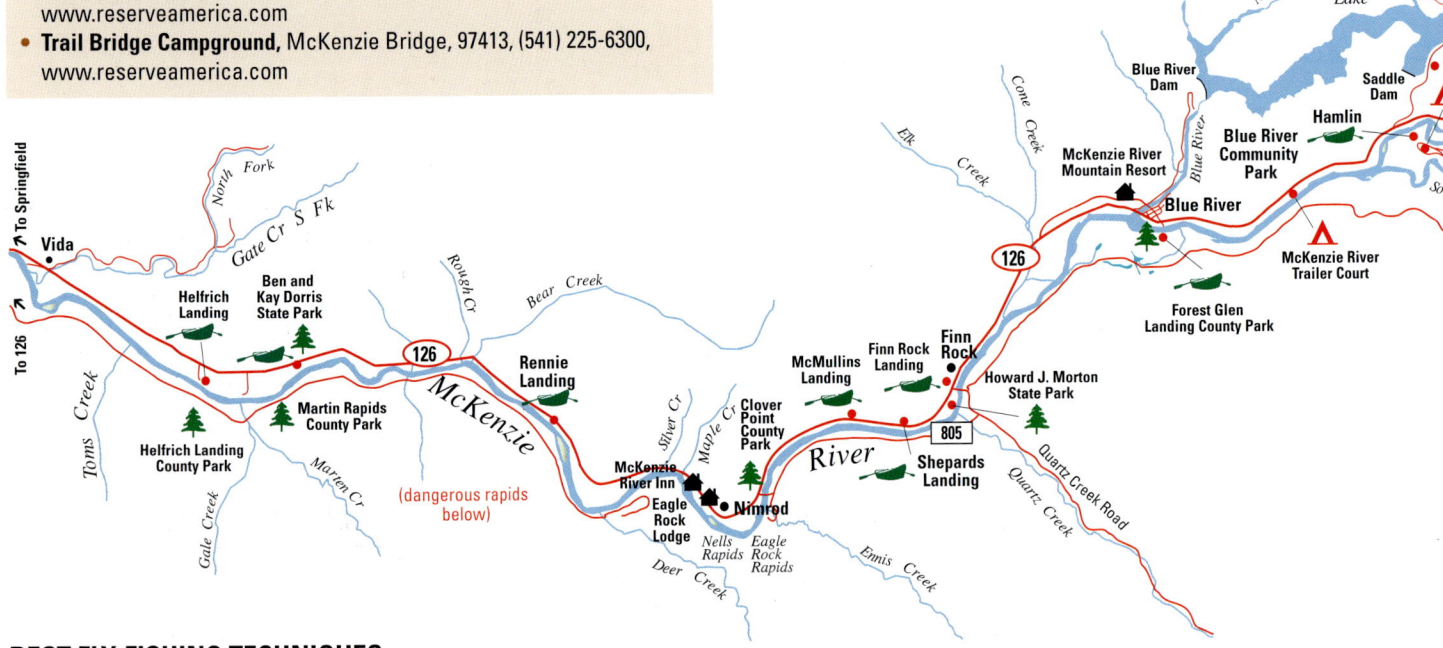

BEST FLY-FISHING TECHNIQUES

Best / Good / Slow	Jan	Feb	Mar	Apr	May	Jun	Jul	Aug	Sep	Oct	Nov	Dec
Summer Steelhead 2000				2,3,4 5,6,7	2,3,4 5,6,7	2,3,4 5,6,7	2,3,4 5,6,7	2,3,4 5,6,7	2,3,4 5,6,7	2,3,4 5,6,7		
Spring Chinook 1000					4,6 7,9	4,6 7,9	4,6 7,9					
Rainbow Trout		1,2,3 5,6,8	1,2,3 5,6,8	1,2,3 5,6,8	1,2,3 5,6,8	1,2,3 5,6,8	1,2,3 5,6,8	1,2,3 5,6,8	1,2,3 5,6,8	1,2,3 5,6,8	1,2,3 5,6,8	
Cutthroat			1,2,3 5,6,8	1,2,3 5,6,8	1,2,3 5,6,8	1,2,3 5,6,8	1,2,3 5,6,8	1,2,3 5,6,8	1,2,3 5,6,8	1,2,3 5,6,8		

1. Dry fly, dead-drift
2. Dry fly, swung
3. Wet fly, swung near surface
4. Wet fly, swung deep
5. Nymph(s), lightly weighted
6. Nymph(s), weighted with indicator
7. Deep drifted fly (with or without indicator)
8. Wet fly retrieved near surface
9. Deep swing with retrieve

McKenzie River, Upper

- **Horse Creek Lodge,** Blue River, 97413, (541) 822-3243, www.horse-creek.com

TACKLE SHOPS
- **Mazama Sporting Goods,** Eugene, (541) 357-4419, www.mazamasportinggoods.com
- **The Caddis Fly Angling Shop,** Eugene, 97401, (541) 342-7005, www.caddisflyshop.com
- **Cabela's,** Springfield, 97477, (541) 349-5760, www.cabelas.com
- **Oregon Rod Reel and Tackle,** Eugene, 97408, (541) 683-4965, www.oregonrrt.com
- **Home Waters Fly Fishing,** Eugene, 97401, (541) 342-6691

VISITOR INFORMATION
- **Lane County Parks,** Eugene, 97408, (541) 682-2000, www.lanecounty.org/parks
- **Willamette National Forest,** Blue River, 97413, (541) 225-6300, www.fs.usda.gov/willamette
- **Springfield City Parks,** (541) 736-4104, www.willamalane.org
- **Springfield Chamber of Commerce,** Springfield, 97477, (541) 746-1651, (866) 346-1651, www.springfield-chamber.org

Fly-anglers love the McKenzie River for her colorful "redside" rainbow trout.

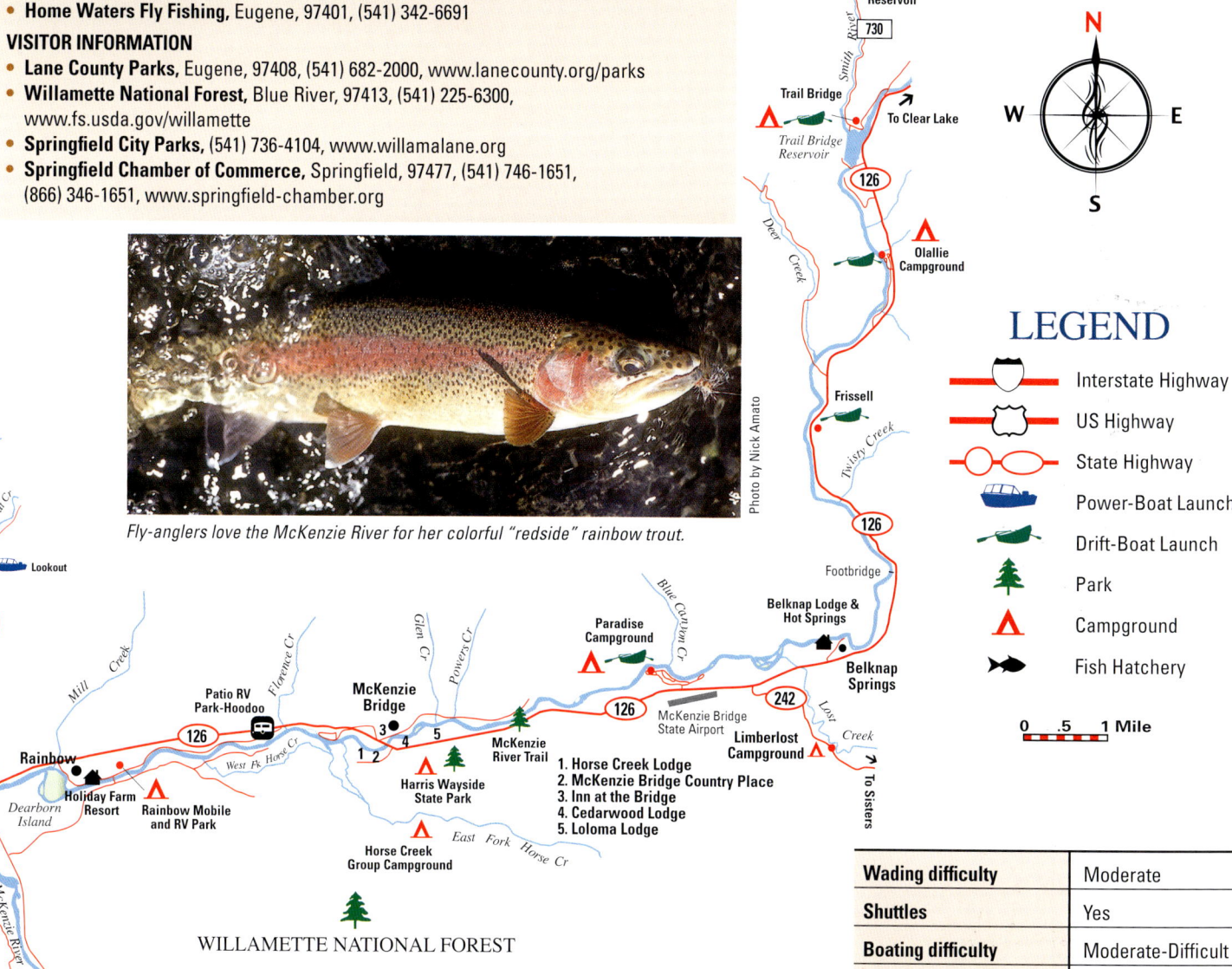

LEGEND
- Interstate Highway
- US Highway
- State Highway
- Power-Boat Launch
- Drift-Boat Launch
- Park
- Campground
- Fish Hatchery

Wading difficulty	Moderate
Shuttles	Yes
Boating difficulty	Moderate-Difficult
USGS river levels on-line	Yes
Water clarity recovery	Moderate
Best river levels	1.5" - 3.5"

BEST GEAR-FISHING TECHNIQUES & ESTIMATED HOOKUPS IN AN AVERAGE YEAR

Best / Good / Slow	Jan	Feb	Mar	Apr	May	Jun	Jul	Aug	Sep	Oct	Nov	Dec
Summer Steelhead 2000				1,2 3,4	1,2 3,4	1,2 3,4	1,2 3,4	1,2 3,4	1,2 3,4	1,2 3,4		
Spring Chinook 1000					1,2,3 4,5	1,2,3 4,5	1,2,3 4,5					
Rainbow Trout		2	2	2	2	2	2	2	2	2		
Cutthroat		2	2	2	2	2	2	2	2	2		

1. Drift fishing (from bank or boat, with or without bait)
2. Casting spinners, spoons, plugs
3. Float fishing (with jigs or bait)
4. Back-trolling (plugs or diver-and-bait)
5. Back-bouncing (boat)
6. Trolling (boat only)
7. Anchor fishing
8. Plunking
9. Jigging

73

Oregon River Maps & Fishing Guide

Middle Fork Willamette River

The Middle Fork of the Willamette River offers almost thirty miles of prime steelhead and salmon water, from Dexter Reservoir downstream to the confluence with the Coast Fork near Glenwood. Spring Chinook salmon and summer steelhead are the main attractions, although the river's resident rainbow trout are also popular among fly-anglers.

Spring Chinook run from late April through July, with the peak of the run occuring from mid-May to the end of June. Every method of fishing can be effective, but casting spinners or float fishing with roe are the most productive. Summer steelhead run from late March through October, with the peak of the run occuring from May through September. Casting float-and-jig combinations, as well as spinners and spoons, either from a boat or from the bank, are the most effective methods.

Rainbow trout inhabit every part of the Middle Willamette, and are a favorite quarry of local fly-anglers. Matching the native insect hatches is the best way to catch these elusive trout. See the hatch guide and list of flies on pages 3 and 4 to prepare for the Middle Willamette's insect hatches.

Most of the Middle Willamette's best bank access is centered around Dexter Park below the reservoir. Drift boats offer the best access to the river below.

LOCATION: Lane County

Wading difficulty	Moderate
Shuttles	Yes
Boating difficulty	Easy-Moderate
USGS river levels on-line	No
Water clarity recovery	Fast

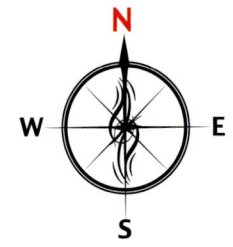

BEST GEAR-FISHING TECHNIQUES & ESTIMATED HOOKUPS IN AN AVERAGE YEAR

Best / Good / Slow	Jan	Feb	Mar	Apr	May	Jun	Jul	Aug	Sep	Oct	Nov	Dec
Spring Chinook 1000					1,2,3 4,5,8	1,2,3 4,5,8	1,2,3 4,5,8	1,2,3,4,5,8				
Summer Steelhead 800				1,2,3,4,5,8	1,2,3 4,5,8	1,2,3 4,5,8	1,2,3 4,5,8	1,2,3 4,5,8	1,2,3 4,5,8	1,2,3 4,5,8		
Rainbow Trout					2 / 2	2	2	2	2	2		

1. Drift fishing (from bank or boat, with or without bait)
2. Casting spinners, spoons, plugs
3. Float fishing (with jigs or bait)
4. Back-trolling (plugs or diver-and-bait)
5. Back-bouncing (boat)
6. Trolling (boat only)
7. Anchor fishing
8. Plunking
9. Jigging

BEST FLY-FISHING TECHNIQUES

Best / Good / Slow	Jan	Feb	Mar	Apr	May	Jun	Jul	Aug	Sep	Oct	Nov	Dec
Spring Chinook					4,6 7,9	4,6 7,9	4,6 7,9	4,6,7,9				
Summer Steelhead				2,3,4,6,7	2,3,4 6,7	2,3,4 6,7	2,3,4 6,7	2,3,4 6,7	2,3,4 6,7	2,3,4 6,7		
Rainbow Trout					1,2,3 4,5,6	1,2,3 4,5,6	1,2,3 4,5,6	1,2,3 4,5,6	1,2,3 4,5,6	1,2,3 4,5,6		

1. Dry fly, dead-drift
2. Dry fly, swung
3. Wet fly, swung near surface
4. Wet fly, swung deep
5. Nymph(s), lightly weighted
6. Nymph(s), weighted with indicator
7. Deep drifted fly (with or without indicator)
8. Wet fly retrieved near surface
9. Deep swing with retrieve

MIDDLE FORK WILLAMETTE RIVER

SERVICES

CAMPING/PARKS
- **Shamrock Village RV Park,** Eugene, 97403, (541) 747-7473, www.shamrockvillagepark.com
- **Deerwood RV Park,** Eugene, 97405, (541) 988-1139, email: info@deerwoodrvpark.com, www.deerwoodrvpark.com
- **Dexter Shores RV Park,** Dexter, 97431, (541) 937-3711, (866) 558-9777, www.dextershoresrv.com
- **Casey's Riverside RV Park,** Westfir, 97492, (541) 782-1906, www.caseysrvpark.com
- **Arbor Inn Motel & Oakridge RV Park,** Oakridge, 97463, (541) 782-2611, www.arborinnmotel.net

ACCOMMODATIONS
- **McKenzie Orchards B&B,** Springfield, 97478, (541) 515-8153, email: mckenzieorchards@yahoo.com, www.mkobb.com
- **The Oval Door B&B Inn,** Eugene, 97401, (541) 683-3160, (800) 882-3160, www.ovaldoor.com

TACKLE SHOPS
- **Mazama Sporting Goods,** Eugene, 97402, (541) 357-4419, www.mazamasportinggoods.com
- **Cabela's,** Springfield, 97477, (541) 349-5760, www.cabelas.com
- **Oregon Rod Reel and Tackle,** Eugene, 97408, (541) 683-4965, www.oregonrrt.com
- **Home Waters Fly Fishing,** Eugene, 97401, (541) 342-6691
- **Caddis Fly Angling Shop,** Eugene, 97401, (541) 342-7005, email: caddiseug@yahoo.com, www.caddisflyshop.com

VISITOR INFORMATION
- **Willamette National Forest,** Springfield, 97477, (541) 225-6300, www.fs.usda.gov/willamette
- **Lane County,** Eugene, 97408, (541) 682-2000, www.lanecounty.org
- **Oregon Fishing Reports,** (503) 377-9696, www.theguidesforecast.com
- **Springfield Area Chamber of Commerce,** Springfield, 97477, (541) 746-1651, www.springfield-chamber.org

Rainbow Trout

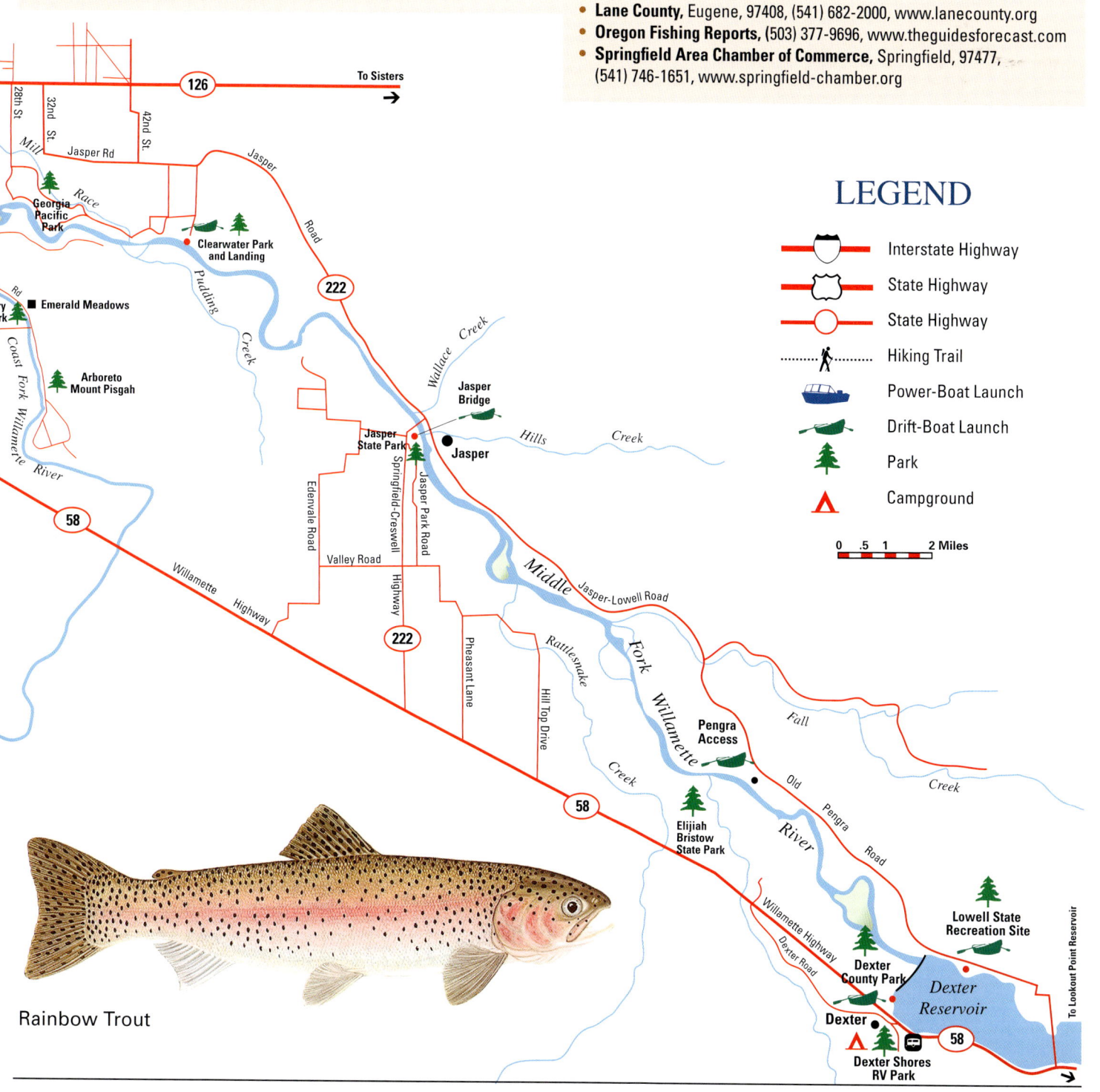

Deschutes River, Lower

The lower Deschutes River is arguably the greatest rainbow trout fishery in the western United States. With over 3000 rainbows per river mile, plus thousands of summer steelhead, the sheer volume of fish in the lower Deschutes is staggering. From the quaint canyon-town of Maupin to the river's confluence with the Columbia River at Moody, anglers can access over 50 miles of blue-ribbon water.

Resident rainbow trout are the main attraction from Maupin down to Mack's Canyon. The rainbow fishing is good year-round, but becomes exceptional from April through September. A variety of seasonal insect hatches spurs the best trout fishing (see the hatch chart on page 3), including the world-famous salmonfly hatch occuring from May to early June. In the summer months, the Deschutes hosts tremendous hatches of caddisflies, creating evening rises that rival any in the world. Fly-fishing is the most popular method of trout fishing on the Deschutes, but fly/bubble combinations work very well with light spinning tackle.

Summer steelhead move into the lower Deschutes from mid-July through October. These hefty sea-run rainbows average six pounds, but occasionally tip the scales at over twenty pounds. In August and September, the main run of steelhead arrives. These fish range from 4 to 12 pounds, and are most aggressive in early morning and late evening (when the sun is off the water). Swinging small to medium steelhead flies across the riffles and runs is an excellent way to attract Deschutes steelhead. Spinners, spoons and plugs are also very effective. No matter the method, all fishing on the lower Deschutes is done from the bank. Fishing from a boat is prohibited.

Spring Chinook salmon run in the lower Deschutes from April through June. These powerful fish can be caught with various lures and flies, but bait fishing below Sherar's Falls is the most productive.

Boating on the lower Deschutes is for experts only. There are numerous Class III and Class IV rapids. Sherar's falls, located 8 miles downriver from Maupin, is unnavigable, and should never be attempted, even by the best oarsman.

From Mack's Canyon to Moody, the river is very remote, with no additional take-outs. Most anglers take three days to float this stretch, though many also run up from Moody in jet boats. Jet boats are only allowed on the river at certain times. Check with the Bureau of Land Management (BLM) or local shops for details.

All boating on the Deschutes requires a boaters pass, issued by the BLM, and available at the tackle shops listed on this page. The BLM limits use on this section of river, and strictly enforces safety rules.

LOCATION: Sherman & Wasco Counties

Wading difficulty	Difficult
Shuttles	Yes
Boating difficulty	Dangerous
USGS river levels on-line	Yes
Water clarity recovery	Moderate

BEST GEAR-FISHING TECHNIQUES & ESTIMATED HOOKUPS IN AN AVERAGE YEAR

	Jan	Feb	Mar	Apr	May	Jun	Jul	Aug	Sep	Oct	Nov	Dec
Summer Steelhead 8000	1,2,3	1,2,3					1,2,3	1,2,3	1,2,3	1,2,3	1,2,3	1,2,3
Spring Chinook 2000				1,2,3	1,2,3	1,2,3	1,2,3					
Fall Chinook 500									1,2,3	1,2,3	1,2,3	
Rainbow Trout 300,000	2	2	2	2	2	2	2	2	2	2	2	2

1. Drift fishing (from bank or boat, with or without bait)
2. Casting spinners, spoons, plugs
3. Float fishing (with jigs or bait)
4. Back-trolling (plugs or diver-and-bait)
5. Back-bouncing (boat)
6. Trolling (boat only)
7. Anchor fishing
8. Plunking
9. Jigging

BEST FLY-FISHING TECHNIQUES

	Jan	Feb	Mar	Apr	May	Jun	Jul	Aug	Sep	Oct	Nov	Dec
Summer Steelhead	1,2,3 4,5,6	1,2,3 4,5,6					1,2,3,4,5,6	1,2,3 4,5,6	1,2,3 4,5,6	1,2,3 4,5,6	1,2,3 4,5,6	1,2,3 4,5,6
Spring Chinook				4,6,7,9	4,6 7,9	4,6 7,9	4,6,7,9					
Fall Chinook									4,6,7,9	4,6 7,9	4,6,7,9	
Rainbow Trout	1,2,3 5,6	1,2,3,5,6 1,2,3,5,6	1,2,3 5,6	1,2,3 5,6	1,2,3 5,6	1,2,3 5,6	1,2,3 5,6	1,2,3 5,6	1,2,3 5,6	1,2,3 5,6	1,2,3 5,6	1,2,3 5,6

1. Dry fly, dead-drift
2. Dry fly, swung
3. Wet fly, swung near surface
4. Wet fly, swung deep
5. Nymph(s), lightly weighted
6. Nymph(s), weighted with indicator
7. Deep drifted fly (with or without indicator)
8. Wet fly retrieved near surface
9. Deep swing with retrieve

DESCHUTES RIVER, LOWER

SERVICES

CAMPING/PARKS
- **Deschutes River State Recreation Area,** Wasco, 97065, (541) 739-2322, Reservations: (800) 452-5687, www.oregonstateparks.org
- **Maupin City Park,** Maupin, 97037, (541) 395-2252, www.cityofmaupin.com

ACCOMMODATIONS
- **The Oasis Resort & Guide Service,** Maupin, 97037, (541) 395-2611, www.deschutesriveroasis.com
- **Imperial River Co.,** Maupin, 97037, (541) 395-2404, (800) 395-3903, www.deschutesriver.com

TACKLE SHOPS
- **Deschutes Canyon Fly Shop,** Maupin, 97037, (541) 395-2565, www.flyfishingdeschutes.com
- **Deschutes Angler Fly Shop,** Maupin, 97037, (541) 395-0995, www.deschutesangler.com
- **The Fly Fisher's Place,** Sisters, 97759, (541) 549-FISH, www.flyfishersplace.com

VISITOR INFORMATION
- **Required Deschutes River Boaters Pass,** (541) 416-6700, www.boaterpass.com
- **Special Rules for Lower Deschutes River Corridor,** www.blm.gov/or
- **Maupin Area Chamber of Commerce,** Maupin, 97037, (541) 993-1708, www.maupinoregon.com

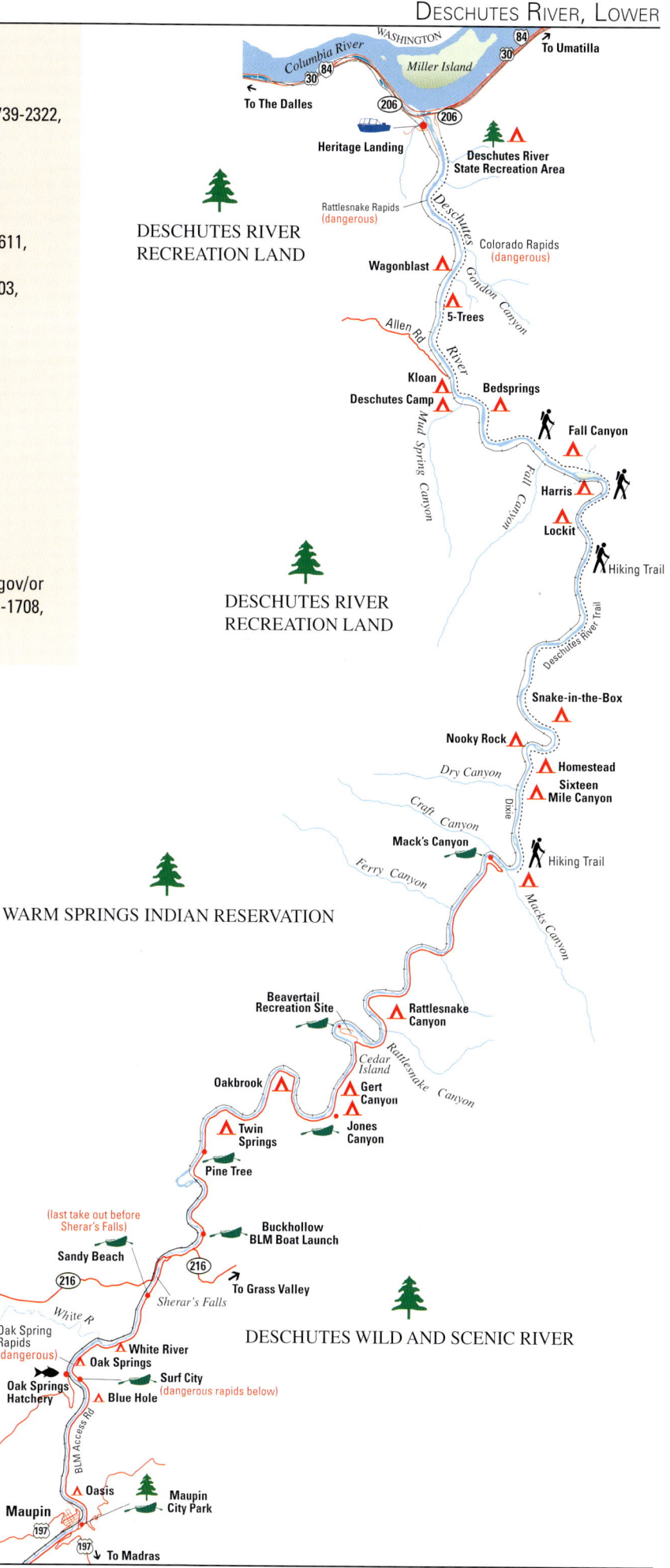

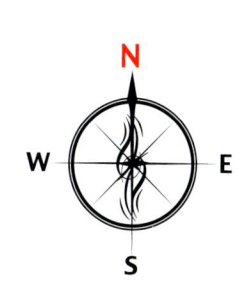

LEGEND
- Interstate Highway
- US Highway
- State Highway
- Hiking Trail
- Power-Boat Launch
- Drift-Boat Launch
- Park
- Campground
- Fish Hatchery

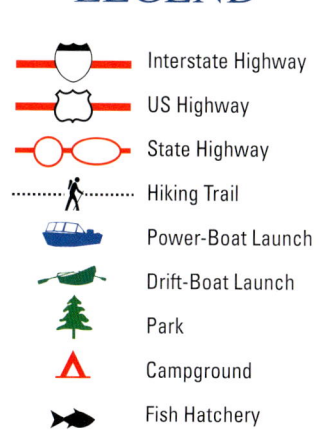

OREGON RIVER MAPS & FISHING GUIDE

Deschutes River, Lower

The spectacular Deschutes River Canyon is a fly-fisher's paradise.
Photo by Rob Crandall

From Warm Springs to Maupin, the Deschutes River carves its way through magnificent canyon country. This is the wildest stretch of the Deschutes, and the most productive for anglers. Rainbow trout are the main attraction, known to Deschutes anglers as "redsides" for their stunning coloration. The trout share the river with thousands of steelhead, spring Chinook salmon and whitefish, all of which are vulnerable to a well-fished fly.

The most popular one-day float trip on the Deschutes goes from Warm Springs to Trout Creek. It is classic fly-fishing water, hosting thousands of trout per mile. This section's popularity makes it a busy area, especially on the weekends, but there are always places to fish. Bank anglers prefer to drive into Upper and Lower Mecca (on the east side of the river), or Dry Creek on the west side. Anglers who wish to fish on Warm Springs Reservation must obtain a permit from the Confederated Tribes of Warm Springs.

Trout Creek to Maupin is reserved for multi-day float trips and experienced boaters. Limited campsites are carefully managed by the BLM, and boating and camping passes are required (www.boaterspass.com). There are some notable rapids along the way, the most dangerous of which is Whitehorse Rapids. Many an inexperienced drift boater has lost his boat here, so be sure to scout the big rapids before attempting to run them, and always wear a life jacket.

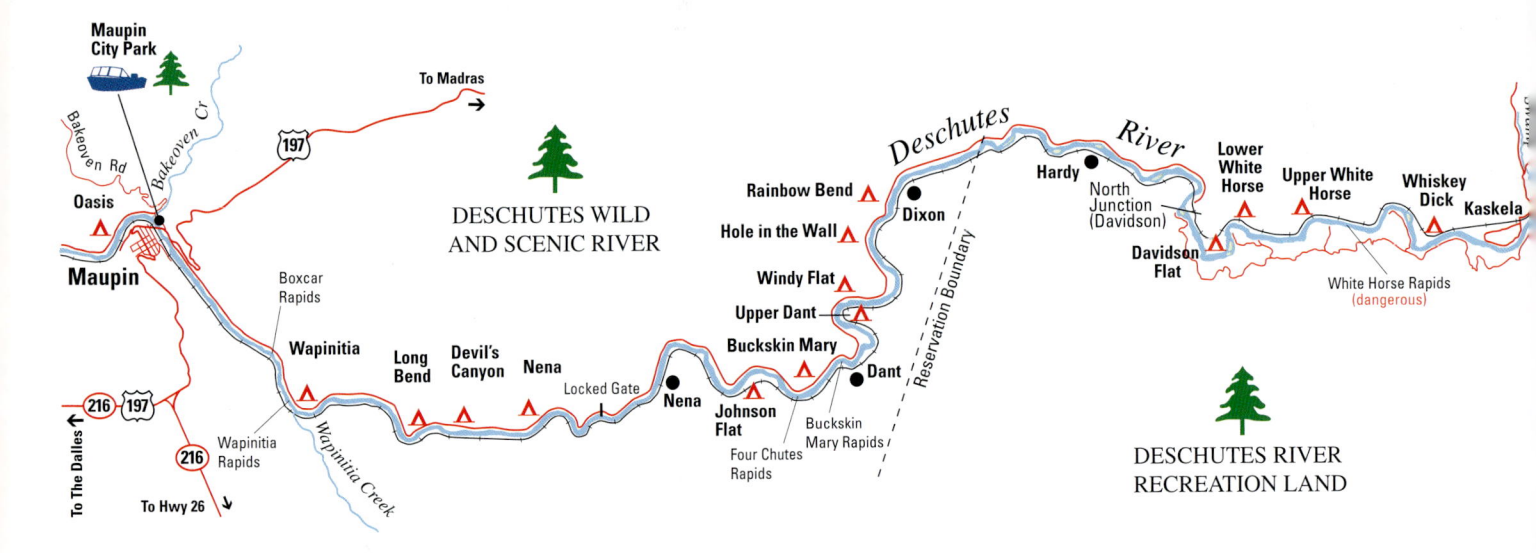

Some of the best fishing in this stretch can be accessed by car. Drive up the east side of the river from Maupin. Automobile access extends to "the locked gate." Anglers are permitted to hike past the gate for day trips.

Trout are available throughout this section of the Deschutes year-round. Summer steelhead arrive from July through October, and stay in the river until the following spring. Fly-fishing is the preferred angling method for Deschutes trout and steelhead (see the hatch chart and fly patterns on page 6 & 7).

LOCATION: Sherman, Wasco & Jefferson Counties

Wading difficulty	Difficult
Shuttles	Yes
Boating difficulty	Dangerous
USGS river levels on-line	Yes
Water clarity recovery	Moderate

78

DESCHUTES RIVER, LOWER

BEST GEAR-FISHING TECHNIQUES & ESTIMATED HOOKUPS IN AN AVERAGE YEAR

	Jan	Feb	Mar	Apr	May	Jun	Jul	Aug	Sep	Oct	Nov	Dec
Summer Steelhead 8000	1,2,3	1,2,3					1,2,3	1,2,3	1,2,3	1,2,3	1,2,3	1,2,3
Spring Chinook 2000				1,2,3	1,2,3	1,2,3	1,2,3					
Fall Chinook 500									1,2,3	1,2,3	1,2,3	
Rainbow Trout 300,000	2	2 / 2	2	2	2	2	2	2	2	2	2	2

Legend: Best / Good / Slow

1. Drift fishing (from bank or boat, with or without bait)
2. Casting spinners, spoons, plugs
3. Float fishing (with jigs or bait)
4. Back-trolling (plugs or diver-and-bait)
5. Back-bouncing (boat)
6. Trolling (boat only)
7. Anchor fishing
8. Plunking
9. Jigging

BEST FLY-FISHING TECHNIQUES

	Jan	Feb	Mar	Apr	May	Jun	Jul	Aug	Sep	Oct	Nov	Dec
Summer Steelhead	1,2,3 4,5,6	1,2,3 4,5,6					1,2,3,4,5,6	1,2,3 4,5,6	1,2,3 4,5,6	1,2,3 4,5,6	1,2,3 4,5,6	1,2,3 4,5,6
Spring Chinook				4,6,7,9	4,6 7,9	4,6 7,9	4,6,7,9					
Fall Chinook									4,6,7,9	4,6 7,9	4,6,7,9	
Rainbow Trout	1,2,3 5,6	1,2,3,5,6 / 1,2,3,5,6	1,2,3 5,6	1,2,3 5,6	1,2,3 5,6	1,2,3 5,6	1,2,3 5,6	1,2,3 5,6	1,2,3 5,6	1,2,3 5,6	1,2,3 5,6	1,2,3 5,6

1. Dry fly, dead-drift
2. Dry fly, swung
3. Wet fly, swung near surface
4. Wet fly, swung deep
5. Nymph(s), lightly weighted
6. Nymph(s), weighted with indicator
7. Deep drifted fly (with or without indicator)
8. Wet fly retrieved near surface
9. Deep swing with retrieve

SERVICES

CAMPING/PARKS
- **Lake Simtustus RV Park & Fish Camp,** Madras, 97741, (541) 475-1085, www.lakesimtustusresort.com
- **Maupin City Park,** Maupin, 97037, (541) 395-2252, www.cityofmaupin.com

ACCOMMODATIONS
- **Kah-Nee-Ta Resort & Spa,** Warm Springs, 97761, (800) 554-4786, www.kahneeta.com
- **Sweet Virginia's B&B,** Metolius, 97741, (541) 546-3031, www.sweetvirginiasbedandbreakfast.com
- **The Oasis Resort & Guide Service,** Maupin, 97037, (541) 395-2611, www.deschutesriveroasis.com
- **Imperial River Co.,** Maupin, 97037, (541) 395-2404, (800) 395-3903, www.deschutesriver.com

TACKLE SHOPS
- **Brad's Bait & Tackle,** Madras, 97741, (541) 475-6892, www.bradsbaitandtackle.com
- **Deschutes Canyon Fly Shop,** Maupin, 97037, (541) 395-2565, www.flyfishingdeschutes.com
- **Deschutes Angler Fly Shop,** Maupin, 97037, (541) 395-0995, www.deschutesangler.com
- **The Fly Fisher's Place,** Sisters, 97759, (541) 549-FISH, www.flyfishersplace.com

VISITOR INFORMATION
- **Required Deschutes River Boaters Pass,** (541) 416-6700, www.boaterpass.com
- **Special Rules for Lower Deschutes River Corridor,** www.blm.gov/or
- **Tribal Fishing Permits, Info: CTWSRO Fisheries Department,** (541) 553-2042, tribalpermit@wstribes.org, www.tribalpermit.com
- **Madras-Jefferson County Chamber of Commerce,** Madras, 97741, (541) 475-2350, (800) 967-3564, www.madraschamber.com

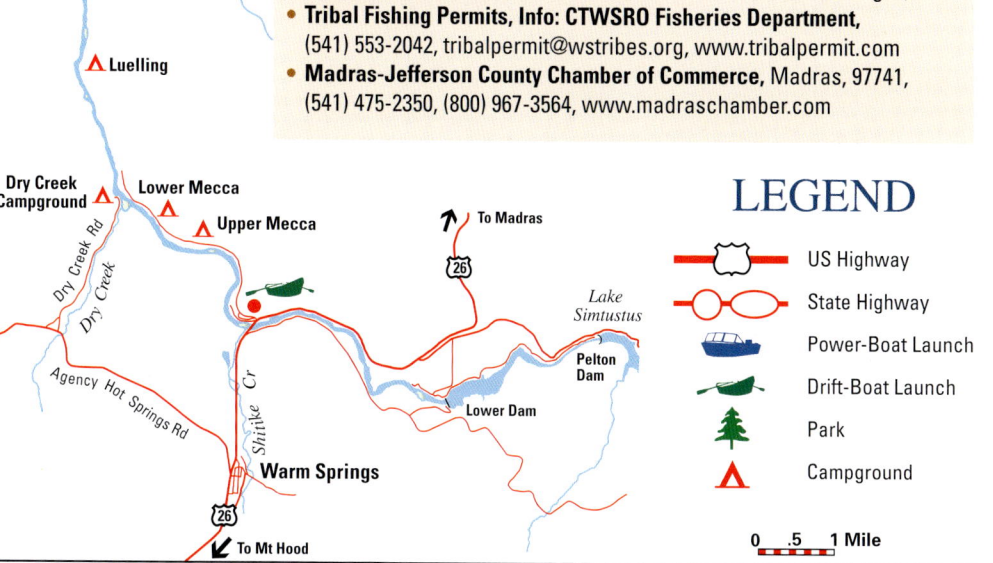

WARM SPRINGS INDIAN RESERVATION

LEGEND
- US Highway
- State Highway
- Power-Boat Launch
- Drift-Boat Launch
- Park
- Campground

0 .5 1 Mile

79

OREGON RIVER MAPS & FISHING GUIDE

Metolius River

Among trout anglers, the Metolius River is regarded as one of Oregon's crown jewels. It stands out as one of the most beautiful spring creeks in the state, and offers trophy-trout fishing year-round. The temperature of the Metolius remains a consistent 40 degrees year-round, rising from a spring at its source near Black Butte. A variety of trout call the Metolius home. Native rainbow trout are still the dominant species, along with bull trout (currently listed as a threatened species). Brown trout and eastern brook trout occur in lesser numbers, and a unique run of kokanee salmon migrate up from the lake each autumn. Bait-fishing is prohibited on the Metolius.

LOCATION: Jefferson County

Wading difficulty	Moderate
Water clarity recovery	Fast

BEST GEAR-FISHING TECHNIQUES & ESTIMATED HOOKUPS IN AN AVERAGE YEAR

Best / Good / Slow	Jan	Feb	Mar	Apr	May	Jun	Jul	Aug	Sep	Oct	Nov	Dec
Rainbow Trout	2	2	2	2	2	2	2	2	2	2	2	2
Brown Trout	2	2	2	2	2	2	2	2	2	2	2/2	2
Bull Trout	2	2	2	2	2	2	2	2	2	2	2	2
Kokanee Salmon									2/2	2	2/2	

1. Drift fishing (from bank or boat, with or without bait)
2. Casting spinners, spoons, plugs
3. Float fishing (with jigs or bait)
4. Back-trolling (plugs or diver-and-bait)
5. Back-bouncing (boat)
6. Trolling (boat only)
7. Anchor fishing
8. Plunking
9. Jigging

BEST FLY-FISHING TECHNIQUES

Best / Good / Slow	Jan	Feb	Mar	Apr	May	Jun	Jul	Aug	Sep	Oct	Nov	Dec
Rainbow Trout	1,2 5,6	1,2 5,6	1,2 5,6	1,2 5,6	1,2 5,6	1,2 5,6	1,2 5,6	1,2 5,6	1,2 5,6	1,2 5,6	1,2 5,6	1,2 5,6
Brown Trout	1,2 5,6	1,2 5,6	1,2 5,6	1,2 5,6	1,2 5,6	1,2 5,6	1,2 5,6	1,2 5,6	1,2 5,6	1,2 5,6	1,2 5,6	1,2 5,6
Bull Trout	1,2 5,6	1,2 5,6	1,2 5,6	1,2 5,6	1,2 5,6	1,2 5,6	1,2 5,6	1,2 5,6	1,2 5,6	1,2 5,6	1,2 5,6	1,2 5,6
Kokanee Salmon									3,4,9 / 3,4,9	3,4,9	3,4,9 / 3,4,9	

1. Dry fly, dead-drift
2. Dry fly, swung
3. Wet fly, swung near surface
4. Wet fly, swung deep
5. Nymph(s), lightly weighted
6. Nymph(s), weighted with indicator
7. Deep drifted fly (with or without indicator)
8. Wet fly retrieved near surface
9. Deep swing with retrieve

Robert Campbell pinned this bull trout while fishing shallow water with a Bunny Leech streamer.

Photo by Gary Lewis

METOLIUS RIVER

SERVICES

CAMPING/PARKS
- **Cold Springs Resort & RV Park,** Camp Sherman, 97730, (541) 595-6271, www.coldspringsresort.com
- **Camp Sherman RV Park,** Camp Sherman, reserve; www.recreation.gov or (877) 444-6777, www.hoodoo.com
- **Area Campgrounds:** Smiling River, Pine Rest, Gorge, Canyon Creek,
- **Allen Springs, Pioneer Ford, Lower Bridge, Candle Creek,** www.hoodoo.com/deschutes-national-forest-or/metolius-river/

ACCOMMODATIONS
- **The Lodge at Suttle Lake,** Sisters, 97759, (541) 595-2628, www.thelodgeatsuttlelake.com
- **Metolius River Resort,** Camp Sherman, 97730, (541) 595-6281, www.metoliusriverresort.com
- **Metolius River Lodges,** Camp Sherman, 97730, (541) 595-6290, www.metoliusriverlodges.com
- **House on the Metolius,** Camp Sherman, 97730, (541) 595-6620, www.metolius.com

TACKLE SHOPS
- **Camp Sherman Store & Fly Shop,** Camp Sherman, 97730, (541) 595-6711, www.campshermanstore.com
- **Brad's Bait & Tackle,** Madras, 97741, (541) 475-6892, www.bradsbaitandtackle.com
- **The Fly Fisher's Place,** Sisters, 97759, (541) 549-FISH, www.flyfishersplace.com

VISITOR INFORMATION
- **Willamette National Forest,** Blue River, 97413, (541) 225-6300, www.fs.usda.gov/willamette
- **Deschutes National Forest Campgrounds,** www.hoodoo.com
- **Madras-Jefferson County Chamber of Commerce,** Madras, 97741, (541) 475-2350, (800) 967-3564, www.madraschamber.com

LEGEND
- US Highway
- State Highway
- NFD — National Forest Road
- Drift-Boat Launch
- Park
- Campground
- Fish Hatchery

0 .5 1 2 Miles

Ryan Young battles a bull trout in swift water on the Metolius.

Photo by Gary Lewis

DESCHUTES NATIONAL FOREST

Head of the Metolius (springs)

81

OREGON RIVER MAPS & FISHING GUIDE

Crooked River

The Crooked River is one of Oregon's most productive trout streams. A major tributary to the Deschutes River, its long, breathtaking canyon makes it one of the most beautiful streams anywhere in the western states. Native redband trout and whitefish inhabit the entire drainage and grow quickly due to the tremendous natural food in the river. The "canyon" is the most popular stretch of the Crooked, referring to the twenty river-miles from Bowman Dam (Prineville Reservoir) to the town of Prineville. Since the water flowing out of Prineville Reservoir remains a constant temperature year-round, insects and fish are very active through the winter. It is for this reason that the Crooked River Canyon has become a popular winter trout fishery. From November through March, while many other streams are too cold to offer good trout fishing, the Crooked sees consistent insect hatches (see hatch chart on page 6).

Jeff Perin and friend on the Crooked River.

Jeff Perin fights a rainbow on the Crooked River

BEST GEAR-FISHING TECHNIQUES & ESTIMATED HOOKUPS IN AN AVERAGE YEAR

Best / Good / Slow	Jan	Feb	Mar	Apr	May	Jun	Jul	Aug	Sep	Oct	Nov	Dec
Rainbow Trout	2	2	2	2	2	2	2	2	2	2	2	2
Brown Trout	2	2	2	2	2	2	2	2	2	2	2/2	2
Bull Trout	2	2	2	2	2	2	2	2	2	2	2	2
Kokanee Salmon									2/2	2	2/2	

1. Drift fishing (from bank or boat, with or without bait)
2. Casting spinners, spoons, plugs
3. Float fishing (with jigs or bait)
4. Back-trolling (plugs or diver-and-bait)
5. Back-bouncing (boat)
6. Trolling (boat only)
7. Anchor fishing
8. Plunking
9. Jigging

BEST FLY-FISHING TECHNIQUES

Best / Good / Slow	Jan	Feb	Mar	Apr	May	Jun	Jul	Aug	Sep	Oct	Nov	Dec
Rainbow Trout	1,2 / 5,6	1,2 / 5,6	1,2 / 5,6	1,2 / 5,6	1,2 / 5,6	1,2 / 5,6	1,2 / 5,6	1,2 / 5,6	1,2 / 5,6	1,2 / 5,6	1,2 / 5,6	1,2 / 5,6
Brown Trout	1,2 / 5,6	1,2 / 5,6	1,2 / 5,6	1,2 / 5,6	1,2 / 5,6	1,2 / 5,6	1,2 / 5,6	1,2 / 5,6	1,2 / 5,6	1,2 / 5,6	1,2 / 5,6	1,2 / 5,6
Bull Trout	1,2 / 5,6	1,2 / 5,6	1,2 / 5,6	1,2 / 5,6	1,2 / 5,6	1,2 / 5,6	1,2 / 5,6	1,2 / 5,6	1,2 / 5,6	1,2 / 5,6	1,2 / 5,6	1,2 / 5,6
Kokanee Salmon									3,4,9 / 3,4,9	3,4,9 / 3,4,9	3,4,9 / 3,4,9	

1. Dry fly, dead-drift
2. Dry fly, swung
3. Wet fly, swung near surface
4. Wet fly, swung deep
5. Nymph(s), lightly weighted
6. Nymph(s), weighted with indicator
7. Deep drifted fly (with or without indicator)
8. Wet fly retrieved near surface
9. Deep swing with retrieve

Crooked River

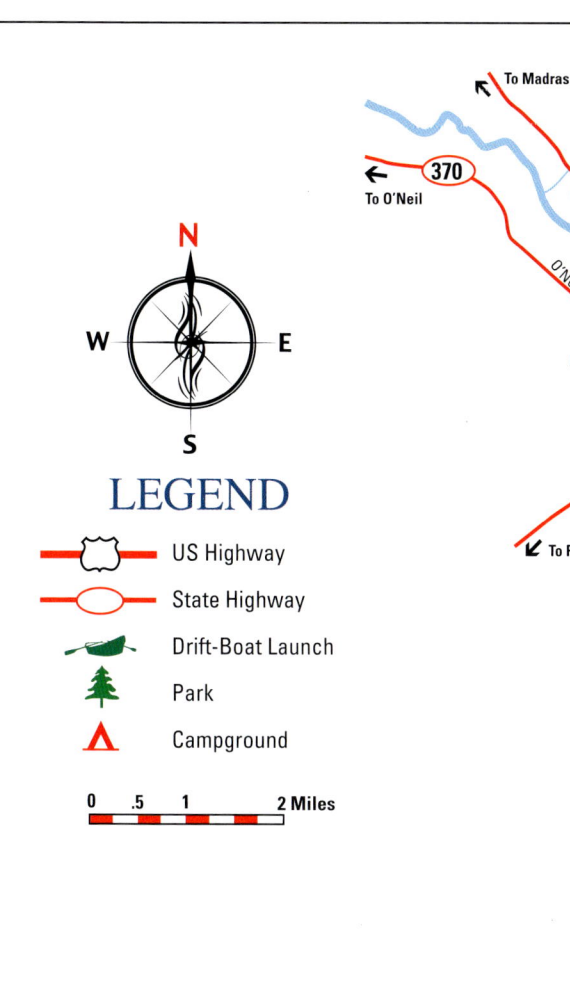

LOCATION: Crook County

Wading difficulty	Easy-Moderate
Boating difficulty	n/a
Water clarity recovery	Fast

SERVICES

CAMPING/PARKS
- **Prineville Reservoir State Park,** Prineville, 97754, Reservations: (800) 452-5687, www.oregonstateparks.org
- **Crook County RV Park,** Prineville, 97754, (541) 447-2599, (800) 609-2599, www.ccprd.org

ACCOMMODATIONS
- **Bellavista B&B,** Prineville, 97754, (541) 416-2400, www.bellavistab-b.com

TACKLE SHOPS
- **Cent Wise Sporting Goods,** Redmond, 97756, (541) 548-4422, www.centwiseredmond.com
- **Patient Angler Fly Shop,** Bend, 97702, (541) 389-6208, www.patientangler.com
- **Brads Bait & Tackle,** Madras, 97741, (541) 475-6892, www.bradsbaitandtackle.com

VISITOR INFORMATION
- **Crook County Parks and Recreation,** Prineville, 97754, (541) 447-7663, www.ccprd.org
- **Prineville-Crook County Chamber of Commerce,** Prineville, 97754, (541) 447-6304, www.visitprineville.org

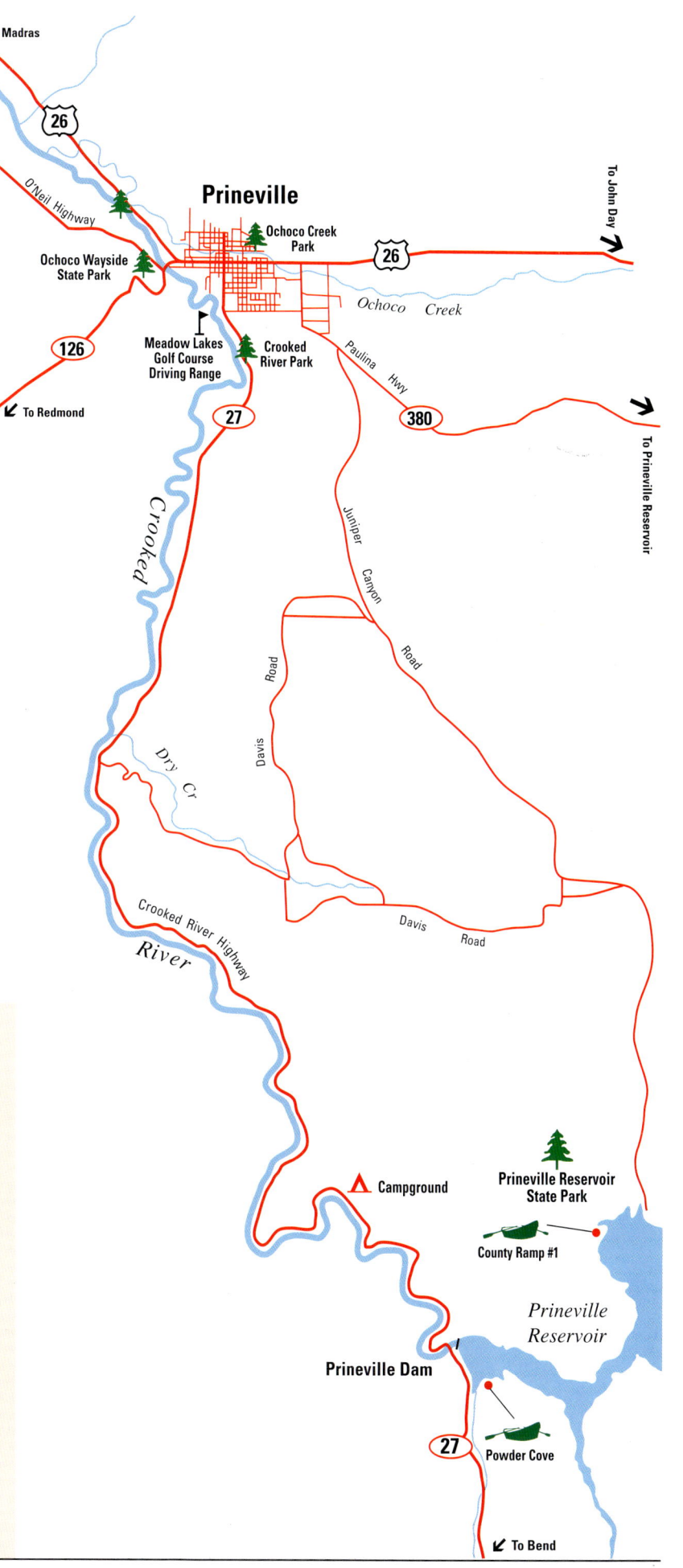

OREGON RIVER MAPS & FISHING GUIDE

Grande Ronde River

This 200-mile-long river drains two significant mountain ranges in the northeast corner of Oregon before flowing into Washington State and, eventually, into the Snake River. It is famous for its steelhead and trout fishing, and for its spectacular scenery. The Grande Ronde and its tributaries offer a wide variety of fishing opportunities, from the tumbling mountain trout streams of the Blue and Wallawa mountains, to the dramatic desert canyon that attracts steelheaders from around the world.

Originating in the Blue Mountains southwest of La Grande, the river winds its way down into the arid Grande Ronde Valley. By late spring, the valley portion of the river heats up to lethal temperatures for trout, and instead supports a number of warm water species. Further downstream, just north of Looking Glass, the Wallawa River enters. This famous trout stream adds clean, cold water from the high Wallawa Mountains, refreshing the Grande Ronde and making it fit for trout and steelhead. From the confluence (an area called Rondowa) downstream to Wildcat Creek, the river is designated as Wild & Scenic. This section is a favorite for boating and summer trout fishing. Below Wildcat Creek, the river is designated as a recreation area, allowing for easier access for bank anglers and boaters. Trout are available here from the opener on May 24th until the end of October.

From late September through December, thousands of summer steelhead move into the Grande Ronde. Steelheading can be excellent from Rondowa all the way to the confluence with the Snake River in Washington. Fly-fishing is the most popular method, but casting lures with conventional tackle is also very effective. Most years, the best steelheading occurs between October 15th and December 1st. Drift boats can access the entire lower river. During the height of steelhead season, boats are discouraged from Wildcat Creek to Troy. Most anglers choose to drive to the numerous access points in this section, since boaters cannot avoid drifting over the best water. At the height of steelhead fishing in November, nighttime temperatures often dip below freezing.

BEST GEAR-FISHING TECHNIQUES & ESTIMATED HOOKUPS IN AN AVERAGE YEAR

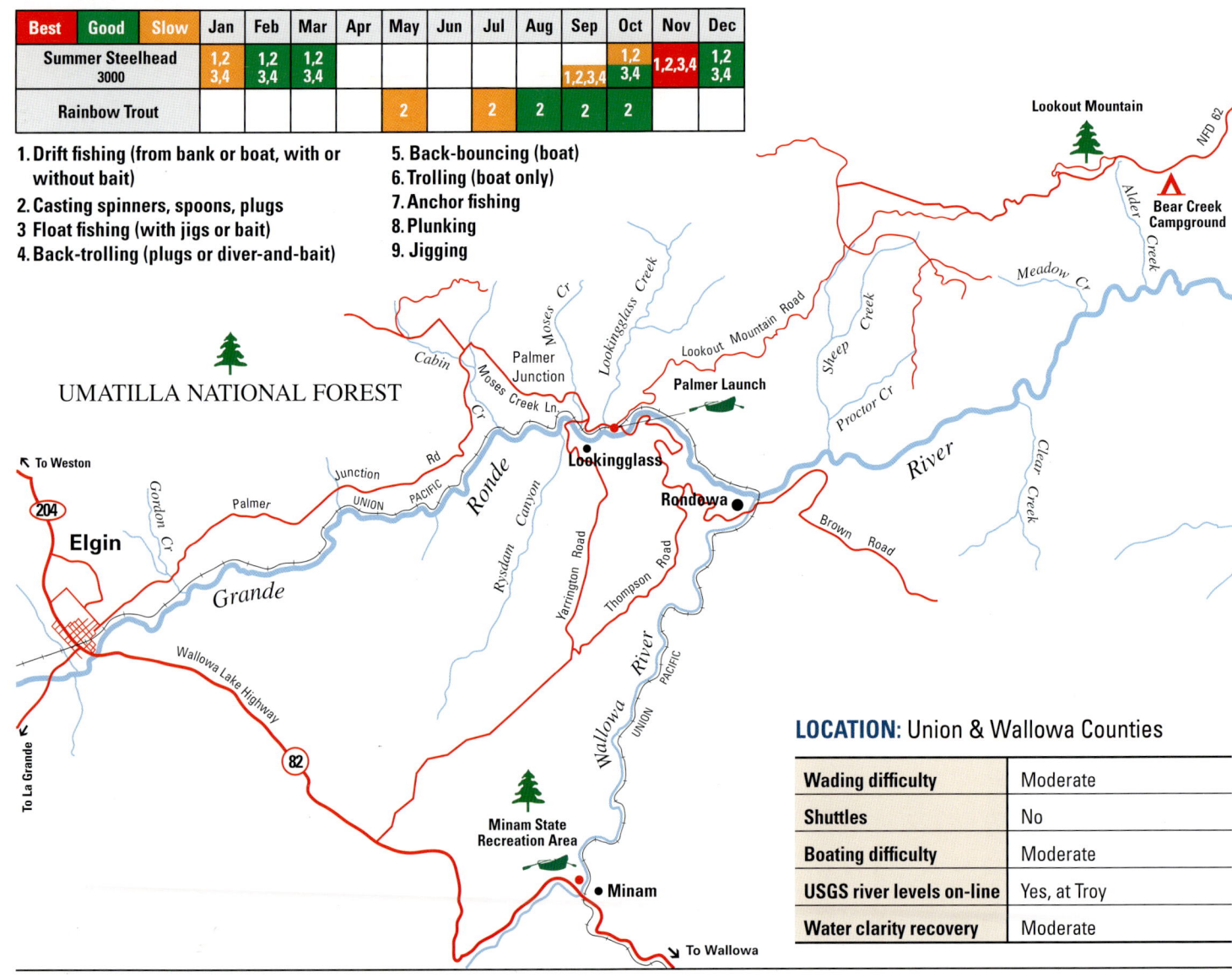

	Jan	Feb	Mar	Apr	May	Jun	Jul	Aug	Sep	Oct	Nov	Dec
Summer Steelhead 3000	1,2 3,4	1,2 3,4	1,2 3,4						1,2,3,4	1,2 3,4	1,2,3,4	1,2 3,4
Rainbow Trout					2		2	2	2			

Legend: Best / Good / Slow

1. Drift fishing (from bank or boat, with or without bait)
2. Casting spinners, spoons, plugs
3. Float fishing (with jigs or bait)
4. Back-trolling (plugs or diver-and-bait)
5. Back-bouncing (boat)
6. Trolling (boat only)
7. Anchor fishing
8. Plunking
9. Jigging

LOCATION: Union & Wallowa Counties

Wading difficulty	Moderate
Shuttles	No
Boating difficulty	Moderate
USGS river levels on-line	Yes, at Troy
Water clarity recovery	Moderate

84

GRANDE RONDE RIVER

SERVICES

CAMPING/PARKS
- **Hu Na Ha RV Park,** Elgin, 97827, (541) 786-1662, www.cityofelginor.org
- **Five Peaks RV Park,** Joseph, 97846, (541) 432-4605, www.5peaksrvpark.com
- **Log House RV Park & Campground,** Enterprise, 97828, (541) 426-4027, (877) 426-4027, www.loghouservpark.com
- **Wallowa River RV Park,** Wallowa, 97885, (541) 886-7002, www.wallowariverrvpark.com
- **Wallowa Lake State Park,** Joseph, 97846, (541) 432-8855, Reservations: (800) 452-5687, www.oregonstateparks.org

ACCOMMODATIONS
- **Bronze Antler B&B,** Joseph, 97846, (541) 432-0230, (866) 520-9769, www.bronzeantler.com
- **Chandler's Inn,** Joseph, 97846, (541) 432-9765, www.josephbedandbreakfast.com
- **Belle Pepper's B&B,** Joseph, 97846, (541) 432-0490, www.bellepeppersbnb.com
- **1910 Historic Enterprise House B&B,** Enterprise, 97828, (541) 426-4238, www.enterprisehousebnb.com
- **Hot Lake Springs B&B,** La Grande, 97850, (541) 963-4685, www.hotlakesprings.com

TACKLE SHOPS
- **Wallowa Lake Marina,** Joseph, 97846, (541) 432-9115, www.wallowalakemarina.com
- **Joseph Fly Shoppe,** Joseph, 97846, (541) 432-4343, email: flyshop@eoni.com, www.josephflyshoppe.com

VISITOR INFORMATION
- **Umatilla National Forest,** Pendleton, 97801, (541) 278-3716, www.fs.usda.gov/umatilla
- **Wallowa-Whitman National Forest,** Baker City, 97814, (541) 523-6391, www.fs.usda.gov
- **Minam State Recreation Area,** www.oregonstateparks.org
- **Wallowa County Parks,** www.wallowacounty.org
- **City of Enterprise,** www.enterpriseoregon.org
- **US Forest Service Campgrounds,** Wallowa Mountain Visitor Center, (541) 426-5546
- **Elgin Chamber of Commerce,** Elgin, 97827, (541) 786-1770, www.visitelginoregon.com
- **Wallowa County Oregon Chamber of Commerce,** Enterprise, 97828, (541) 426-4622, (800) 585-4121, www.wallowacounty.org

BEST FLY-FISHING TECHNIQUES

	Jan	Feb	Mar	Apr	May	Jun	Jul	Aug	Sep	Oct	Nov	Dec
Summer Steelhead	2,3,4 5,6,7	2,3,4 5,6,7	2,3,4 5,6,7						2,3,4,5, 6,7	2,3,4 5,6,7	2,3,4 5,6,7	2,3,4 5,6,7
Rainbow Trout					1,2,3 4,5,6		1,2,3 4,5,6	1,2,3 4,5,6	1,2,3 4,5,6	1,2,3 4,5,6		

Legend: Best / Good / Slow

1. Dry fly, dead-drift
2. Dry fly, swung
3. Wet fly, swung near surface
4. Wet fly, swung deep
5. Nymph(s), lightly weighted
6. Nymph(s), weighted with indicator
7. Deep drifted fly (with or without indicator)
8. Wet fly retrieved near surface
9. Deep swing with retrieve

LEGEND
- State Highway
- Railroad
- Drift-Boat Launch
- Park
- Campground

OREGON RIVER MAPS & FISHING GUIDE

John Day River, Lower

The John Day is the longest free-flowing river in Oregon, and the second longest free-flowing river in the continental U.S. It boasts the healthiest population of wild summer steelhead in the Northwest, and a significant population of wild spring Chinook. In spite of the good steelheading, smallmouth bass have become the John Day's most popular attraction since their introduction in 1971.

Summer bass fishing is the main draw to the John Day from April through September. From Kimberly to the mouth, rafters can choose from a variety of float-trips. Fly-fishing is the most popular method, although casting small lures with light spinning gear is also very effective.

John Day summer steelhead arrive in the fall and winter. From mid-September through February, thousands of native steelhead move into the 200-mile-long watershed, spawning from March through May. They are joined by hatchery steelhead which stray into the John Day from other Columbia tributaries. November and December are the peak months. Fly-fishing and casting lures are the most popular techniques.

Some of the best trophy-bass fishing of the year takes place in early March when the flows are stable and the water is beginning to warm. A slight upward temperature change can spark a strike.

Photo by Gary Lewis

LOCATION:
Sherman & Gilliam Counties

Wading difficulty	Easy
Shuttles	Yes
Boating difficulty	Moderate
USGS river levels on-line	Yes
Water clarity recovery	Fast

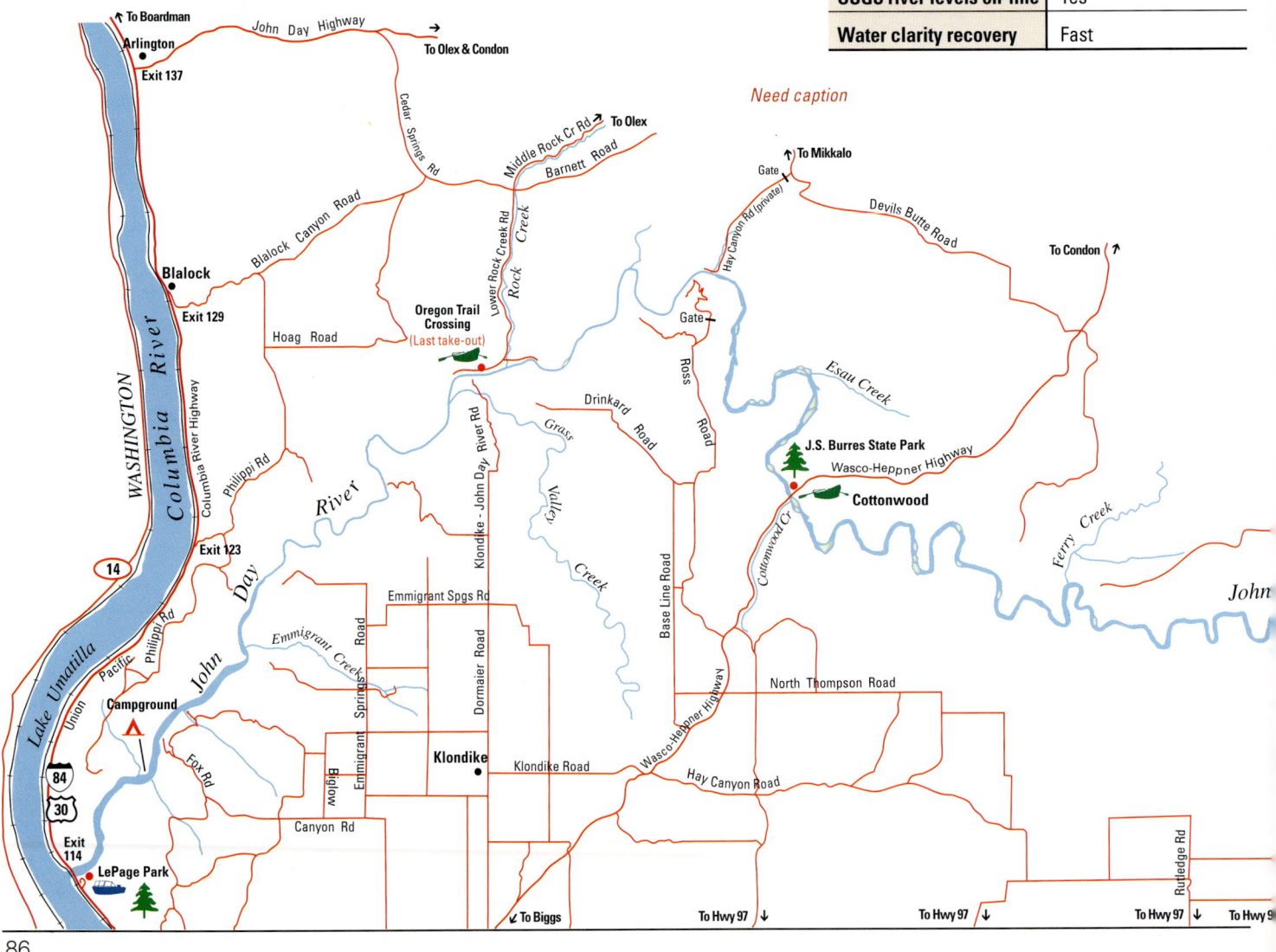

Need caption

86

John Day River, Lower

BEST GEAR-FISHING TECHNIQUES & ESTIMATED HOOKUPS IN AN AVERAGE YEAR

Best / Good / Slow	Jan	Feb	Mar	Apr	May	Jun	Jul	Aug	Sep	Oct	Nov	Dec
John Day Arm Summer Steelhead 1500	3,6,8									3,6,8	3,6,8	3,6,8
Summer Steelhead (River) 3000	1,2 3,4	1,2 3,4								1,2 3,4	1,2 3,4	1,2 3,4
Smallmouth Bass					2	2	2	2	2	2		

1. Drift fishing (from bank or boat, with or without bait)
2. Casting spinners, spoons, plugs
3. Float fishing (with jigs or bait)
4. Back-trolling (plugs or diver-and-bait)
5. Back-bouncing (boat)
6. Trolling (boat only)
7. Anchor fishing
8. Plunking
9. Jigging

BEST FLY-FISHING TECHNIQUES

Best / Good / Slow	Jan	Feb	Mar	Apr	May	Jun	Jul	Aug	Sep	Oct	Nov	Dec
Summer Steelhead (River)	2,3,4 5,6,7	2,3,4 5,6,7								2,3,4 5,6,7	2,3,4 5,6,7	2,3,4 5,6,7
Smallmouth Bass					8,9	8,9	8,9	8,9	8,9	8,9		

1. Dry fly, dead-drift
2. Dry fly, swung
3. Wet fly, swung near surface
4. Wet fly, swung deep
5. Nymph(s), lightly weighted
6. Nymph(s), weighted with indicator
7. Deep drifted fly (with or without indicator)
8. Wet fly retrieved near surface
9. Deep swing with retrieve

Photo by Tony Amato

Tony Amato displays a beautiful native winter steelhead caught with a black jig and slip bobber on the Lower John Day River in late fall.

LEGEND

- Interstate Highway
- US Highway
- State Highway
- Power-Boat Launch
- Drift-Boat Launch
- Park
- Campground

0 .5 1 2 Mile

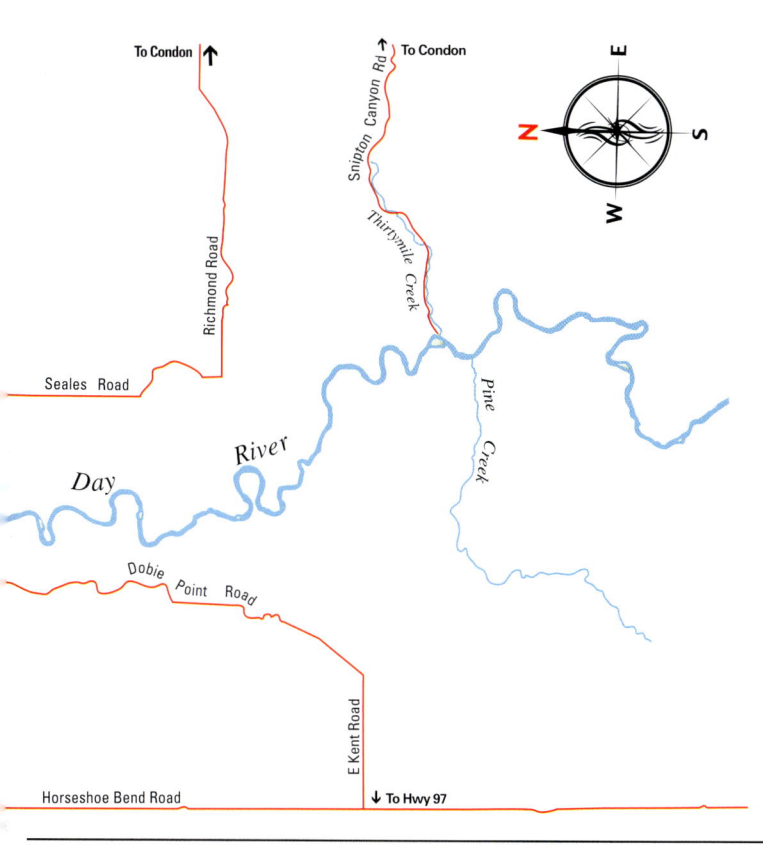

SERVICES

CAMPING/PARKS
- **LePage Park,** Rufus, 97050, (541) 506-4807, www.reserveamerica.com
- **J.S. Burres State Park,** www.co.gilliam.or.us
- **Cottonwood Canyon,** www.cottonwoodcanyon.wordpress.com
- **Rufus RV Park,** Rufus, 97050, (541) 739-2272, www.rufusrvpark.com
- **Burns Park,** Condon, 97823, (541) 384-5395, www.co.gilliam.or.us

ACCOMMODATIONS
- **Hotel Condon,** Condon, 97823, (541) 384-4624, www.hotelcondon.com
- **Wilson Ranches Retreat B&B,** Fossil, 97830, (541) 763-2227, (866) 763-2227, www.wilsonranchesretreat.com

TACKLE SHOPS
- **Dinty's Market,** Wasco, 97065, (541) 739-2236
- **Gorge Outfitters Supply,** Rufus, 97050, (541) 739-2222

VISITOR INFORMATION
- **U.S. Army Corps of Engineers,** (541) 296-1181
- **Sherman County Parks,** www.sherman-county.com
- **Campgrounds near John Day Fossil Beds,** www.nps.gov
- **Condon Chamber of Commerce,** Condon, 97823, (541) 384-7777, www.condonchamber.org

OREGON RIVER MAPS & FISHING GUIDE

JOHN DAY RIVER, LOWER

John Day River, Lower

Trout fishing in the upper John Day and its forks can be good, but because so many juvenile wild steelhead share the river with hatchery trout, it is often discouraged.

Summer bass fishing is the main draw to the John Day from April through September. From Kimberly to the mouth, rafters can choose from a variety of float-trips. From Kimberly to Service Creek, Highway 19 offers ideal access for bank and boat anglers. Experienced whitewater rafters enjoy the popular drift from Service Creek to Cottonwood Bridge. This section includes several Class III and one Class IV rapid (Clarno Rapids). Fly-fishing is the most popular method, although casting small lures with light spinning gear is also very effective.

SERVICES

CAMPING/PARKS

- **Fossil Motel and RV Park,** Fossil, 97830, www.facebook.com/fossilmotelrvpark
- **Shelton Wayside Park,** Fossil, 97830, (541) 763-2010, www.orparks.org
- **Big Sarvice Corral,** Fossil, 97830, (541) 468-2121, www.big-sarvice-corral-fossil-or.oregon.usa.camille-adair.com
- **Grant County Fairgrounds RV Park,** John Day, 97845, (541) 575-1900, www.grantcountyfairgrounds.com
- **Spray Riverfront Park,** Spray, 97874, (541) 468-2069, www.sprayoregon.us
- **Muleshoe Campground,** Spray, 97874, (541) 416-6700, www.campgroundsoregon.com
- **Campgrounds near John Day Fossil Beds,** www.nps.gov

ACCOMMODATIONS

- **Service Creek Lodge,** Fossil, 97830, (541) 468-3331
- **Up The Lazy River B&B,** John Day, 97845, (541) 575-5612, www.upthelazyriver.net

TACKLE SHOPS

- **John Day True Value Hardware,** John Day, 97845, (541) 575-0632, ww3.truevalue.com/johndaytruevalue

VISITOR INFORMATION

- **Wheeler County Parks,** Fossil, 97830, (541) 763-2010, www.orparks.org
- **Campgrounds near John Day Fossil Beds,** www.nps.gov
- **Grant County Chamber of Commerce,** John Day, 97845, (541) 575-0547, (800) 769-5664, www.grantcountychamber.com

LEGEND

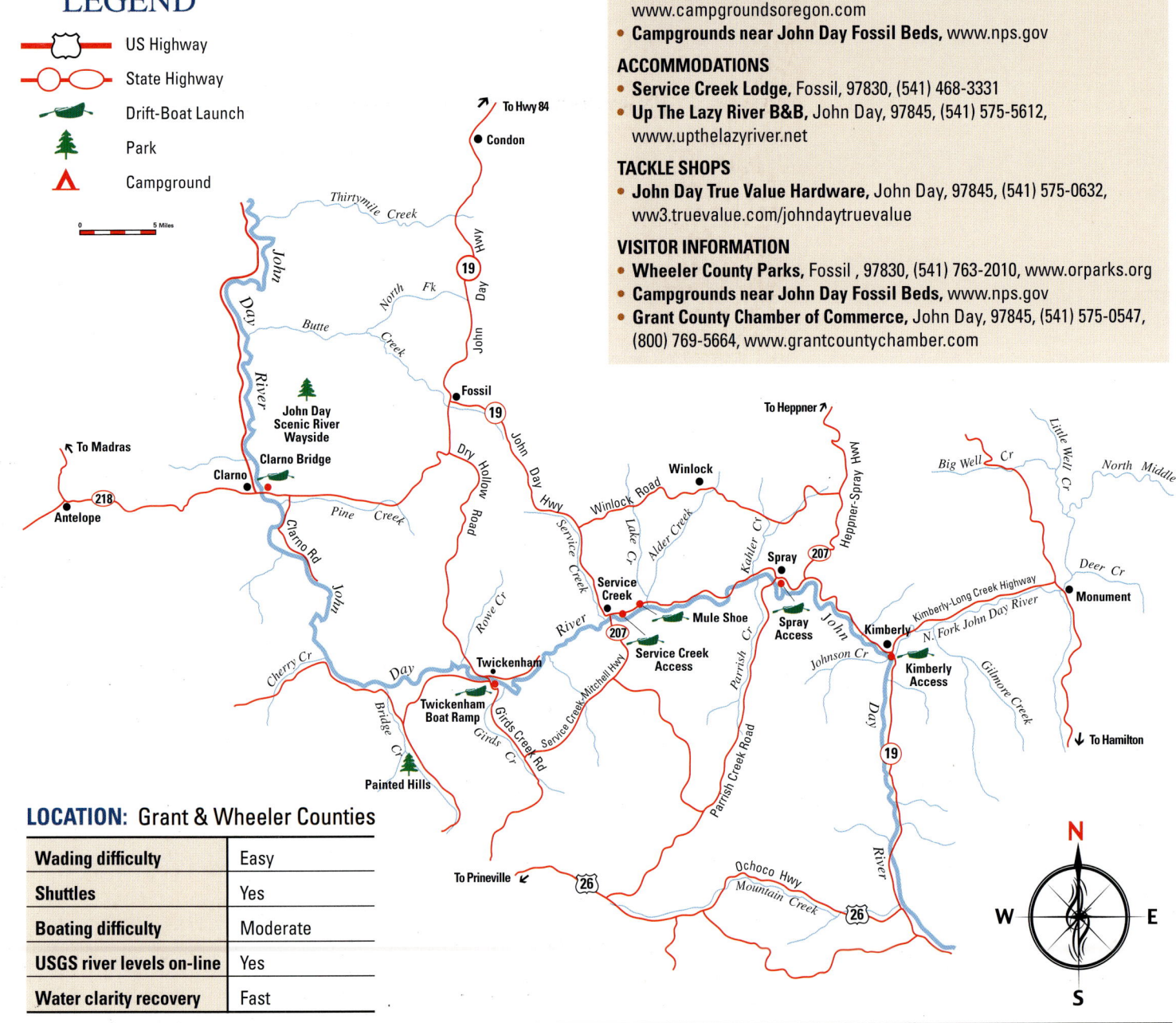

- US Highway
- State Highway
- Drift-Boat Launch
- Park
- Campground

0 — 5 Miles

LOCATION: Grant & Wheeler Counties

Wading difficulty	Easy
Shuttles	Yes
Boating difficulty	Moderate
USGS river levels on-line	Yes
Water clarity recovery	Fast

88